# Empire and Antislavery

## PITT LATIN AMERICAN SERIES

Billie R. DeWalt, General Editor
Reid Andrews, Associate Editor
Jorge I. Domínguez, Associate Editor

# EMPIRE

## ❧ AND ❧

# ANTISLAVERY

## Spain, Cuba, and Puerto Rico, 1833–1874

### Christopher Schmidt-Nowara

UNIVERSITY OF PITTSBURGH PRESS

Published by the University of Pittsburgh Press, Pittsburgh, Pa. 15261
Copyright © 1999, University of Pittsburgh Press
All rights reserved
Manufactured in the United States of America
Printed on acid-free paper
10 9 8 7 6 5 4 3 2 1

ISBN 0-8229-4089-2 (cl)
ISBN 0-8229-5690-x (pb)

A CIP catalog record for this book is available from the Library of Congress
and the British Library.

I dedicate this work to my family
and to the memory of my grandparents,
Emily and Robert Ebert.

# CONTENTS

# TABLES

# ACKNOWLEDGMENTS

Just as I was entering graduate school in 1988, a cartoonist popularized the image of the graduate student as a miserable wretch. Despite popular opinion, I found researching and writing this dissertation and manuscript to be an adventure well worth living. My thanks to the following for the generous financial assistance that provided the opportunity and leisure to travel and write over the years: the Department of History, the Program for the Comparative Study of Social Transformations, the Rackham School of Graduate Studies, and the Mellon dissertation program, of the University of Michigan; the Fulbright program; the Program for Cultural Cooperation between Spain and the United States; the Department of History, Stanford University; the American Historical Association; the Office of the Dean of Graduate Studies at Fordham University; and the Lydia Cabrera Award from the Conference on Latin American History. Special thanks also go to the staffs of the Biblioteca Nacional, the Hemeroteca Municipal, the Archivo Histórico Nacional, and to Carmén de Labra in Madrid; the Biblioteca de Catalunya, the library of the Fomento del Treball Nacional, the Biblioteca Arús, and the Arxiu Municipal in Barcelona; the Museu-Biblioteca Víctor Balaguer in Vilanova i la Geltrú; the Biblioteca Nacional José Martí and the Archivo Nacional in Havana; and the Colección Puertorriqueña, the Centro de Investigaciónes Históricos, and the Archivo General in San Juan; and the Archivo Histórico Municipal in Ponce.

This work had its origin in my encounter with the dynamic intellectual community at the University of Michigan, Ann Arbor. I especially want to express gratitude and admiration for my four great mentors there, Geoff Eley, Ann Stoler, Fred Cooper, and above all Rebecca Scott. Their advice and example have inspired me from start to finish. Many others in Ann Arbor provided important support and friendship during those exciting years: Ada Ferrer, Karen Robert, Teo Ruiz, Steve Soper, Rafe Blaufarb, Erik Seeman, Victoria Wolcott, Leila Hudson, Lora Wildenthal, Andrew Diamond, and Elizabeth Horodowich. Dorothy Marschke and Brenda Apstis of the History Department helped keep me on track throughout. The early encouragement and advice of Robert Kern of the University of New Mexico was also important.

During my research in Spain I was lucky to meet great friends, advisors, and colleagues: Luis Miguel García Mora, Stephen Jacobson, Joan Casanovas, Magdalena Chocano, Josep María Fradera, and especially Jim Amelang and our fellow basketball players. I would also like to thank Mario Padilla, Inés and Elena Sánchez de Madariaga, Clara Cerón, Patricia Zahniser, Tomás Rodríguez, Mary Coffey, Manuel Pérez Ledesma, Jordi Maluquer de Motes, Angel Duarte, Astrid Cubano, Juan Pan-Montojo, Elena Hernández Sandöica, Consuelo Naranjo, Pamela Radcliff, Andrew Davis, and David Ortiz.

Luis Figueroa and Francisco Scarano gave me invaluable advice for my research in Puerto Rico. In Puerto Rico, I would also like to thank Nelly Vázquez Sotillo, María Dolores Luque, Gladys Tormes, and especially Luis Ferrao and Libia González for being great hosts.

In Cuba, thanks go to Oscar Zanetti, Reynaldo Funes Monzote and his family, Leida Fernández Prieto, Sergia Martínez, and the staffs of the Biblioteca Nacional José Martí and the Archivo Nacional for their generous help. Within the field of Cuban studies in the United States, I have received helpful advice from Alfonso Quiroz and especially from Laird Bergad, Lou Pérez, and Alan Dye.

As I revised this manuscript, encouragement came from several colleagues at Stanford, especially my fellow post-docs— Stephen Hastings-King, Bob Batchelor, Isaac Miller, Lisa Rothrauff, Jennifer Selwyn, Alastair Bellany, and Krystyna von Henneberg—in our collective effort to survive Silicon Valley. Thanks also to John Wirth, Paula Findlen, Richard Roberts, Michael Predmore, Carolyn Lougee, and to fellow members of the Bay Area Iberian History Tertulia and the Spain, Europe, and the Americas workshop sponsored by the Stanford Humanities Center.

Presenting papers and discussing interpretations with many colleagues between 1995 and 1998 helped me get revisions under way: Javier Morillo-Alicea, Adrian Shubert, Arcadio Díaz Quiñones, Fred Cooper, Antonio Sánchez Cazorla, Richard Kagan, John Tone, Juan Pan-Montojo, Juan Pro Ruiz, José Alvarez Junco, Manuel Pérez Ledesma, and Carlos Serrano all gave insightful comments along the way. Again, my close friends and colleagues Ada Ferrer, Joan Casanovas, Stephen Jacobson, and Luis Miguel García Mora provided invaluable support and inspiration.

Turning the cumbersome dissertation into a readable manuscript was made easier by the advice of distinguished colleagues in the field. Seymour Drescher of the University of Pittsburgh generously reviewed the dissertation soon after its completion, and his comments have guided me from the start. He also steered me toward the University of Pittsburgh Press, and as the reader will quickly note, his work has significantly influenced my own. Robert Paquette of Hamilton College bravely reviewed the manuscript twice and his comments made this a far more presentable piece of writing and helped me rethink what it was about. Thanks also to another anonymous reader for the University of Pittsburgh Press and to Eileen Kiley, Kathy Meyer, Jennifer Flanagan and Jane Flanders at the Press for seeing this project through with timely advice and careful editing.

My biggest inspiration has always come from my family, without whom I could do nothing, so to them I dedicate this work. Joy Conlon has made the study of Spanish and Latin American history truly joyous. My parents, Wolfgang and Betsy, my siblings, Peter and Molly, and my extended family, especially John Ebert and Barbara Ebert, have supported me constantly, always with great humor. Finally, my late grandparents, Emily and Robert Ebert, were and continue to be my models for much of what I do. To their memories in particular I dedicate this book.

# Empire and Antislavery

# Introduction

## SPAIN IN THE ANTILLES
## AND THE ANTILLES
## IN SPAIN

"We reformists . . . want *a single and identical Spain* on both sides of the ocean without dictators, without monopolies, and without slaves."[1] Joaquín María Sanromá, a leader of the Spanish Abolitionist Society (Sociedad Abolicionista Española, established in 1865), issued that challenge to Antillean slavery and the Spanish colonial order in 1872 during a time of revolution and civil war in Spain and Cuba. At the time, there were more than 300,000 slaves in Cuba and Puerto Rico, and while the metropolitan government had passed a law providing for gradual abolition in 1870, Cuban slaveowners in particular clung tenaciously to their slaves because of the centrality of slave labor to all forms of primary production. Slavery and the slave trade to Cuba were vital and lucrative enterprises until their final abolition (the slave trade in 1867, slavery in 1886).[2] Cuban planters reaped tremendous wealth from slave-produced sugar and continued to expand the slave system until it was politically nonviable. Moreover, metropolitan interests were deeply implicated in the colonial economy and fiercely opposed any challenge to the status quo, especially to the institution of slavery.[3] The effort by the Spanish Abolitionist Society to abolish Cuban and Puerto Rican slavery met with massive resistance, both in the colonies and in Spain, as it threatened the very basis of economic and political hegemony within the imperial system. The origins of that challenge, and the goals and strategies adopted by metropolitan and colonial abolitionists, are the subject of this study.

My research strategy is two-pronged. On the one hand, I explored the archives of Spain's colonial administration, the Overseas Ministry (Ministerio de Ultramar) and related bodies, located in Madrid, Havana, and San Juan.[4] These sources enabled me to follow the interests of Hispano-Antillean political and economic elites as they maneuvered through the complicated geopolitics of the Atlantic world to sustain the slave trade and slavery against abolitionist pressures at home and abroad.

Second, I consulted a wide range of personal papers, newspapers, pamphlets, memoirs, and parliamentary debates produced by activists, politicians, and planters on both sides of the Atlantic. These sources throw light on the interests and strategies of local actors throughout the empire who mobilized to attack or to defend slavery. They give some insight into how transatlantic political struggles disrupted or dovetailed with the hegemony of the Spanish state and the colonial slaveowning class. This approach enabled me to show how the actions and ideas of locally situated historical actors intersected with and transformed the broader political economy of slavery and colonialism in the Atlantic world.

I treat these sources as political acts carried out by motivated individuals who were seeking both to interpret and to influence their social world. In other words, I believe that all texts are highly ideological: they capture not an objective historical reality but a partial interpretation made by situated individuals who write for interested reasons. This is not to say that all history is interpretation divorced from material forces. It is rather to say that no individual can comprehend the totality of a historical moment; thus everyone writes from a limited perspective. My strategy is to explain the limitations of perspective and capture the clash of ideological projects of local actors who constantly altered an overdetermined historical reality through their actions.[5]

Four interrelated arguments frame this work. First, I argue that one must reassess the power and complexity of the Spanish colonial project in the nineteenth century as a backdrop for understanding the dynamics of the growth and destruction of Antillean slavery. Spanish colonialism did not end with the Spanish American revolutions. Powerful commercial, agricultural, and military interests in the metropolis were reconcentrated on Cuba and Puerto Rico in the first half of the nineteenth century. Moreover, despite the loss of certain prerogatives gained in the late eighteenth century, the Antillean elite found inclusion within the Spanish Empire to be generally beneficial and convenient, as Spain was the last European power to abolish the transatlantic slave trade. Representing nineteenth-century Spain as a feeble relic of its former greatness fails to capture the renewal of the colonial project after the 1820s and the complexity of the bonds linking Spain and its colonies.

Second, by focusing on the Abolitionist Society and related antislavery initiatives, I hope to reconstruct the breadth of the political stage on which the battle over Antillean slavery was fought. In this I am following Rebecca Scott's emphasis on the role of popular political mobilization, in relation to economic changes, in bringing slavery to end in Cuba.[6] This emphasis on the politics of antislavery, as well as proslavery mobilizations, draws new attention to the spatial dimensions of Antillean slavery's demise. Spain, Cuba, and Puerto Rico were parts of an integrated, though fractured, political unit. To comprehend fully the destruction of Cuban and Puerto Rican slavery, one must look beyond the boundaries of each society to capture the range of interested actors within the broader imperial context.

Third, Spanish and Antillean elites always perceived political and economic transformations through a racial lens. Cuban and Puerto Rican slavery exploded in the aftermath of the Haitian revolution (1791–1804), the Atlantic world's only successful slave rebellion. After the birth of Haiti, Caribbean slaveowners and metropolitan officials lived in constant terror of rebellion and race war. However, while the specter of racial violence haunted all members of the elite, they disagreed dramatically over the meaning of race and the consequences of racial difference for the timing of slave emancipation.

Fourth, concerning the historiography of Atlantic slavery and abolition, I advocate studying the interaction of colony and metropolis in the formation of antislavery movements. The dominant paradigms of antislavery studies generally emphasize the central role of social and cultural changes either in the colonies or in the metropolis in producing attacks on slavery. Instead, I seek to demonstrate that one cannot separate colony from metropolis in understanding the origins and interests of abolitionist movements.

## The Second Slavery and the Second Empire

Reevaluating Spain's nineteenth-century colonial project casts new light on the rise and fall of Antillean slavery. Cuba and Puerto Rico were part of the Atlantic world's "second slavery,"[7] societies that responded to expanded European demand for staple goods through the mobilization of slave labor in the nineteenth century. Moreover, this second slavery forced Spain to refashion its centuries-old colonial regime, in effect constructing a "second empire."[8] Spain was not merely a feeble and decadent drain on Antillean resources, but an active player in refashioning Atlantic slavery.[9]

TABLE 1.
**Slaves Imported to Cuba, 1791–1870**

| | |
|---|---|
| 1791–1800 | 69,500 |
| 1801–1810 | 74,000 |
| 1811–1820 | 168,600 |
| 1821–1830 | 83,100 |
| 1831–1840 | 181,600 |
| 1841–1850 | 50,800 |
| 1851–1860 | 121,000 |
| 1861–1870 | 31,600 |
| *Total* | 780,200 |

*Source:* Eltis, *Economic Growth,* 249.

TABLE 2
**Cuban Cane Sugar as Percentage
of World Production, 1820–1900**

| | |
|---|---|
| 1820 | 13.64 |
| 1830 | 18.53 |
| 1840 | 20.87 |
| 1850 | 28.19 |
| 1860 | 31.44 |
| 1870 | 42.31 |
| 1880 | 32.90 |
| 1890 | 24.47 |
| 1900 | 5.85 |

*Source:* Moreno Fraginals, *El Ingenio,* 3 : 35–38 .

The scale of Spanish rule in the nineteenth-century Caribbean was unique in the long history of Spanish colonialism in the Americas. The number of slaves brought to Cuba between 1790 and the closing of the trade in 1867 is revealing (see table 1). In that period, Cuba imported approximately 780,000 slaves, whereas all of Spanish America between 1520 and 1780 imported approximately 700,000.[10] That unprecedented number of slaves produced sugar in vast quantities. By 1870, Cuba was producing fully 40 percent of the world's cane sugar (see table 2). The massive scale of sugar production and slavery in the Caribbean helps explain the allegiance of the planter class to the metropolis. Though Spain did not import colonial sugar in substantial quantities, it provided a political and economic framework that stimulated colonial production. This was in contrast to rival European metropolises that were abolishing the transatlantic slave trade and colonial slavery in the early and mid-nineteenth century.

Hispano-Antillean planters and slave traders were not the only interests implicated in the second slavery and the second empire. At the end of the eighteenth century, Spanish America was far and away Spain's largest export market, receiving nearly 40 percent of Spanish exports. After the Spanish American revolutions, Spanish manufacturers and agricultural producers had to search out new markets, and many turned to continental Europe. Many others, however, reconcentrated their interests on the Caribbean. Throughout the nineteenth century, Cuba remained Spain's third largest export market, behind Great Britain and France (see tables 3 and 4). Protecting colonial markets was thus a high priority for the Spanish state and the Spanish bourgeoisie until the very end of the century.[11]

Maintaining protected markets was also a source of conflict with Antillean planters, who favored free-trade policies, both to lower the cost of imports and to ship their exports more cheaply to their largest markets, Great Britain and the United States. Indeed, the growing importance of the North American market for Cuban sugar and the virtual irrelevance of the Spanish market heightened tensions between colony and metropolis (see table 5). Nonetheless, the priority of the slave trade and the necessity of controlling the slave population generally ensured the loyalty of the planter class and cemented Spanish hegemony. Though economically weak, Spain was still an effective colonial power. Historians who represent Spain as

TABLE 3
**World Markets for Spanish Exports, 1792 and 1827 (in percentages)**

|  | 1792 | 1827 |
|---|---|---|
| Spanish America | 39.2 | 0.1 |
| Cuba, Puerto Rico, Philippines | 4.4 | 16.6 |
| Britain | 15.5 | 28.3 |
| France | 12.5 | 27.9 |

*Source:* Prados de la Esocosura, *De imperio a nación,* 76.

TABLE 4
**World Markets for Spanish Exports, 1827–1913
(in percentages)**

|  | 1827 | 1855–59 | 1875–79 | 1890–94 | 1910–13 |
|---|---|---|---|---|---|
| Cuba | 16.6 | 19.4 | 15.2 | 14.7 | 5.3 |
| Britain | 28.3 | 25.6 | 36.9 | 23.0 | 21.4 |
| France | 27.9 | 26.4 | 22.2 | 37.9 | 24.9 |

*Source:* Prados de la Esocosura, *De imperio a nación,* 202.

TABLE 5
Exports of Cuban Sugar to Spain
and the United States, 1840–1900 (in percentages)

| | | |
|---|---|---|
| 1840 | 10.60 | 17.16 |
| 1850 | 7.65 | 26.96 |
| 1860 | 7.70 | 58.47 |
| 1870 | 5.33 | 46.24 |
| 1880 | 2.90 | 81.58 |
| 1890 | 8.17 | 80.68 |
| 1894 | 2.18 | 91.49 |
| 1900 | – | 99.86 |

*Source:* Moreno Fraginals, *El Ingenio*, 3:75–77.

"seigneurial" or "unable to fulfill the economic role of a modern imperial power" box the historical process into teleological narratives of modernity that gloss over the reshaping of the colonial project and diminish the powerful economic and political interests served by Spanish rule.[12]

## The Space of Antislavery

Not only did Spanish colonial retrenchment facilitate the growth of Antillean slavery, it also paradoxically created new sites for antislavery and anticolonial initiatives. The centrality of colonialism to political and economic changes in Spain made it a prime target for metropolitan reformers and radicals; change the colonies and metropolitan change would follow, they argued. As Rebecca Scott notes in her study of emancipation in Cuba, the tight connection between metropolitan and colonial politics opened opportunities for creoles and slaves to force changes in their societies.[13] Therefore, I discuss colonialism not only as a series of repressive mechanisms but also as an enabling political framework, one that permitted not only the growth of slavery but also certain kinds of mobilization against slavery and the political status quo.[14]

Two crucial changes within the empire fueled the antislavery movement. First, the transformation of the public sphere in mid-nineteenth-century Spain, especially in Madrid, created the possibilities for antislavery mobilization. I understand *public sphere* to be a domain that "mediates between society and state, in which the public organizes itself as the bearer of public opinion."[15] Two transformations in Spanish political life facilitated the rise of antislavery: the development of a vibrant middle-class associational culture in mid-nineteenth-century Madrid and the concurrent debate throughout the Peninsula over national economic policy. The first created a public receptive to colonial criticisms of Spanish rule, and moreover a public organized in associations—dedicated to working-class education and free trade, among other causes—that were models for the Abolitionist Society. The second mobilized economic and political groups throughout Spain around the issue of economic protectionism, which was also one of the central axes of conservative hegemony in the colonies. Indeed, the battle over slavery in Spain would follow the contours of the national public sphere carved out in the struggle over protectionism.[16]

Second, the rise of antislavery sentiment in Puerto Rico was fundamental to the founding of the Abolitionist Society in Spain. Antislavery arose in Puerto Rico not because of slavery's marginality to the island's economy and society, as one classic interpretation holds,[17] but as a projected solution—and one that faced stiff opposition from slaveowners—to the island's economic decline and political subordination. As Puerto Rican slavery stagnated in the mid-nineteenth century, a faction of creole society came to argue that an immediate transition to free labor would benefit the island's sugar sector. Operating within the context of broader changes in imperial politics in the 1860s, Puerto Ricans like Julio de Vizcarrondo were able to put the issue of immediate abolition on the political agenda, not just for Puerto Rico but for Cuba and Spain as well.[18]

In short, this work reconsiders the locations from which Antillean slavery could be attacked and defended, in effect rethinking the Spanish dimension of slavery and antislavery. It will also reconsider the Antillean dimension of Spain's "bourgeois revolution" and Spanish politics in the nineteenth century. Both approaches will call into question conventional notions of the boundaries between colony and metropolis by examining how political interests and alliances cut across the Atlantic.[19]

## Race, Slavery, and Colonial Identities

If the boundaries between colony and metropolis were permeable, racial boundaries within Antillean society were also shifting. Scholars have begun to uncover the profound preoccupation with racial differences that hobbled the nationalist projects in both Cuba and Puerto Rico. It is clear that Cuban and Puerto Rican nationalism were not fixed phenomena but shifting political projects contested by diverse groups profoundly divided over the question of race. My work will follow these recent revisions by concentrating on the Antillean elite's changing identification with the Spanish metropolis and how race shaped elite attitudes toward slavery and abolition.[20]

First I will spell out how I define *race* and the politics of racial identity in a colonial context. Borrowing from Sidney Mintz and Joan Wallach Scott, I understand *race* as knowledge about physical, especially phenotypical, and/or cultural differences.[21] Race is not a biological reality but a category of perceived differences, skin color being one of the most common markers. That knowledge refers not only to others, but to the self as well; for instance, by describing Cuban slaves as black, Spanish abolitionists were implicitly describing themselves as white. In other words, the politics of racial difference in the Spanish colonial empire involved the construction of blackness and whiteness—and whiteness not only in the metropolis, but also in the colonies, as the Antillean elite sought to articulate their difference from the slave population and the free population of color. One strategy for representing that difference was through identification with the "white" metropolis.[22]

In nineteenth-century Cuba and Puerto Rico, race and slavery heavily influenced colonial identities and interests. Among the colonial elite, the boundary between colonizer and colonized, between Spain and Cuba or Puerto Rico, was contingent. Fear of racial conflict decisively shaped elite attitudes toward slavery and colonialism. If the second slavery was powerful and flexible, it was also vulnerable on innumerable political and ideological fronts in an increasingly abolitionist age. The Haitian revolution (1791–1804) and emancipation in the British colonies (1834–1838) gave Antillean planters an opportunity to fill the vacuum in world sugar production. Yet these events also filled them with dread and a sense of permanent crisis and conflict.[23]

Their own slaves were a source of peril. So were British initiatives against the slave trade and slavery. Moreover, in both Cuba and Puerto Rico there were substantial numbers of free people of color—about 16 percent of the total population in mid-nineteenth-century Cuba and almost 40 percent in Puerto Rico.[24] Though the categories of race in the Spanish colonial world were complex and recognized degrees of racial mixture, the division between white and nonwhite was nonetheless jealously guarded by the colonial state and the white elite.[25] White Antilleans in particular closely monitored this racial distinction with the increase in the slave population and the growing crisis in Atlantic slavery. They saw themselves as surrounded by a nonwhite population, both in their own countries and the Caribbean more broadly, and on the brink of race war.[26] The perception of impending racial conflict thus strongly shaped the political options of the Antillean elite. Though creoles like the Cuban publicist José Antonio Saco at times expressed odium for Spain, fear of the growing slave population also led him to seek greater inclusion for Cuba in the Spanish liberal regime as the surest bulwark against race war.

Racial categories were not static, however, and they changed significantly over the course of the nineteenth century. The crisis of the Spanish Empire set off by the Napoleonic invasion in 1808 had forced peninsular and creole elites to rethink the nature of the colonial bond during the Cortes of Cádiz (1810–1814). During the Cortes, Spanish liberals had succeeded in excluding from electoral censuses all male members of colonial society who had African origins as a means of ensuring the numerical superiority of peninsular delegates in the Cortes. Antillean deputies at Cádiz were chiefly concerned with quieting any open discussion of slavery and abolition, which they feared would lead to unrest among the slave population. In short, at the opening of the nineteenth-century debate over the nature of empire, the Spanish and Antillean elite not only defended slavery but also explicitly marginalized people of African origin from active membership in the Spanish nation. Nonetheless, changing political circumstances and necessities forced Hispano-Antillean elites to rethink the relationships linking race, nation, and empire. By 1868, the Spanish and creole liberals gathered in the Abolitionist Society were fighting not only for immediate slave emancipation but also for a vision of nation and empire that was multiracial. One purpose of this study will be to suggest how the struggles over colonial slavery transformed the racial boundaries of empire and nation, not just in Cuba and Puerto Rico, but in Spain as well.[27]

## Antislavery, Hegemony, and Counterhegemony

The centrality of racial ideologies in shaping attitudes toward slavery and colonialism raises the question of the role of ideology in determining antislavery mobilization. This issue has been thoroughly interrogated by scholars of Atlantic antislavery movements. Classic works such as Eric Williams's *Capitalism and Slavery* and Seymour Drescher's *Capitalism and Antislavery* seek to establish the relationship between European, primarily British, capitalist development and the demise of American slavery. Subsequent studies place greater emphasis on cultural and political transformations within the broader context of global capitalist development, both in Europe and the Americas.[28] This study will try to straddle both models by looking at forms of ideology and political action, both in the metropolis and the colonies, and the impact of capitalist development in the Spanish colonial empire on the politics of slavery and antislavery.

Historians of British antislavery argue that abolitionism and abolitionist ideology played crucial roles in consolidating the political and ideological hegemony of a rising capitalist class in the industrializing nations of the late eighteenth and early nineteenth centuries. Eric Williams was a pioneer in those studies. In 1944, Williams broke with the historiographical tradition that had portrayed British abolitionists as "saints" concerned only with humanitarian aims by arguing that a desire for free trade and more productive forms of labor within an emerging capitalist world system moved Britain to abolish slavery and the slave trade. Slavery, in Williams's interpretation, was an archaic and unproductive institution by the nineteenth century, an institution supported by monopolistic trade policies that were destroyed by British capital in its march toward economic liberalization. According to Williams, the drive of the British capitalist classes toward worldwide capitalist social relations and free trade impelled British abolitionism. Though he admitted their humanitarian aims, he also portrayed the "saints" as mouthpieces or pawns of capital. Economic, not humanitarian, concerns were the primary causal factors in British antislavery.[29]

Many scholars have challenged the Williams thesis. Using economic and quantitative methods, Seymour Drescher and David Eltis argue that British colonial slavery was a booming concern and that Britain was poised to carry through a major reorganization of sugar (and cotton) production in relatively underdeveloped colonies like Trinidad and Demerara just as abolitionists cut off the supply of labor by forcing the abolition of the slave trade in 1806–1807. Eltis, moreover, contends that British initiatives against the Atlantic slave trade in general cannot be explained by purely economic motives because Britain depended on American exports that were most profitably produced by slave labor. The title of Drescher's work captures the gist of this revisionist interpretation of British antislavery: econocide. In other words, for Drescher and Eltis, British antislavery was at odds with Britain's objective economic interests. The causes of the antislavery movement had to lie elsewhere.[30]

Drescher has been one of the major participants in that search and he has written much of his work in dialogue with another investigator: David Brion Davis. Davis has pursued both the Williams thesis and the earlier version of the "saints," valorizing and revising both interpretations. On the one hand, he explores the importance of religious evangelicalism in fostering antislavery thought and politics in both Great Britian and the United States, showing how members of religious and economic groups, especially the Quakers, in both societies came to see slavery as a violation of moral and material progress.[31] On the other hand, Davis follows the broader ideological function of British antislavery apart from its religious origins. In this field, he recasts Williams's argument about the relation between capitalism and slavery by shifting the nexus away from the level of objective economic interests to that of perceived economic and class interests.

In Davis's interpretation, British antislavery provided an ideological justification for the new forms of social exploitation developing within the industrializing metropolis. Seen through the "perceptual lens" of the antislavery movement, any form of labor that was not bonded was "free."[32] This austere conception of freedom and free labor, defined largely through its opposition to slavery, legitimated the rise of market society and the misery that accompanied the proletarianization of the English working population. In this view, antislavery was one of the ideological linchpins of metropolitan capitalism. Antislavery was thus an expression of economic interests, but as a displacement of metropolitan conflicts onto a distant struggle.[33]

Davis not only calls attention to the centrality of slavery and antislavery to the Atlantic world's transition to a modern capitalist economy, but also demonstrates that this transformation was a political and ideological, as well as an economic, process. Abolitionists did not act out a prescribed historical script of modernity and capitalism but mobilized in particular ways and fought for particular beliefs. Davis's emphasis on the displacement of metropolitan struggles captures both the interplay between material and ideological forces in historical action and the contingency of the battle against slavery in the Atlantic world.

Drescher broadens the concept of antislavery as a political and cultural phenomenon. He modifies Davis's interpretations by exploring the diverse social and religious bases of antislavery and the multiple uses and appropriations of antislavery within the British metropolis, stressing the *counterhegemonic* function of abolitionism and antislavery ideology. While Davis argues that antislavery was the ideological expression of a rising industrial and political class, Drescher responds that antislavery was also an oppositional ideology, particularly in the later phases of the movement in the 1830s, adopted by classes threatened by proletarianization and the industrial economy to criticize their "wage" slavery and loss of autonomy.[34] As for the religious base, popular sects like Methodism were crucial sources of antislavery sentiment and activism. In fact, the importance of religious organizations was, according to Drescher, one of the elements that made British antislavery so powerful and distinctive: religious associations in Britain, especially nonconformist sects, served as essential mediating bodies linking different classes and regions. Such a mediating structure was absent, for instance, from French social and political life in the same period, which mitigated the extent of antislavery mobilization in France.[35]

The comparative focus has led Drescher to question the usefulness of exploring the relation between capitalism and antislavery. For instance, why did capitalism produce a mass antislavery movement in Britian in the late eighteenth and early nineteenth centuries, but not in the Netherlands? The answer for Drescher leads away from understanding antislavery sentiment as an expression of and a response to capitalist development and toward the study of particular political possibilities for abolitionist action. He writes:

> Antislavery seems to have been more dependent on the invention of new forms of collective behavior and on communal expansions of the rights of individuals, of social roles, of public membership, which accompanied the rise of Britain and its settler societies to prominence and world primacy. As the discussion broadens, the rise of antislavery has to be imagined less as a correlate of expanding new class domination than as one of the new modes of social mobilization.[36]

Both the focus on capitalist development and on political and ideological transformations are useful for comprehending the origins and interests of the Abolitionist Society. On the one hand, the society's actions were shaped by the peculiar structure of capitalism in the Spanish colonial empire. While staunch defenders of the market economy, Spanish and Antillean abolitionists criticized the dominant strategies of capital accumulation in Spain and the Antilles and sought to transform them by abolishing slavery and opening free markets. In short, the battle over the nature of Hispano-Antillean capitalism, of which slavery was an integral part, produced a counterhegemonic abolitionist movement.[37]

On the other hand, also crucial to the rise of abolitionism were the new forms of political action that developed in Madrid at midcentury, as well as ideological challenges to Spanish liberalism and colonialism made by Antillean reformers beginning in the 1830s. Here, Drescher's recent arguments about political mobilization and Davis's emphasis on ideological transformations as laying the foundations for attacks on colonial slavery provide important insights.[38]

This study departs from the work of Drescher and Davis in focusing on the transatlantic nature of antislavery ideology and mobilization.[39] Davis's work is suggestive but ambiguous on this point. While he highlights the interaction of North American and English abolitionists, especially Quakers, in attacking slavery in the British Empire, he also, along with Drescher, locates the origins of abolitionism in metropolitan political and social struggles that were then displaced onto colonial society.[40] While I agree that

Spanish abolitionists did indeed apply their ideal social vision to the colonies, they generally did so in response to political pressures not just from Spain but, more significantly, from Cuba and Puerto Rico.

Moreover, seeing the Abolitionist Society as a metropolitan association is insufficent because the original impulse for abolition came from Puerto Rico, and Puerto Rican reformers were instrumental in founding the society. Instead, I believe it is more helpful to see the Abolitionist Society as a "hybrid" political association, in that it amalgamated colonial and metropolitan actors and their interests and political strategies.[41] Mobilization against slavery was a transatlantic phenomenon, and abolitionism and the overthrow of slavery resulted from the dialectic between colonial and metropolitan initiatives. Local actors had limited social visions, yet they made calculated responses to the distant intiatives made by similarly locally circumscribed actors. That uneven clash of interests and ideologies was the motor of antislavery.[42]

# I

# The Limits of Revolution

## SLAVERY AND LIBERTY
## IN SPAIN AND CUBA,
## 1833–1854

The death of the Spanish monarch Fernando VII and the restoration of constitutional government in Spain in 1833 raised the hopes of Antillean
creoles for significant political and economic liberalization in the colonies.
These events also raised the thorny question of the status of slavery and the
slave trade. During Spain's previous constitutional periods, 1810–1814 and
1820–1823, metropolitan and American deputies had made proposals for
abolishing the trade and the gradual abolition of slavery. Writing from Havana in 1836, the creole slaveowner José Luis Alfonso urged his friend José
Antonio Saco, the elected deputy to the Estatuto Real for Santiago de Cuba,
to protect the interests of Cuban slaveowners:

> In the first Cortes, they will deal with our great problem: *the blacks*. We
> have learned from a relative of Alcalá Galiano, who lives in Havana, that
> he will propose the emancipation of our slaves. We have also learned
> that an Abolitionist Society has been established in Madrid that will
> propose the same measure. Though this is a holy and just cause, it is
> urgent to reconcile this measure with the interest of the slaveowners.
> That is to say, it is urgent to do it gradually, with prudence and discre-
> tion.[1]

Alfonso's tacit acknowledgement of the conflict between slaveowners' interests and the "holy and just cause" of abolition reflected the dilemma of
the Antillean slaveowning elite in the 1830s: while slave labor was productive for Antillean planters, it was becoming politically and ideologically in-

defensible in the broader Atlantic world, as slave rebellions and abolitionist movements challenged not only the legitimacy but also the very existence of slavery and the slave trade.[2]

Alfonso need not have worried about the Spanish Cortes in the 1830s,
however. Spain did abolish slavery, but only in the Peninsula, where it had
been defunct for some time.[3] Though the Spanish government signed a new
treaty with Great Britain banning the slave trade to Cuba in 1835, in general it acted tacitly to stimulate and encourage slavery and the slave trade.
Indeed, more slaves were imported into Cuba during the 1830s than in any
other decade in its history. (See table 1.) The Cortes's most radical actions
regarding the colonies were to tighten Cuba's and Puerto Rico's political
and economic subordination, crushing the hopes of creoles for reform.

In 1837, a commission in the newly elected Cortes voted to expel the
Cuban, Puerto Rican, and Filipino deputies from the assembly. The commissioners, including some of the most notable figures in Spanish liberalism, such as Agustín Argüelles and Salustiano de Olózaga, argued that the
heterogeneous populations of the colonies, especially Cuba, required "special laws" to rule them. Until those laws were determined, the colonies
would have no representatives in the Cortes.[4]

The decision of the Spanish Cortes arose from the centralizing tendencies of Spanish liberalism and the growth of Antillean slavery. The Spanish
revolutions of the first half of the nineteenth century (1810–1814, 1820–
1823, 1833–1840) consolidated a centralized state, with a strong executive
in the form of the Bourbon monarchy and a legislature with an extremely
limited franchise, and together they set the foundations for a capitalist
economy based on private property and free wage labor. Centralization and
capitalist property relations set off centrifugal effects throughout the Peninsula and the Americas. In Spain, for instance, peasants, clergy, and landowners in the northern regions, especially the Basque provinces and Catalonia,
opposed efforts to break up communal, aristocratic, and ecclesiastical properties throughout the nineteenth century. Indeed, the civil war of the 1830s
between liberals and the Carlists (so named for their allegiance to Don
Carlos de Bourbon, Fernando VII's reactionary brother) was a major obstacle to consolidating the liberal regime. To finance it, liberals relied
heavily upon Spain's wealthy Antillean colonies.[5]

The crucial importance of colonial wealth pushed Spanish liberals to
seek greater political and economic control in the Antilles, although long-
term trends also shaped liberal colonial policies. During the earlier constitutional periods (1810–1814, 1820–1823), Spanish revolutionaries had
sought to incorporate American elites into the liberal state by giving them

political representation and by claiming the equality of all "Spaniards" on both sides of the Atlantic. This was a significant break from the traditional view of the American colonies as separate and dependent societies.[6] Yet metropolitan liberals also sought to maximize Spanish control by limiting the number of American representatives to the Spanish Cortes and by creating a colonial administration that preserved the metropolitan-colonial hierarchy. American desires for self-rule, however, were at odds with state formation in Spain, and most of the American colonies successfully fought for their independence from Madrid in the 1810s and 1820s.[7]

Cuba had remained loyal not only because of Spain's military predominance, but also because of the singular place of the Cuban elite within the empire. Cuban creoles, unlike most of their American counterparts, were accustomed to significant local control in the late eighteenth and early nineteenth centuries. During the French and the Spanish American revolutions, the Cuban planter class had successfully pacted with the Spanish state, trading loyalty for limited self-rule and free trade.[8] Moreover, the precipitous growth of slavery in an age of slave rebellions and abolitionism made Cuban planters eager to stabilize local society. (See table 6.) Their ideal was the United States' South, where slaveowners enjoyed local dominance and national representation. Inclusion within the Spanish state potentially offered them such an arrangement.[9]

Yet Spanish revolutionaries acted instead to exclude creoles from the liberal regime that was being consolidated in the 1830s and to assert Spain's preeminence in Antillean affairs. Whereas Cuban planters had enjoyed tremendous bargaining power in the late eighteenth and early nineteenth centuries, given the extent of Spain's military commitments, by the 1830s Spain was able to bring substantial military force to bear upon Cuba. The political ambitions of Antillean planters conflicted with those of Spain's fledgling constitutional regime, which acted to consolidate the "second empire," a colonial order that would reign until the Cuban and Spanish

### TABLE 6
### Population of Cuba, 1817–1862

|      | White   | Free Colored | Slave   | Total     |
|------|---------|--------------|---------|-----------|
| 1817 | 239,830 | 114,058      | 199,145 | 553,033   |
| 1827 | 311,051 | 106,494      | 286,946 | 704,491   |
| 1846 | 425,767 | 149,226      | 323,759 | 898,752   |
| 1862 | 793,484 | 232,433      | 370,553 | 1,396,470 |

*Source:* Pérez, *Cuba: Between Reform and Revolution,* 86.

revolutions of 1868. The defining structures of that system were slavery and the slave trade, centralized, nonrepresentative rule, and protected colonial markets for Spanish producers and carriers.[10]

This chapter discusses the defeat of Cuban constitutionalism in the 1830s and analyzes responses by the Cuban elite to the Spanish clampdown. Despite the political backlash of the 1830s, Spain still found many supporters in Cuba. Some creoles, especially the major planters of sugar-rich western Cuba, adopted a pro-Spanish strategy because of their desire to maintain slavery and the slave trade. But others, especially urban professionals and landowners from less-developed regions, paradoxically turned toward Spain because of their fear of slavery and the slave trade. For them, Spanish rule was the safest alternative to revolution and race war. Rather than passively accept Spanish dominance, however, creole intellectuals like José Antonio Saco and Domingo del Monte sought to exploit fractures within Spanish political life to gain inclusion for the Cuban elite in the new constitutional regime. Although this strategy took time to pay off, creoles' engagement with oppositional factions within Spain's liberal regime ultimately brought about significant, though unexpected, transformations within the colonial order. It also stimulated major attacks on Cuban slavery in the form of the Spanish Abolitionist Society.

## Revolution and Revanche: Spain and Cuba in Conflict, 1833–1837

Fernando VII's death in 1833 set off a long-simmering civil war in Spain between supporters of continued absolutist rule and those of constitutional government that lasted until 1840.[11] Supporters of the new liberal regime saw themselves under siege from all sides, not just in the metropolis but in the colonies as well. The captain general of Puerto Rico, Miguel López de Baños, wrote that the majority of the great landowners, the clergy, and the colonial bureaucracy supported the Carlist cause. Though he claimed that separatism enjoyed little support, neither did the new liberal government.[12]

In Cuba, by contrast, Captain General Miguel Tacón, one of the so-called *ayacuchos*, fiercely anticreole Spanish officers who had participated in the Spanish American revolutions,[13] believed himself to be surrounded by separatist threats, both domestic and foreign. He reported to the secretary of state:

> The situation is critical and compromised. To convince yourself of this, consider the number of interior and exterior enemies. There is a het-

erogeneous and dangerous population. There is a propensity in many of the natives of this country to separate themselves from the metropolis, a propensity that apparently (as I have had to report on other occasions) is in their blood. Even the major landowners suffer from it. They led, with few exceptions, the uprisings in the Americas.

The external enemies include the republics that were previously ruled by Spain and the Methodists, who try to proselytize among the slaves and encourage them to rebel against their masters. . . . The former seek the emancipation of the country; the latter that of the slaves. All work against the interests of Spain.[14]

Tacón's report expressed not only the distrust of creoles and the American republics typical of the *ayacuchos,* but also the fear of slave emancipation or rebellion. This fear was strengthened by the proximate experience of slave emancipation in the British Caribbean and was shared by the creole elite he so despised. Tacón's fear of foreign abolitionists arose not only from the threat of slave rebellion, but also from the threat posed by abolitionism to the still vibrant Cuban slave trade. In the 1830s, despite two Anglo-Spanish treaties banning the trade in 1817 and 1835, 181,600 slaves were introduced into Cuba.[15] (See table 1.) Thus Tacón's evaluation of threats to Spanish sovereignty was not merely the paranoid ravings of an *ayacucho.* It also represented tacit encouragement to slavetrading interests in Cuba against the antitrade policies that some creoles, led by José Antonio Saco, sought to push through the new Spanish Cortes.

### José Antonio Saco's Opposition to Spain and the Slave Trade

In 1834 Saco was elected to represent the eastern city of Santiago de Cuba in the Estatuto Real, the limited assembly convened after the death of Ferdinando VII. Though eventually he was identified with major creole planters in western Cuba through his education in Havana, Saco (1797–1879) was born in Bayamo in eastern Cuba, a region very different from the sugar and slave-rich west. Spain found few supporters in the east, which remained unevenly developed for most of the nineteenth century; indeed, after 1868 many active opponents in the east turned to armed resistance to Spanish rule.[16] Though politically connected to Havana's planter class, Saco was something of an outsider; he owned no slaves and thus had no clear economic stake in sustaining Spanish rule and maintaining the slave trade. He did, however, vigorously defend slavery itself as a necessary evil, given his fear of race war.[17]

Saco's criticisms of the slave trade and Spanish rule in the 1820s and

José Antonio Saco (1797–1879). Cabrera,
*Cuba and the Cubans.*

1830's led to his virtually permanent exile from Cuba in 1834. His arugments antagonized not only the Spanish authorities but also slaveowners, regardless of their ethnic identity. When Saco was elected to represent the city of Santiago de Cuba in 1834, Tacón had just banished him from Cuba for defending the defunct Cuban Academy of Literature (Academia Cubana de la Literatura), a branch of Havana's Royal Patriotic Society (Real Sociedad Patriótica).[18] Indeed, by the time of his exile, Saco was already a notorious figure in colonial society, not only for his attacks on the slave trade but also for his major polemic carried on with a Spanish scientist and colonial official, Ramón de la Sagra, in which Saco bitterly denounced both Sagra's scientific credentials and Spain as a colonial overlord.[19]

For Saco, the key to Cuban liberty and the reform of Spanish colonial rule was abolition of the slave trade and "whitening" the slave population. In that strategy, he was following patrician reformers from western Cuba, such as the planter Francisco Arango y Parreño, who believed that "whitening" was the long-term solution to Cuba's political subordination and so-

cial instability.[20] Arango's 1832 report on immigration and slavery captured
this reformist tendency.[21] Arango argued that the key to Cuba's problems
lay in abolition of the slave trade, large-scale immigration by European
workers, and miscegenation among the laboring classes so as to lessen, but
not eradicate, the racial differences between Cuban workers and the elite
that threatened to tear Cuba apart. Only when miscegenation had led to the
"erasure or destruction of the preoccupation with color," Arango believed,
would Cuba be ready for major political and economic reforms, including
one day the abolition of slavery.[22]

Like Arango, Saco believed that the growth of the slave population undermined Cuban liberty. First, the increasing number of slaves threatened
to destroy Cuba by inviting rebellion or abolition, as was currently happening in the neighboring English colonies. Saco had been among the first
Cubans to speak out openly against the slave trade. In 1832 he published a
review of a new book on Brazil in the Royal Patriotic Society's *Revista
Bimestre Cubana* in which he argued that the expansion of Cuba's black
population could prove to be the island's doom. He went so far as to pose
the possibility of a war of extermination waged by the Caribbean's black
population against the region's European population, basing his claim on a
statistical study of the racial balance throughout the Caribbean.[23]

Second, Saco argued, slavery and the slave trade led to nonrepresentative rule. The Spanish government legitimated its military control in Cuba
by pointing to the threat of slave rebellion—a fear that led the slaveowning
class to compromise with the regime, thus ensuring the marginalization of
all creoles. In a prizewinning essay on vagrancy in Cuba, Saco argued for
the urgent necessity of "whitening" Cuba lest it remain subordinate to
Spanish rule because of the threat of race war. Racial boundaries had to be
erased by planned miscegenation between European laborers and free
people of color. Saco also encouraged white Cubans to throw off their
prejudice toward manual labor caused by its association with slavery and
to learn artisanal skills so that the work of Cuban society would be less
dependent upon the labor of slaves and free Cubans of color, who filled
most urban trades. European immigration was thus the key to his long-term
solution to political marginalization, for it would both "whiten" Cuba and
wean Cuban society from its dependence on slave labor.[24]

Creole reformers like Saco responded to the restoration of constitutional government by calling for political reforms and by attacking the slave
trade and its effects on Cuban society. Havana's Royal Patriotic Society
published memorials on white immigration and speculated on the viability

of using free labor for cultivating sugar cane.[25] Saco's close friend and political associate, Domingo del Monte, defended the Cuban Academy as a
necessary institution for cultivating Cuba's national genius.[26] Del Monte
also published a pamphlet in which he deplored the debasement of
Havana's aristocratic creole society by parvenu Spaniards made rich
through the slave trade.[27] Arango y Parreño drafted a plan for local government in which military and political power would be separated and creoles
would enjoy representation in the Cortes.[28]

The figurehead for that discontent with colonial slave society was Saco,
serving as an elected deputy in Madrid. Among the vicissitudes of peninsular political changes, Saco militated for the Cuban elite's inclusion in the
new constitutional regime and for abolishing the slave trade, arguing that
Cuba had suffecent slaves to work its plantations and that the importation
of slaves was bringing the island ever closer to race war.[29]

### Tacón, Lorenzo, and the Santiago Regime, 1836

The cause of creole constitutionalism embodied by Saco found both adher-
ents and opponents within the colonial administration back in Cuba,
though the opponents proved to be far more powerful. Saco had a bitter
enemy in Tacón, who sought to counter his public campaign in Madrid with
reports of the negative effects of Saco's work in Cuba. He referred to Saco
and the two other Cuban deputies in Madrid as the "Club of Disloyal Cubans" and insisted that this "club" was a threat to Spanish sovereignty in
Cuba. Tacón told Madrid that his authority, and Spanish rule, were being
undermined by the unchecked circulation of Saco's pamphlets in Cuba.
Referring to Saco's admiring description of the United States in an article
comparing Cuba to several English colonies, "Paralelo entre la isla de Cuba
y algunas colonias inglesas," Tacón bridled at the fact that such literature
could be produced in Madrid itself:

> This is the paper that the Club of Disloyal Cubans sends from the Court
> to circulate in the overseas provinces. The seditious ideas that it devel-
> ops, and the subversive allusions it contains can have no other object
> than to incite rebellion in this country and separate it from Spain. And
> this is written in the very Court! This is published shamelessly and
> circulated through these dominions. My complete vigilance is incapable
> of stopping its introduction, and the author has not the least difficulty
> in flaunting his crime and in insulting the government of H. M.!!! *[sic]* I
> despair at seeing such pernicious impunity. I see with deep pain that my
> position is surrounded every day with new embarrassments.[30]

The most threatening "embarrassment" surrounding Tacón was the constitutional regime declared in Santiago de Cuba (the city that elected Saco) by the Spanish governor of Oriente Province, General Manuel Lorenzo, in 1836.[31] Lorenzo arrived in Santiago in 1835. In August 1836, Spain's so-called Sergeants' Revolt, a palace revolt at the royal family's summer retreat in Aranjuez, had forced the queen regent, María Cristina, to proclaim Spain's 1812 constitution, replacing the far more restrictive assembly, the Estatuto Real, with a broader franchise and a more powerful legislature. The first notice of the new constitution arrived in Cuba through Santiago. Without waiting for orders from Madrid or from Tacón in Havana, Lorenzo declared the constitution in force in Santiago and called municipal and regional elections for the first time in fifteen years. In the new elections for the Cortes, Saco was returned by an overwhelming majority.[32] For Lorenzo, Oriente's self-government under the 1812 constitution would serve as an example for the rest of the island: "CUBANS: the sun has risen in the eastern provinces of the island of Cuba, and all of its inhabitants turn their gazes to watch it rise, radiant, tranquil, and majestic. A few more days, and its vibrant splendor will disperse the dark and gloomy clouds of the West."[33]

Lorenzo's optimism, however, clashed with the complex interests at play in western Cuba and Spain in the 1830s. First, an *ayacucho* like Tacón, who had already revealed his antagonism toward creole patriotism by exiling Saco, Santiago's representative in Madrid, was unlikely to support colonial constitutionalism. Second, the Santiago regime clearly represented interests antagonistic to the slave trade, as Saco was campaigning against it in the Peninsula. Such a position was hostile to the increasingly powerful Spanish slave traders of Havana and Matanzas—as well as to planters, Spanish and creole alike, who depended on the trade as a source of labor.[34] Finally, the major slaveowners of the western provinces viewed a liberal regime with some trepidation, especially at a time when the neighboring British colonies were freeing their slaves. For instance, in a government report on the decline of Santiago's economy written in 1849, the official Ramón Arango traced the origins of the crisis back to 1836: "The lamentable events of 1836 in this department are, in my opinion, the beginning of our decadence. That occurrence alarmed everyone and caused a flight of capital estimated at 2 million pesos."[35]

The supporters of the Santiago regime tried to address these fears. Saco's arguments in Madrid about the advantages of abolishing the slave trade and the compatibility of slavery and political liberty were part of such an effort. On the ground in Cuba, municipal governments swore to the tranquility they enjoyed under the new constitution. The municipal government of Santiago stated that public order and commerce, "the happiness of well-organized peoples," continued, especially "under the command of the worthy general Don Manuel Lorenzo, who with untiring zeal has demonstrated his loyalty, his patriotism, and his determined interest in the prosperity of this territory."[36] Baracoa's municipal government similarly testified to the political and commercial tranquility of the province. However, it also requested reinforcements for its garrison, not because of any political disorders, which it averred did not exist, but because of the constant threat posed by *palenques*, communities of escaped slaves, and by Haiti, eastern Cuba's close neighbor.[37]

### Slavery, Liberty, and Race: Madrid, 1836–1837

The Baracoa government's concern over slave resistance and the racial balance of power in the Caribbean resonated both in Cuba's western provinces and in the Peninsula. The eastern experiment in constitutionalism was intolerable to Tacón and the main sugar planters of western Cuba. They believed that only a unified political authority could contain the dangers posed by Cuba's own slave population and the growing free black population of neighboring islands. Tacón quickly mounted a military expedition to supress Lorenzo's regime. He also continued to send reports to the Peninsula that forecast the loss of Cuba if all political dissent in the island were not quelled. According to Tacón, constitutionalism could only lead to disaster.[38]

Tacón's warnings were heeded. The new government acted to protect its most valuable colony from the perceived threat of separatism. A special committee was formed in the constituent assembly to discuss the status of the colonies under the new regime. In discussing the particular case of Cuba, the commission pointed to the problems raised by the heterogeneity of the island's population. The 1812 constitution contained measures to ensure the numerical hegemony of Spanish deputies over American deputies in the Cortes, a concern that was obsolete after the 1820s. One of those measures excluded from electoral censuses all males who were not of proven Spanish lineage on both sides of the family. Thus in Cuba and Puerto Rico, slaves and free people of color not only were not elegible to vote or to stand for office, but technically they were not *represented* either. The Spanish commissioners found this fact problematic in two ways: first, this exclusion from political representation could breed resentment among the population of color, which given the balance of Cuba's population had to be avoided.[39] Second, remedying the situation required special laws that took into account the specific intricacies of racial difference in Cuba: "It is urgently necessary to decide how all of the Spaniards of different colors will represent and be represented."[40] Until that decision was reached, the captain general should be given absolute authority to govern, for political liberty in a slave society posed too many dangers. The Cortes as a whole agreed with the commission's recommendations and voted 128 to 12 to exclude the colonial deputies.[41]

While the actions of the commissioners and the Cortes were decisive, their language was ambiguous. By pondering the political and civil rights of all "Spaniards" regardless of color, the Spanish commissioners raised the possibility that Spanish liberalism would extend citizenship to people of color—a major change from the exclusionary policies of the Cortes of Cádiz. Though in the immediate context of the 1830s Spanish liberals might only have been paying lip service to the question of race and citizenship, their words foreshadowed the strategies articulated by subsequent generations of Spanish and Antillean liberals in the battles over slavery.[42]

The Cuban deputies to the Cortes were less ambiguous regarding both the commission's recommendations and the relationship between slavery and political liberty. Saco and his fellow Cuban deputies, Fransisco de Armas and Juan Montalvo y Castillo, immediately challenged the commission's report in a protest to the Cortes on February 21, 1837, and in a public objection published in the Madrid newspaper *El Mundo* the following day. They argued that Cuba—as well as Puerto Rico and the Philippines—did indeed require special laws, but that only delegates already elected from those provinces were suited to draft them.[43]

Saco expanded on those protests by arguing that liberty and slavery were indeed reconcilable, as had the municipal governments of Oriente Province, and that their coexistence did not lead inevitably to race war. Saco stated that Cuba deserved representation based on its entire population, which did not preclude the exclusion of the black population from active citizenship. Breaking strategically from his usual emphasis on the threat of race war, which would have played into Spanish hands, Saco claimed that there was little to fear from the population of color claiming political and civil rights because slavery had instilled in them a notion of inferiority. Indeed, even free people of color would gladly accept being banned from voting and holding office if they "have the satisfaction of knowing that they are not excluded from the electoral census."[44]

To dispel the fear of race war, Saco held that newly arrived Africans were usually sent to the sugar plantations and they spoke such a variety of languages that they could not form a cohesive group with shared interests;

thus they were easily dominated. Moreover, Cuba's white population was proportionally much greater than that of other slave societies, like the U.S. South and the British West Indies, which enjoyed considerable political liberty without disaster. The example of the Haitian revolution, invoked by the Spanish representative Vicente Sancho to demonstrate the danger of allowing political liberties in a slave society, was misguided. St. Domingue, unlike Cuba, had an uneven black/white ratio, and the revolution was triggered by meddling French radicals who had formed Les Amis des Noirs to abolish colonial slavery. No such group existed in Spain. In short, there was no reason to "enslave" all Cubans because of the large slave population in Cuba. Slavery and liberty had always existed together: "There were slaves in famed Athens, but treated gently they never disturbed the republic's peace."[45]

Saco's protest went unheeded. Ironically, one of the conditions he had cited as favorable to the exercise of colonial constitutionalism, the absence of a metropolitan abolitionist association, was symptomatic of the political conditions that made Saco's protest against powerful metropolitan and colonial interests so feeble. Despite Tacón's repeated warnings about the "Club of Disloyal Cubans," the truth was that Saco and other colonial deputies had no recourse to autonomous political resources so as to challenge the Cortes's decision. Though isolated members of the new liberal regime believed that the colonies could be most effectively ruled by including the creole elite in the constitutional pact, most sought to assert Spanish control by concentrating power in the hands of the captain general as part of the broader effort to consolidate the centralized liberal state. For the time being, the Antillean elite was excluded from the political pact of the new liberal regime.[46]

As Tacón had suppressed the Santiago regime in Cuba, so too the Spanish deputies voted to delay colonial constitutional government indefinitely. Powerful interests and forces shaped these decisions: military revanchism, peninsular economic interests, civil war in Spain, slave rebellion and emancipation in the Caribbean. Added to the constitution of 1837—and to that of 1845—was an amendment saying that the overseas provinces were to be ruled by special laws to be determined at a later time. For the rest of the nineteenth century, Cubans and Spaniards would struggle over the nature of colonial government.[47]

## Annexationism or Loyalty?

Saco concluded a pamphlet on colonialism in the Atlantic world by arguing that Cuba would realize its potential wealth by becoming part of the United

States.[48] The peace and prosperity of the U.S. South proved that liberty and slavery could flourish together. Many creoles agreed with him, and in response to Spain's consolidation of nonrepresentative rule and the slave trade they sought Cuba's incorporation into the United States. In 1849, the creole slaveowner José Luis Alfonso described to Saco, in exile, the overt expressions of resistance to Spanish rule as annexationist sentiment grew in Cuba: "Matanzas has given clear proof of its hostility. The Philarmonic Society held a dance in honor of the queen's saint's day. Only two ladies and the society's dance commission attended, while outside, the Plaza de Armas was filled with people looking at the deserted salons. Can it be any clearer?" He predicted, "If Spain does not sell us, a revolution will explode here within a year, with or without an American expedition."[49]

Writing to Saco from Havana in 1878, almost thirty years later, Alfonso looked back to the annexationist movements of the 1840s and 1850s as a missed opportunity to settle the fate of Cuban slavery peacefully. By 1878, Cuba had lived through ten years of war and slave emancipation in the eastern provinces, and eight years of gradual slave emancipation throughout the island.[50] The end of slavery, the means by which it would be achieved, and the reorganization and supply of labor were still uncertain.[51] According to Alfonso, bloodshed, chaos, and uncertainty could have been avoided had a plan he drafted in 1851 concerning Cuban slavery and political sovereignty been accepted by the governments of Britain, France, and Spain. Dismayed by the capture and execution of the annexationist leader Narciso López in 1851, Alfonso (then in Washington, D.C.) sought other means by which creoles could carry out the social and political goals of the annexationist movement. He submitted a plan to the British diplomat Joseph Bulwer that he believed would assure Cuba's tranquility and prosperity. In his words:

> Following Bulwer's advice, I wrote up a brief plan entitled *Une solution a toutes les questions de Cuba.* I proposed to the three governments [Britain, France, and Spain] that they sign a treaty by which England and France guaranteed to Spain the tranquil possession of the island of Cuba *until the last day of the century.* They would also prevent any foreign invasion as well as any internal rebellion by whites or by blacks. Spain, for its part, would give the Island, within a year's time, a political constitution *in its spirit* similar to those of the English colonies. It would also decree slavery abolished on the last day of the century in all of the Spanish dominions without indemnity for the slaveowners.

> What degree of prosperity would the Island have attained in those
> 50 years of work and perfect security?[52]

Alfonso conceived his plan immediately after the defeat of Cuban
creoles' best hope for separation from Spain in the forties and fifties: the
annexationist movement led by Narciso López. In the years preceding 1851,
annexationist sentiment had run high among the creole elite. The Venezu-
ela-born Spanish general Narciso López became the figurehead for the
movement, launching two failed military expeditions in 1850 and 1851.[53]
Even after López's capture and execution, the annexationist machinery was
kept in motion, fed by southern American enthusiasm for the endeavor
(John Quitman, former governor of Mississippi, replaced López as the
movement's military leader) and by further Cuban fears of abolition caused
by Britain's pressure on Spain to abolish the slave trade and to free all
slaves introduced after the 1817 treaty. The return of José Gutíerrez de la
Concha—López's captor and executioner—to Cuba as captain general in
1854 quieted Cuban slaveholders' fears.[54]

Although the annexationist movement was the most dramatic political
project of the period and has received considerable scholarly attention, an
important loyalist project existed in dialogue with annexationism. Surprisingly, the most outspoken proponent of redrawing the political pact with
Spain was José Antonio Saco, one of the most virulent critics of Spanish
rule. This section focuses on Saco's political prescriptions for Cuba and
Spain. His vision of "Spanish" Cuba decisively shaped reformist attitudes
in the mid-nineteenth century and helped lay the ideological groundwork,
unwittingly, for the Spanish Abolitionist Society. Moreover, his idea of
"Spanish" Cuba demonstrates how anxiety over the racial boundaries of the
nation and the fate of colonial slavery was always present in the Spanish
and Cuban debates over representation and citizenship.

### The Politics of "Whitening" in the 1840s

Why did Saco urge loyalty to Spain? In doing so, he responded not only to
the debate initiated in the Spanish Cortes in 1836–1837, but also to the instability of Cuban slave society in the 1840s. Creating that sense of crisis
was the unpredictability of Spanish policy vis-à-vis the slave trade and slavery. During the 1840s Britain exerted intense pressure on the Spanish
government to respect the antitrade treaties signed in 1817, 1835, and 1845
and to release all slaves illegally introduced into its colonies after 1820.
While Spain never acquiesed to British demands, unlike the Brazilian gov-

ernment, which abolished the slave trade in 1850, the uncertainty of the situation led slaveowners to flirt with annexation to the United States.[55] It also led planters to begin a trade in indentured Chinese laborers, many of whom were quickly reduced to practical slavery, in case the African slave trade was abolished.[56] Once again, a liberalizing revolution in Spain, this time in 1854, had the paradoxical effect of reaffirming the metropolitan government's commitment to colonial slavery. Not only did Narciso López's nemesis, José Gutiérrez de la Concha, return as captain general, but also the foreign minister avowed in the constituent Cortes: "The Government . . . is convinced that slavery is a necessity and an indispensable condition for the maintenance of the territorial property of the island of Cuba."[57]

The question of "whitening" was another issue over which the tensions of the 1840s between Spain and Cuba were played out. For example, a general panic erupted in Spain and the Antilles in 1841 when it was rumored that Britain's pressure on the Spanish government to abolish the slave trade would lead to the abolition of slavery as well. One major fear was that the government would comply with British demands to free the 260,000 slaves introduced into Cuba after 1820.[58] In response, an official of the Royal Patriotic Society submitted a proposal for encouraging white immigration and abolishing the slave trade.[59] He defended slavery as a necessary institution for the forseeable future to preserve Cuban prosperity and tranquility, though he saw abolition of the slave trade and white immigration as methods for the gradual elimination of slavery itself:

> If at the same time we fulfill the treaties of 1817 and 1835 and adopt extraordinary means to augment the white population, if we substitute free laborers *[brazos]* for the blacks, . . . the island of Cuba's happiness will reach the highest point. For, if we halt the introduction [of slaves], slavery will slowly be extinguished. In this manner, we will reconcile our interests with the humane sentiments that distinguish us.[60]

Such proposals generally met with official disapproval, for several reasons. First, many Spanish officials, especially the *ayacuchos,* distrusted the intent of the creoles' racial arithmetic, seeing it as an expression of separatist tendencies. Second, merchants and slaveowners still had a tremendous interest in the survival of the slave trade. Finally, some officials were concerned with the question of public order and immigration.[61] For instance, in 1841, the captain general of Cuba, Gerónimo Valdés, an *ayacucho,*[62] denounced to the metropolitan government a project for white immigration made by Havana's Junta de Fomento. He objected particularly to the proposal to allow freedom of religion in Cuba as a means of attracting European immigrants. Valdés recommended to Madrid that he and his succesors as captain general be appointed head of the Junta so as to monitor more closely such potentially reckless plans.[63]

The conflict over the slave trade and white immigration was fought not just within official institutions but within informal political spheres as well. In a series of letters to Saco written from Havana, Alfonso warned that it was too dangerous for Saco to return to Cuba and that his only chance of returning depended on his remaining silent on the question of the slave trade. Spaniards hurled the charge of abolitionism at all creoles who opposed the slave trade. Alfonso claimed that he, Domingo del Monte, and Miguel de Aldama (all brothers-in-law) and their families were particular targets of Spanish wrath—first because of the ostentatious palace that the family patriarch, Domingo de Aldama, was constructing in Havana,[64] second, because of the Aldama clan's success in winning railroad concessions,[65] and finally, because of their refusal to buy *bozales*, slaves brought from Africa through the illegal trade.[66]

Another manifestation of hostility between Cuban creoles and Spaniards was the conflict over the membership of David Turnbull in the Royal Patriotic Society. Turnbull, an abolitionist, was the British consul in Havana in the early 1840s. Some creole members supported his membership, while Spaniards fiercely resisted it.[67]

David Turnbull was also at the heart of the most violent conflict in mid-nineteenth-century Cuba: the Escalera conspiracy, a complex and conflicting series of initiatives advanced by elite creoles, free people of color, slaves, and British abolitionists that exploded into massive repression by the colonial state against all who opposed the slave trade and Spanish rule.[68] In 1842, Turnbull and his assistant Francis Ross Cocking had helped to organize an alliance of creole patriots such as Domingo del Monte and free people of color and slaves to fight for Cuba's political independence under British protection and for abolishing slavery and the slave trade. The clearly divergent interests of the unstable coalition soon led creoles like del Monte to withdraw his support and to reveal the conspiracy to a North American diplomat, Alexander Everett—a move that eventually alerted the Spanish government to the conspiracy or conspiracies.[69] When slave rebellions broke out in Matanzas in December 1843, Captain General Leopoldo O'Donnell carried out a vicious persecution of suspected conspirators. Thousands of slaves and free people of color were tortured, executed, and exiled, and elite creoles implicated in the original conspiracy were banished from Cuba.[70]

La Escalera convinced many creoles that they could expect only a con-

tinuation of repression and the slave trade; however, they also believed that
Cuba was unprepared for political independence because of its large and
volatile slave population. A strong state was needed to preserve public order and production, and many creoles believed that annexation to the
United States would offer peace and prosperity.[71]

Some scholars treat annexationism as an important phase in the development of Cuban nationalism, especially among the Cuban elite, seeing it
as a partial affirmation of Cuba's separate identity.[72] However, creole political identities and interests in the mid-nineteenth century were volatile and
uncertain. On the one hand, even the most ardent Cuban patriots and
champions of "whitening," such as the annexationist Gaspar Betancourt
Cisneros, expressed doubt about their own claim to whiteness. For instance,
in a letter to his friend Saco, Betancourt Cisneros exclaimed:

> What origins! . . . do not tell me that you desire that *nationality* for your
> country! No! Give me Turks, Arabs, Russians. Give me Demons, any-
> thing but the product of Spaniards, Congos, Mandingas and now (though
> luckily the plan has been frustrated) Malays to complete the mosaic of
> population, ideas, customs, institutions, habits, and sentiments of de-
> generate, enslaved men who sing and laugh to the sound of chains, who
> tolerate their own degradation and vilely prostrate themselves before
> their masters.[73]

Like Saco, Betancourt Cisneros was a creole from a relatively underdeveloped region, Puerto Príncipe, that was marginalized by the sugar complex of the western regions and the conditions of Spanish rule. He believed
that allegiance to Spain promised nothing but a continued threat of race
war and the gradual undermining of creole whiteness. For annexationists
like Betancourt Cisneros, attachment to the United States was the best
guard against race war and the anxiety caused by fear of racial mixing. As
one critic of Saco put it, the United States would shield Cuba "from Spain,
and England, Europe, negro-traders, or abolitionists—in a word, from enemies within and without."[74]

On the other hand, Spain remained a crucial pole of identity and a locus of political and economic interests for many creoles, especially within
the slaveowning class. Carlos Drake y del Castillo, the count of Vega-Mar, is
illustrative. Vega-Mar was from a Havana slaveowning family that had risen
to prominence in the late eighteenth and early nineteenth centuries.[75]
Though members of this class had lost some political and economic privileges in the 1830s, their ties to Spain were still complex. In a pamphlet writ-

ten for the Spanish government in 1868 on the question of political and social reforms, Vega-Mar introduced himself in the following manner:

> Born in Havana of one of the oldest families in the country, I am the owner of an *ingenio* with nearly 400 slaves. For the last twenty-three years, I have been the permanent deputy in this court for Havana's municipal government, as well as its proxy. Married in Spain, with children, and resident in Madrid, I own several urban and rural properties of some consideration in various parts of the Peninsula. I raise various crops in the province of Guadalajara, and I direct my vast flour factory in Aranjuez, as well as a salt factory in Salinas del Trocadero in Cádiz. Thus, I am a taxpayer of no small consideration in Cuba and in the Peninsula, a Cuban by origin and peninsular by interests and familial bonds.[76]

Vega-Mar no doubt accentuated his ties to Spain in this instance, given his intended audience, the Spanish government. Whether he believed himself to be more Cuban or Spanish is not the point; rather, Vega-Mar illustrates the viability of Spain as an imperial power in the nineteenth century, ideologically, politically, and economically. Spain did more than protect slavery and property in the Caribbean. As Angel Bahamonde and José Cayuela demonstrate, Cuban planters received titles of nobility from the Spanish Crown throughout the nineteenth century, and many invested heavily in peninsular properties and ventures.[77] Moreover, Spain was a central political and ideological resource; even at the height of annexationism, some creoles chose to emphasize Cuba's Spanish origins in part to further their hopes for reforms initiated within the metropolis. Saco, with the help of del Monte, was the most eloquent spokesman for that political and ideological project, one that reflected not only Spanish colonial hegemony but also the complexity of creole identities and interests.

In dialogue with the annexationists in the 1840s and 1850s, Saco insisted that Spain offered the best protection against race war and that it was more efficacious to fight for inclusion in the constitutional pact than to seek separation.[78] Armed intervention from the United States might trigger the very revolution the annexationists hoped to prevent, while incorporation into the United States would lead to Cuba's loss of identity.[79] Spain, he argued, was at a political conjuncture that boded well for the Cubans. Liberty was the spirit of the age, and it had finally triumphed in Spain after years of revolution and civil war. With constitutional government safely consolidated after the end of the civil war in 1840, Cuban reformists could work in cooperation with both the Moderate (Moderado) government and the opposition Progressive (Progresista) Party, the natural allies of Cuban liberalism on an ideological level (though they were the party that expelled the colonial deputies from the Cortes in 1837):

> The opposition party in the Cortes would seize upon our just cause; the despotism that oppresses us would make a terrible weapon against the government. Despite initial resistance, the government would succumb to the combined blows of the opinions of Cuba and the peninsular opposition. . . . If one or more wealthy, educated and important persons came to Madrid to denounce . . . the disorders of the current political and administrative system that rules [Cuba] before the government and the metropolis's public opinion I am sure that he would meet with great success.[80]

### Saco and Del Monte: Creating the Reformist Alternative

Saco certainly practiced what he preached. During and after this period of the annexationist debate, he and Domingo del Monte (until the latter's sudden death in 1853)—both in exile, Saco for his criticism of the slave trade, del Monte for his suspected involvement in the conspiracy of La Escalera—engaged in public polemics in Spain over the nature of Spanish rule in Cuba, and both sought to influence government officials through private meetings and discussions. Through these efforts, Saco and del Monte established the model of reformist political action that elite creoles turned to in the late 1850s and 1860s after the collapse of annexationism as an alternative.

Del Monte said of the annexationists: "What they will achieve is not annexation, nor liberty, . . . but persecution, firing squads, prisons, and disgrace and ten more years of a state of siege and special laws."[81] Like Saco, he favored working through the Spanish state. Del Monte was a pivotal figure in Cuban political and intellectual life from the early to mid-nineteenth century. His Havana salon was one of the centers of creole patriotism in the 1830s, and he had been the driving force behind the short-lived Cuban Academy. Del Monte's salon captured some of the ambiguities of Cuban reformism during this period. Not only had it hosted white writers like Saco and the poet José Heredia, but also the former slaves and poets Plácido (later executed for his alleged involvement in La Escalera) and Juan Francisco Manzano (imprisoned during the repression of La Escalera and freed by the intervention of the del Monte group). Though a patron of former slaves and implicitly a critic of slavery, del Monte was nonetheless connected by marriage and patronage to two of the most prominent slaveholding families in Cuba: the powerful Aldama and Alfonso families, important creole planters. In other words, although a friend and patron to individual slaves or free people of color, he firmly defended the interests of slaveowners and feared Cuban slaves and free people of color in general.[82]

Del Monte's link to patriotic circles and former slaves made him sympathetic to reformists and a figure distrusted by Spanish officials and slave traders in Cuba; however, his relationship to powerful slaveowners gave him access to metropolitan officials whom he privately lobbied for the Cuban elite's inclusion in the constitutional regime. A letter from del Monte to Saco in 1850 gives some sense of his modus operandi:

> I had an interview with Minister Sartorius [the Moderate interior minister]. Pepe Mora, the editor of *El Heraldo,* a deputy and chief of the Havana desk in the Ministry of Interior, set it up for me. [Sartorius] gave me a warm reception. I told him that I wanted to dispel the calumnies made by the slave traders and their friends against me. I told him that I was and always have been a man of order, that I have never conspired against the government and that I was tired of being called *rebellious* when to the contrary I wanted to take an active part in the management of public affairs *[la cosa pública]* in Spain and as a Spaniard, etc.[83]

Saco, in contrast, worked in the limited colonial public sphere that existed in Madrid in the forties and fifties. Though he advocated reform within Spain rather than annexation to the United States, his public polemics carried on with Spaniards reflected his essential agreement with the annexationists concerning Spanish misrule and the dangers posed by the slave population. In his Spanish debates, he insisted on the need for white immigration to Cuba, suppression of the slave trade, and political liberty for creoles.

Saco's debate with the Spanish colonial official Vicente Vázquez Queipo is an example.[84] As was often the case in the debates between creole reformers and the colonial state, Saco demanded abolishing the slave trade and encouraging white immigration as urgently needed reforms, while Vázquez Queipo argued that Cuba's wealth indicated the benefits of Spanish rule. For instance, replying to Vázquez Queipo's negative report on European immigration, Saco insisted: "I want families and single colonists; I want artisans, merchants, writers and scholars: in a word, I want all kinds of people as long as they have white faces and know how to work honorably."[85] Vázquez Queipo consistently denounced Saco as a racist and a subversive.[86]

The Saco–Vázquez Queipo debate attracted attention in Madrid. Saco's arguments, however, still bristled with the anti-Spanish sentiment that had characterized his works of the 1820s and 1830s. His antiannexationist pamphlets, in contrast, while still critical of Spanish rule, struck a more moderate chord. Saco aimed the latter not only at Cuban annexationists and slaveowners, but also at metropolitan politicians and colonial officials. To solicit that public more effectively, del Monte coached and edited Saco's work, tailoring his writings to suit peninsular sensibilities. His main advice was to downplay the differences between Spaniards and Cubans. In a letter from del Monte to Saco written in 1851, he commented on the revisions he made to one of Saco's works:

> My dear Saquete: I have received your paper. It looks good to me, though I have made two corrections to the original because they sounded bad: "and though both ills are very grave, they fortunately have a simple remedy that the *Spanish* government can apply, etc." I have erased *Spanish*, as I have done before in your other writings, because they give you the air of a *foreigner* or *rebel.* "Under attack, . . . the Spanish fleet would have to seek refuge (that is, *flee*) in the island's ports or be *battered* by superior forces." I have erased these two sentences because they would mortify the national pride. In their place, I have written the generalization: "We would have to fight at a disadvantage against naval forces double or triple the size of ours."[87]

Thus, one part of del Monte's and Saco's antiannexationist and reformist strategy was to emphasize Cuba's "Spanishness," a tactic used by reformers in the 1860s once the U.S. Civil War had put an end to annexationism and forced the Spanish government to take serious action on the colonial question.

Despite his appeal to a Spanish public under del Monte's guidance, Saco's reformist arguments more or less revived the debates of 1836–1837, provoking the same responses from Spanish commentators as they had in the 1830s: Cuba's heterogeneous population made the introduction of political liberty too perilous; Cuba was wealthy and prosperous under the current administration; and constitutional reforms for the colony would lead to annexation.[88]

There was, however, increasing interest in the colonial question in Spain in the 1850s. The Moderate president Juan Bravo Murillo created an Overseas Council, the Consejo de Ultramar, in an attempt to coordinate the colonial administration, which was scattered among various ministries. (The Overseas Ministry was finally created in 1863 during a period of intensive state-sponsored reformism, a response to the crisis set off by the American

Civil War.) Periodicals dedicated to the colonies made brief appearances in this period—*Revista de España y sus provincias de Ultramar* (1850–1851), *Revista española de ambos mundos* (1853–1855), modeled on the French *Revue des deux mondes,* and the more consequential *La Crónica* (1853–1877), sponsored by the Spanish government and published in New York, and eventually the influential *La América* (1857–1886)—while major dailies carried some news and debate as well. Saco and del Monte thus maneuvered within that small opening as well as they could: del Monte pursuing government officials in Madrid, Saco publishing pamphlets and responding to the Spanish press from France.[89]

In contrast to the 1830s, by the mid-1850s Cubans had gained some listeners who, if their actions were largely ineffectual, would later have a decisive impact on the colonial question. The revolution of 1854 brought the Progressive Party back to power in Spain after ten years of increasingly repressive Moderate rule. The Progressive colonial policy at that moment consisted of appeasing the Cuban slaveholders who had been thrown into a panic by rumors of abolition, sale to the United States, and the annexationist adventures.[90]

On the other hand, advocates of liberal reforms in the colonies made their appearance in Spain. José María Orense, marquis of Albaida, one of the founders of the Democratic Party, proposed in the constituent assembly a plan for the abolition of slavery to check the annexationist plotting in the U.S. South: "Although it will not obtain a majority, like all ideas it will spread little by little; . . . the manner in which to save ourselves from American preponderance is to declare the abolition of slavery in our Antilles."[91] Salustiano Olózaga, a leader of the Progressive Party and a member of the committee that had voted to expel the colonial deputies in 1837, disagreed with Orense's proposal for abolition, but now he recanted his decision of the 1830s by arguing that the time had come to include creoles in the constitutional pact: "We must attract the will of the islanders *[isleños],* . . . allowing their enlightened men some participation in their own administration."[92] Even Ramón de la Sagra, a staunch supporter of Tacón in the 1830s, voiced support for some of the reforms long sought by Saco and Arango, though he argued that they should be put off until thorough data had been collected for the proper study of the question.[93]

Orense and Olózaga were both future presidents of the Abolitionist Society, and their political parties would play major roles in colonial politics in the 1860s and 1870s. For the present, their proposals went unheeded, but Saco's reformist plan to form alliances with peninsular liberalism, first established in this period, would eventually lead to profound challenges to the Spanish colonial system. The ideological linchpin of that alliance would be the vision of a "Spanish" Cuba—a vision defended by Saco throughout the 1840s and 1850s against the annexationists and revived by the next generation of Cuban reformers. But Saco's loyalist option did not merely address the question of Cuba's inclusion in the Spanish liberal regime. For Saco, as for the annexationists, the question of representation and political rights was inextricably linked to the fate of Cuban slavery and the fear of race war.

# 2

# "Cuestión de brazos"

## THE RISE OF PUERTO RICAN
## ANTISLAVERY, 1840–1860

For the first four decades of the nineteenth century, critics of slavery and the slave trade among the Cuban and Puerto Rican elite converged in demanding abolition of the trade and advocating white immigration and miscegenation. In short, they shared a commitment to "whitening" as the solution to the social instability and political marginalization of the two colonies.[1]

Distinct social, political, and economic conditions by midcentury, however, produced divergent attitudes toward slavery. Puerto Rico rose to prominence as a sugar producer somewhat later than Cuba. While sugar cultivation and slavery were firmly entrenched in Cuba by the late eighteenth century, sugar and slavery did not become major features of Puerto Rican economic life until the early nineteenth century. Puerto Rican planters responded primarily to increased demand in the North American market, whereas Cuba also found important markets in Europe. While Cuba continued to import slaves until the trade was abolished in 1867, and supplemented them with Chinese indentured laborers between 1847 and 1874, in Puerto Rico the slave trade came to an effective end in the 1840s, while the total population of the island continued to grow. (See table 7.) By the mid-nineteenth century, slaves in Puerto Rico formed a much lower percentage of the population than in Cuba.[2] Moreover, with the end of the trade in the 1840s, the question of alternative forms of labor became a live topic. As Seymour Drescher observes, ending the slave trade to a particular slave society generally (with the obvious exception of the United States) in the long run brought the abolition of slavery itself.[3]

TABLE 7
Population of Puerto Rico, 1820–1860

| | White | Free Colored | Slave | Total |
|---|---|---|---|---|
| 1820 | 102,432 | 106,460 | 21,730 | 211,622 |
| 1834 | 190,619 | 126,399 | 41,818 | 358,836 |
| 1846 | 216,083 | 175,791 | 51,265 | 443,139 |
| 1860 | 300,430 | 241,015 | 41,736 | 583,308 |

*Sources:* Bergad, *Coffee,* 69; and Kinsbruner, *Not of Pure Blood,* 29.

To say, however, that the end of the trade to Puerto Rico automatically spelled the end of slavery is to treat the question with too much benefit of hindsight. I agree with Francisco Scarano's judgment that in Puerto Rico a "*smooth* transition to free labor did not occur."[4] While a major explanation for the abolition of Puerto Rican slavery holds that the institution was never central to the island's economy, recent studies have found the opposite.[5] Even if the slave population stagnated and diminished as a percentage of the total population of Puerto Rico, coerced labor still remained central to plantation labor until its abolition. Between 1850 and the abolition of slavery in 1873, Puerto Rican sugar planters clamored for measures that included revival of the slave trade, introduction of African and Asian indentured laborers, and coercion of the free agrarian population. Even after the abolition of slavery, planters still demanded that the colonial state greatly restrict the freedom of laborers so as to force them into plantation labor.[6]

Even though slave labor continued to be essential to sugar production, some Puerto Rican planters came to see abolition with indemnity as a possible solution to the stagnation of the sugar sector, although their commitment to abolition was tenuous.[7] A group of creole intellectuals sought to exploit that breach within the planter class by arguing that Puerto Rico was ready to abolish slavery and other forms of bonded labor and to make the transition to free labor. They believed that racial difference had been sufficently overcome in Puerto Rico and that the land-to-labor ratio now favored the formation of a free-labor market. As I will show, although Puerto Rican abolitionism was steadfastly reformist, it nonetheless posited and eventually brought about a profound shift in the colonial status quo. Indeed, the origins of the Abolitionist Society lay not so much in Spain, nor in the Caribbean's major slave society, Cuba, but in Puerto Rico.

Before beginning this evaluation of Puerto Rican antislavery activists, I should note that while I often make comparisons with Cuba, my framework is not strictly comparative. Rather, one must understand the rise and fall of Antillean slavery as happening within an imperial and an Atlantic context.

The unit of analysis is the imperial system as it existed in relation both to local factors and to the broader Atlantic world. In other words, changes in Puerto Rican slavery and politics, which shaped and responded to both endogenous and exogenous forces, were crucial not just for Puerto Rico, but for the empire as a whole.[8]

## "A Healthy Terror": Resistance, Repression, and Labor in the First Half of the Nineteenth Century

In 1849, the captain general of Puerto Rico, Juan de la Pezuela (the count of Cheste), established the Special Regulation for Day Laborers (Reglamento Especial de Jornaleros), which required all landless laborers and smallholders to enter into contracts with employers. All "free" workers had to carry a workbook (libreta) that demonstrated that they were gainfully employed.[9] The regulation also called for a yearly lottery to reward "worthy" workers. In each district, the local government chose approximately one hundred candidates to enter the competition. On a particular day, local political officials, hacendados, and the chosen laborers gathered to pick one name out of an urn. The prize was fifty pesos.[10]

Several weeks after the winner was chosen, dignitaries and laborers gathered again for the giving of the prize. Part of the ritual was an "exhortation" by a local official to the winner and the other workers, reminding them of the importance of hard work and respect for property and government. The exhortation was delivered in the familiar tú and vosotros (rather than the formal usted and ustedes), a further reminder that this ceremony was not only a reward for hard work, but also a spectacle of domination and subordination:

> This is the prize that the Government grants to the laboring class to stimulate work and respectability. This is the prize with which fortune has graced you. Receive it in the name of her Sacred Majesty the Queen . . . and of his Excellency the Governor and Captain General who thus reward your laboriousness and good habits. Make yourself deserving of this grace. Continue to hold a sound attitude and try to rise even further through hard work and impeccable conduct. And workers, all of you, see how the authorities [la superioridad] reward the efforts of the honorable man, observe that it knows how to compensate merit in your class, and that with its paternal vigilance procures your well-being. Never forget that work is the source of public wealth and of a people's greatness and fame.
>
> Long live her Sacred Majesty! Long live the Captain General![11]

The workbook and the accompanying ritual ceremony celebrating hierarchy and hard work captured the problem of labor in Puerto Rico in the mid-ninteenth century. Whereas in Cuba *hacendados* disposed of enough capital to keep the slave trade booming until its final abolition in 1867, in Puerto Rico, *hacendados* had to rely on government coercion of the "free" population to recruit labor.[12]

The death of the slave trade and the greater reliance on intermediary forms of forced labor in the 1840s and 1850s occasioned debates within Puerto Rican society over slavery and free labor. While *hacendados*, especially in Ponce, the island's most important sugar region, clamored for more slaves, indentured laborers, or tighter enforcement of the *libreta* system,[13] a group of creole intellectuals and professionals in San Juan sought to convince them that Puerto Rico was ready for the abolition of slavery and the *libreta* system and prepared for the transition to free labor. What forces led to the rise of antislavery sentiment in Puerto Rico?

The consolidation of the second slavery and the second empire in the Antilles during a time of increasing attacks on slavery in the Atlantic world provoked resistance and anxieties in Puerto Rico similar to those in Cuba. For instance, in 1838, two soldiers from the regiment of Granada stationed in San Juan informed the administration of a separatist plot spearheaded by creole military officers. The creoles implicated in the aborted uprising were prominent figures in Puerto Rican intellectual and political life during the first third of the nineteenth century. Andrés Vizcarrondo was an active member of the local Royal Economic Society (Real Sociedad Económica) and José San Just was the Puerto Rican representative to the Cortes when the exclusion of the colonial deputies was voted in 1837. The captain general imprisoned seventeen soldiers, sergeants, and corporals, as well as leaders such as Buenaventura Quiñones, San Just, and Lorenzo Vizcarrondo. The captain general reported to Madrid that suppression of colonial constitutionalism and special taxes levied to fund the civil war in Spain were at the root of the planned uprising.[14]

Moreover, fear over slave rebellion and abolitionism had as long a history in Puerto Rico as it did in Cuba.[15] For instance, during the Cortes of Cádiz (1810–1814), the mayor of San Juan, Pedro de Yrizzary, recommended to Ramón Power y Giralt, the Puerto Rican representative, that Puerto Rico should resist becoming dependent upon slave labor because African slaves were "inhuman by nature" and implacable enemies of any colony's white population. Hence, increasing the island's African population would be suicidal on the part of the creole elite: "They are few for now, people will say. There is nothing to fear. But introducing more and more every day . . . will they not come to form a multitude, which if not now, will one day be an exterminating thunderbolt?" Furthermore, Yrizarry predicted that Puerto Rico's slave population would not struggle against its masters alone, but with the aid of Haiti's trained and seasoned revolutionaries.[16]

Fear of Haiti and pan-Caribbean race war persisted. In 1841, the captain general reported to Madrid that an agent provocateur from Haiti had entered Puerto Rico to stir up a slave rebellion.[17] Creoles denounced British abolitionism as a hypocritical plot to ruin the colonies of other European nations.[18] The most notorious example of this anxiety was the ban issued by Captain General Juan Prim y Prats (the count of Reus) in reaction to unrest in Martinique following emancipation of the slaves in the French colonies in 1848.[19] The ban called for the brutal punishment of any person of color, free or slave, charged with a crime, particularly against a white person. Prim reported to Madrid that his intention "was not to oppress individuals of the African race, nor to bother them in the least as long as they remain submissive and obedient, but to impress upon them a healthy terror."[20] When the unrest in Martinique spread to the Danish colony of St. Croix, however, he argued that Madrid should declare Puerto Rico to be in a permanent state of war so as to protect it against the menace of free blacks in the surrounding colonies:

> Allow me to repeat what on other occasions I have reported to your excellency concerning the situation in which a series of circumstances have placed this island. At present, one may consider [Puerto Rico] blockaded by the African race, which is dominant in Santo Domingo, Venezuela, the French and lately the Danish Antilles. Puerto Rico should be considered in a permanent state of war, the same as Ceuta, Melilla, or any other town on the frontier with barbarians.[21]

The creole elite and colonial administrators in Cuba and Puerto Rico shared a similar resistance to Spanish military rule and anxiety over slavery. Yet the two islands experienced very different patterns of population growth and economic change between 1840 and 1860, differences that in part led to different attitudes toward slavery. Significantly, Prim's successor as captain general, Juan de la Pezuela, not only lifted Prim's ban against people of color but also instituted the *libreta*. In other words, even in the midst of continued anxiety over slave or abolitionist conspiracies, the search for alternative ways of controlling labor was already under way in Puerto Rico.

Early criticism of slavery and the slave trade had gone unheeded by Puerto Rican *hacendados*. The slave population grew significantly in the first half of the nineteenth century. However, slaves always made up a much lower percentage of the population than in Cuba. (See table 7.) The Puerto Rican slave population reached its peak in 1846, and by 1860 there were 41,736 slaves in a total population of 583,308.[22] The virtual end of the slave trade had struck a serious blow to Puerto Rican slavery, as had a cholera epidemic in 1855, which according to Díaz Soler may have claimed the lives of as many as 6,000 slaves.[23] Puerto Rican *hacendados* were apparently as helpless as their Cuban counterparts in their attempts to increase the slave population by any other means but importation. In Ponce, for instance, in the 1860s, the slave population hovered consistently around 4,700. The number of Puerto Rican workers registered with *libretas,* in contrast, grew from 2,348 in 1862 to a peak of 3,370 in 1865, an increase of 43 percent.[24] The need for labor remained constant; where laborers would come from and how they would be organized, however, was a matter of debate.

### Puerto Rican Slavery in Crisis: Abolition as a Way Out

By the 1850s, the Puerto Rican sugar sector was in trouble. Laird Bergad reports that between 1851 and 1868 sugar exports barely increased from 118.8 million pounds to 123.4 million.[25] Planters saw labor as the key problem. Slavery was in crisis, and planters sought various means to recruit labor, one of which was the *libreta.* Another method they advocated was to introduce contract laborers from Asia or Africa. In 1860, for instance, San Juan's Royal Economic Society considered a proposal to import 20,000 African contract laborers into Puerto Rico.[26] The proposal met with adamant resistance. Román Baldorioty de Castro, in a report for the Ecomomic Society, argued that Puerto Rico had no need for such immigration. The report "reasons forcefully against the project, arguing that the island has enough laborers to sustain its agriculture and that the immigration of a savage race will cause grave problems. Instead, [Castro] proposes the introduction of moral peasants from Galicia who will not require the vigilance that the African race requires but instead will teach our people about agriculture."[27]

Baldorioty de Castro's preference for Spanish over African immigration had a long history in Puerto Rico. Pedro Yrizzary had advocated the same measures in 1809.[28] In 1822, José Espaillat, in the Royal Economic Society, had similarly argued against the slave trade.[29] In 1856, a report on immigration written for the society concluded: "Africa and Asia, repugnant in their stupidity and depravities, are not the sources of the immigration that will improve our situation." Rather, Puerto Rico needed an immigration that was "national, Christian, intelligent, and laborious, like the artisans and peasants of the Peninsula and the Canary Islands."[30] Baldorioty's criticism of African immigration resembled all the earlier opinions on the subject: he favored white, especially Spanish, immigration over immigration from Africa or Asia. Unlike the others, though, Baldorioty argued that Puerto Rico already had enough laborers to work its fields, even without immigration. How had this change come about?

Baldorioty was a member of a group of creole intellectuals who had studied in Europe or the United States and who had come of political age during the crisis of Puerto Rican slavery. Having studied Puerto Rican history and the island's contemporary political economy, Baldorioty and others concluded that the formation of a free-labor market held the answer to Puerto Rico's labor problems. For them, Puerto Rico had a large enough agrarian population that needed only the stimulus of the market to transform it into a productive working class. Their arguments were abolitionist in their logic, but only implicitly so. Only in more open political conditions would they actually be able to speak of abolition.[31]

**José Julián Acosta (1825–1891).**
**García,** *Fotografías.*

Baldorioty was one of four students—the others were José Julián Acosta, Eduardo Micault Pignateli, and Julián Aurelio Núñez[32]—who received a grant from the Spanish government in the 1840s to travel to Madrid under the tutelage of the priest Rufo Manuel Fernández. The youths were to be trained as professors for a projected secondary school in San Juan. The Spanish government selected children of poor families in the hope of making men who would be permanently loyal to Spain.[33]

While studying in Madrid, Baldorioty and Acosta found themselves a part of a large group of Puerto Rican and Cuban students and exiles. The most prominent Antillean figure in Madrid in the 1840s was Domingo del Monte, whose home served as a meeting place for Antilleans and Spaniards interested in colonial history and politics.[34] Puerto Ricans living in the Peninsula dedicated themselves to retrieving Puerto Rico's long colonial history so as to better understand its present social and economic state. Acosta, for instance, developed a passionate interest in Spanish natural historians and histories of colonial America. In a letter to a Cuban colleague, Acosta wrote: "I am consumed by the desire to undertake a series of historical studies of the privileged individuals of our race who devoted their faculties to the progress of the sciences."[35]

The most significant work that resulted from Acosta's interest in colonial history was his updated and annotated edition of Fray Iñigo Abbad y Lasierra's natural history of Puerto Rico (originally published in 1788), a first-edition copy of which he had found in Domingo del Monte's personal library.[36] In his prologue, Acosta noted the importance of the community of Puerto Rican intellectuals in Madrid during the forties and fifties for the revival of interest in Puerto Rico's history.

In addition to Acosta and Baldorioty, also studying in Madrid at the time were Segundo Ruiz Belvis, one of Puerto Rico's first abolitionists and separatists; Ramón Emeterio Betances, the most prominent and active advocate of Puerto Rican independence; and Alejandro Tapia y Rivera, whose multivolume *Biblioteca Histórica de Puerto-Rico,* a collection of colonial documents culled from Spanish archives, was one of Acosta's main inspirations and scholarly sources.[37] Other important works to emerge from this group of intellectuals were a first edition of Manuel Alonso's *El gíbaro,* a collection of poems, dialogues, and essays on the archetypal Puerto Rican agrarian figure, published in Barcelona in 1849,[38] and Julio de Vizcarrondo's translation of a study of Puerto Rico by the French naturalist Andrés Pedro Ledru (1797). Although Vizcarrondo published his translation in 1863, Acosta had unearthed a copy of the original at a bookseller's stand along the Seine in Paris in the early 1850s.[39]

This outpouring of scholarly and literary works by Puerto Ricans can be seen partly as a response to the crisis in Puerto Rican slavery and labor organization. The appeal to history and political economy and their interest in the island's agrarian population were all part of an exploration of alternatives to slavery. In Puerto Rico in the forties and fifties, the question of alternatives to slave labor was predominant, and like annexationism in Cuba, it attracted the attention of Puerto Rico's leading creole intellectuals.

Acosta entered the debate soon after his return to Puerto Rico. In 1853, he traveled around the island to report on the organization of labor in various sectors of the Puerto Rican economy. His findings stood in interesting contrast to the writings of Pedro de Yrizzary from the first decade of the century. Yrizarry argued that the greatest hindrance to Puerto Rico's economic growth was the uneven ratio of land to labor. Because labor was so scarce, landowners had no choice but to cede usufruct rights to unproductive *agregados* (roughly, sharecroppers) who farmed only for subsistence instead of for export. If landowners tried to coerce them, *agregados* could simply move to new empty lands. It was thus urgently necessary to populate Puerto Rico, he wrote, so as to provide landowners with enough labor, to reduce *agregados* to wage labor, and to create a class of export-oriented farmers.[40]

By the 1850s, Acosta observed dramatic transformations in Puerto Rico's land use and labor supply. First, free labor was already widely used in Puerto Rico. Second, the *jíbaro,* for Acosta a term that encompassed Puerto Rico's free rural work force, was perfectly adaptable to wage labor.[41] Finally, Puerto Rico had enough laborers and had only to incorporate them into the labor market to solve chronic labor shortages. For instance, in Mayagüez, an important sugar region in western Puerto Rico, Acosta held a long conversation with a *hacendado* who employed free wage laborers in his sugar refinery. He reported to Acosta that the *jíbaro* was a perfectly sound worker who responded productively to wage labor. In fact, Acosta saw *jíbaros* carrying out tasks previously thought to be suitable only for Africans, a testament to the stimulus of the market. Given that *jíbaros* could be induced to perform any kind of labor as long as they were well and justly compensated, Acosta concluded, "There is no lack of labor for this industry."[42]

Acosta put forward his free-labor convictions in a debate with Ponce landowners over immigration. In a series of articles published in the newspaper *El Ponceño* in 1853, *hacendados* called for stricter regulation of the rural population and for the immigration of Chinese laborers to supplement their declining work force. They reported that Cuban *hacendados* were importing Chinese contract laborers with great success.[43]

Acosta intervened in this discussion to persuade *hacendados* that instead of seeking to import labor, they should work to perfect the island's free-labor market and improve the education and moral condition of Puerto Rico's actual working population. Slavery was a dying institution in Puerto Rico, argued Acosta, pointing to the transfer of slaves from Puerto Rico to Cuba as proof.[44] Furthermore, Puerto Rico was in a propitious situation for the creation of alternative labor systems. First, Puerto Rico had a large white population—in fact, whites were in the majority, as was not true of other slave societies.[45] Indeed, Acosta and his colleagues frequently pointed not only to white numerical superiority but also to the coexistence of white and black workers on Puerto Rico's plantations as proof that racial conflict had been overcome in Puerto Rico, unlike Cuba.[46] Second, Puerto Rico benefited from considerable population density, according to Acosta, 1,515 persons per square league, versus 269 in Cuba (in 1840), 750 in Spain, and 1,300 in France. Only England and Ireland had more dense populations, with 2,100 persons per square league.[47] Finally, Puerto Rico already enjoyed a partially functioning free-labor market, a fact reflected in the relative cheapness of wages. For instance, in Puerto Rico, the average monthly wage was 6.5 pesos, versus 10 pesos in Cuba.[48] In sum, the threat of race war was a thing of the past, slavery was dying, and the island's land-to-labor ratio was already stimulating the formation of a free-labor market. There was no need for immigration. Rather, Acosta wrote, *hacendados* should turn their attention to the present agrarian population:

> The respectable class of property owners should not waste its time on sterile complaints or in discussing the importation of a race more indo-lent than our own. Instead, it should exercise its influence . . . to benefit the general interest, though always in harmony with their true particu-lar interests, and teach the proletarians the advantages of well-paid work, and cooperate to moralize that class.[49]

When *hacendados* from different parts of the island responded through the pages of *El Ponceño* that the decline of sugar production indicated the need for more and cheaper laborers,[50] Acosta argued that labor was not the principal problem that afflicted the Puerto Rican sugar industry. He pointed to Puerto Rico's weak position in an increasingly competitive world market. Producers around the globe were opening new lands to sugar cultivation, new crops—especially beets—were yielding sugar in major quantities, and new production methods reaped higher yields.[51] Acosta believed that world sugar production was bound to outstrip consumption, a process that boded ill for Puerto Rico: "If the island continues along the same road it follows today regarding sugar production, it will suffer a profound crisis that will be its ruin."[52] Acosta argued that Puerto Rican planters could not afford to imitate the strategies of their Cuban counterparts by investing capital in new land and labor. Puerto Rican planters needed to limit the scale of production and modernize the current production process by investing in new technology that would increase the yield of Puerto Rico's sugar harvests. Investing in immigration, therefore, was a mistake, one that would only hasten the decline of sugar production by diverting capital from new technology.[53]

The alternative articulated by Acosta as a way out of Puerto Rico's labor and production problems took on increasing power during the 1860s, not only because slave emancipation in the United States menaced the existence of Antillean slavery, but also because discontent with the *libreta* system was growing.[54] In 1863, Captain General Messina ordered a survey of the *libreta* throughout the island. The administration sent questionnaires to commissions composed of local governments and leading taxpayers concerning the functioning and future of the *libreta*. Individuals were also invited to write letters.[55]

Messina's successor, Marchesi, collected the responses in 1866. Two letters from Guayama, a sugar region on the south coast, argued that the *libreta* burdened landowners with the population's worst workers. Those who worked hard were probably property owners or renters exempt from the *libreta*. If the *libreta* were abolished, a free-labor market would develop, giving *hacendados* the flexibility of hiring and firing seasonal laborers and drawing small property owners into part-time plantation labor.[56] The report from San Germán, in southwest Puerto Rico, advocated abolishing the *libreta* and erecting in its place tighter vagrancy laws and policing the countryside more effectively by garrisoning the Civil Guard (Guardia Civil, the Spanish rural gendarmerie) at strategic points. The report also recommended the forced concentration of scattered laborers.[57] A letter from Carlos Cabrera of Ponce, in contrast, lauded the morally improving effects of the *libreta*, noting the moral degradation of the region's rural laborers: "I must confess that this class, though improved, has yet to achieve the degree of morality which would make this healthy intervention unnecessary." With some sort of emancipation process staring Puerto Rico in the face, Cabrera argued that abolition of the *libreta* would lead to severe labor shortages.[58]

In summarizing the reports and letters, Marchesi's secretary, Carlos de Rojas, found that a slight majority favored abolishing the *libreta*. Those who defended it feared the loss of workers. Rojas himself vigorously argued for suppression of the *libreta*. He criticized *hacendados* for drawing laborers into debt peonage through the *libreta* and the inefficent distribution of labor encouraged by the system. Like the San Germán commission, he favored abolishing the *libreta* and maintaining public order and steady labor through strict vagrancy laws and vigilant policing and knowledge of the working population.[59]

During this period of debate over forced labor and uncertainty about the fate of slavery, Acosta continued to argue for creating a free-labor market and improving the sugar production process as the answers to Puerto Rico's labor problems and declining output. In his 1866 annotated edition of Abbad y Lasierra's natural history of Puerto Rico, Acosta hammered away at the point that Puerto Rico was already well along the way to creating a market economy. According to his statistics, workers who were issued the *libreta* outnumbered slaves by 56,554, a figure that did not include the large number of small proprietors in Puerto Rico. Regarding the prominence of free labor, Acosta concluded, "The immense majority of our agricultural production is carried out by free labor. This convinces one that we can easily achieve the evolution demanded of us by religion, morality, and our future."[60]

In his original (1788) work, Abbad had noted the indolence of Puerto Rican laborers and property owners brought on by the heat and the ease with which one could produce subsistence goods in a tropical clime.[61] In his notes to Abbad's text, Acosta refuted the Spanish cleric's interpretation, admitting that owing to the legacy of slavery Puerto Ricans were still among the "'races that are made to work.'" However, Puerto Rico's considerable economic and population growth since 1788 had stimulated ever greater industry and productivity among Puerto Rican workers. Any shortcomings were caused not by climate or race—immutable barriers to progress for a European writer like Abbad—but by the lack of "civilizing" institutions in Puerto Rico such as schools or an independent and active press—more historical or political barriers that colonial authors like Acosta, or Saco in Cuba, stressed against European "materialism."[62]

Thus Acosta reiterated his critique of the 1850s: labor or human capital was not the impediment to the revival of Puerto Rican sugar production or the economy in general. Though labor reforms were necessary, Acosta believed that once they were carried out, Puerto Rico would make a successful transition to a free-labor market. As to the more difficult problems confronting the Puerto Rican economy, Acosta pointed to the suffocating effects of Spain's protectionist trade policies implemented in 1836 that hindered Puerto Rican producers' access to foreign markets.[63] He also reemphasized the need to reorganize and modernize production in the island. He advocated a greater division of labor in the sugar sector, separating cane growing from processing so as to make Puerto Rican sugar cheaper and more competitive by allowing processors to invest in modern refining technology instead of land and labor.[64] For the island as a whole, he favored diversifying agricultural production so as to reduce Puerto Rico's dependence on a single crop and to make it self-sufficent in its food production.[65]

## Conclusion: Back to Madrid

When the Spanish state was goaded into action concerning colonial reform by the United States' Civil War and empancipation of the slaves, as well as an Anglo-American initiative against the Cuban slave trade, the creole elite in Puerto Rico and Cuba occupied quite different positions.[66] Though Puerto Rican reformers like Acosta and Baldorioty never openly uttered the word *abolition,* the implicit logic of their arguments concerning the future of labor in Puerto Rico was clear: free wage labor held the answer to Puerto Rico's labor problems. Free labor was widely used, slavery was stagnant, the *jíbaro* had proved to be an available and reliable wage laborer. Moreover, they believed that the racial balance in Puerto Rico boded well for the transition to free labor. Though there had been considerable anxiety about race war in Puerto Rico in the early nineteenth century, by the 1860s some elite creoles were arguing that racial stability (that is, white hegemony) had been achieved.[67] This stood in marked contrast to Cuba. In short, Acosta and others believed that Puerto Rico had come a long way along the path to free labor since Yrizzary's time.

When Acosta was elected to the Junta de Información convened by the Spanish government in Madrid in 1866–1867 to discuss labor, political, and economic reforms, he and two of his fellow Puerto Rican commissioners, Segundo Ruiz Belvis and Francisco M. Quiñones, requested the immediate abolition of slavery and advocated full civil and political rights for the free population of color.[68] Meanwhile, Acosta's friend and colleague, Julio de Vizcarrondo, helped to found the Abolitionist Society in 1865.

A group of well-organized and active abolitionists had arisen in Puerto Rico. Why is it important to focus on the ideas and actions of a small nucleus of intellectuals? Two reasons stand out. First, Acosta and others had obviously won enough proponents within Puerto Rican society to be elected to represent Puerto Rico in Spain. Some planters faced by the stagnation of the slave population and the shortcomings of the *libreta* were willing to consider an indemnified transition to free labor.[69] Second, the antislavery activists in Puerto Rico decisively shaped the mobilization against slavery in Spain's entire colonial empire. The initial impulse for immediate abolition that fired the Hispano-Antillean elite came from Puerto Rico. Puerto Rican abolitionist ideology was a response to Puerto Rican problems, but eventually it influenced the politics of slavery and colonialism throughout the empire. Until slavery was abolished in Puerto Rico in 1873, Puerto Rican abolitionists negotiated the political possibilities open to them in Puerto Rico and Spain against stubborn resistance from metropolitan and colonial authorities. On the one hand, they sought to convince Puerto Rican slaveowners of the potential efficacy of abolition, and on the other they formed alliances with metropolitan associations and political parties to carry out their program. In the long run, then, Puerto Rican abolitionism mobilized and dovetailed with significant antislavery initiatives that resonated throughout the empire.

The Cuban elite sought to carry out a very different program regarding slavery. When the Puerto Rican commissioners proposed immediate abolition in Puerto Rico, they threw their Cuban colleagues into a panic. The Cuban commissioners sought a much more gradual extinction of slavery, a process to be left in the hands of slaveowners. They feared not only a disruption of the sugar industry caused by a dramatic change in labor organization, but also the possibility of race war. For them, slavery preserved not only Cuban productivity, but also white hegemony. Whereas a Puerto Rican like Vizcarrondo had helped to found the Abolitionist Society, Cubans like Saco shunned abolitionism, preferring in their public political discourse to focus on abolishing the slave trade and including the creole elite in the liberal regime—measures that elicited considerable sympathy from metropolitan liberals, as Saco had consistently predicted. They preferred to leave the discussion of slavery in the closed corridors of power. Nonetheless, the divergent interests of Puerto Rican reformers and planters placed the issue of immediate slave emancipation squarely on the public political agenda.[70]

Puerto Rican and Cuban elites entered a new political and intellectual world in Madrid in the 1860s.[71] Whereas in the 1830s colonial deputies had found themselves politically isolated, by the 1860s they had discovered a new universe of political perspectives and resources for mobilizing metropolitan support for colonial reform. Metropolitan liberals addressed the question of colonial slavery through their own experiences with social reform and political action in Spain. Indeed, like Cuban and Puerto Rican reformers, they were seeking to remake the revolutionary settlement of the 1830s. Chapters 3 and 4 discuss the transformation of liberal ideology and political culture in Madrid and Spain during the 1850s and 1860s so as to sketch the context in which Spanish and Antillean reformers established the Abolitionist Society and the conditions under which slave emancipation and colonial reform became pressing issues in the metropolis after three decades of neglect.

# 3

# Free Trade and Protectionism

## THE TRANSFORMATION OF THE METROPOLITAN PUBLIC SPHERE, 1854–1868

### The Idea of the Public in Madrid

When the Spanish Cortes expelled the colonial deputies in 1837, public life in the capital city, Madrid, was slowly developing after years of absolutist rule. Prominent observers of the time noted the paucity of public spaces and forums. In one of his most famous essays of the 1830s, the Madrid writer Mariano José de Larra asked, "Who is the public and where does one find it?" After exploring the capital, Larra's answer to his own question was that the *public* was a chimera. Ramón de Mesonero Romanos, the great chronicler of nineteenth-century Madrid, reminisced that his first writings appeared in 1832 in the city's lone newspaper.[1]

Madrid was a different city by midcentury, when the colonial question returned to the capital. After decades of war and revolution, the city's population began to increase significantly, attaining sustained growth by 1850. (See table 8.) The periodical press also increased. The nineteenth-century dramatist Eugenio Hartzenbusch compiled a record of the number of periodicals published in Madrid between 1661 and 1870 in which he estimated that there were nearly seven times as many periodicals being published in 1868 as there were in 1837.[2] According to Hartzenbusch, there were 36 periodicals in 1837; 139 in 1854; 192 in 1865; and 236 in 1868. Moreover, by the 1850s, twenty years of constitutional rule and institution building, even if limited, had led to a new sense of political possibilities in Madrid. The rise of the idea of the *public,* and the growth of associations that claimed to

TABLE 8
Population of Madrid, 1799–1860

| 1799 | 195,000 |
|------|---------|
| 1821 | 160,000 |
| 1842 | 200,000 |
| 1850 | 220,000 |
| 1860 | 300,000 |

*Source:* David Ringrose, *Madrid and the Spanish Economy,* 28.

mobilize and represent the public, created a style of politics that boded well for Antillean reformers.[3]

Reflecting on the changes that had taken place in Madrid between the 1830s and the 1850s, Mesonero pondered what remained of the earlier period. He answered, "Almost nothing."[4] To take one instance of change, Mesonero noted the new prominence of educational and intellectual institutions created since the 1830s. Whereas the first edition of his guide to Madrid, published in 1831,[5] describes public intellectual life in cafe *tertulias* (literary gatherings), theaters, and royal academies, by the 1850s Mesonero found institutionalized public forums, many of which served as bases for Spanish and Antillean reformers to establish an abolitionist movement. The central university was moved from Alcalá de Henares to Madrid in 1836, and by the 1853–1854 academic year had more than 5,000 students, according to Mesonero. The Medical School (Facultad de Medicina) had opened in 1843. Other professional schools included the Royal Industrial Institute (Real Instituto Industrial, 1850), the School of Mines (Escuela Especial de Ingenieros de Minas, 1835), and the School of Fine Arts (Escuela Especial de Bellas Artes, 1844). And perhaps most important, the Madrid Ateneo, the city's leading intellectual forum, established in 1835, flourished in the 1840s and 1850s.[6] Theaters, important venues for abolitionist meetings in the 1860s, had also proliferated. In addition to the eighteenth-century Teatro de la Cruz (built in 1737) and the Teatro del Príncipe (1745, rebuilt 1806), Madrileneans now attended the Teatro del Instituto (1845), the Teatro de Variedades (1843), the Teatro Lope de Vega (1852), and the biggest theater in Madrid, the Teatro Real (1850).[7]

The meaning of the word *public* also underwent changes in this period. In 1832, the Spanish Academy's *Diccionario de la lengua castellana* defined it as follows:

PÚBLICO, CA. adj. Notorious, patent, manifest, something that everyone knows. *Publicus.* Vulgar, common and noticed by everyone; so they

say: a public thief, a public woman etc. *Publicus.* Applies to power, jurisdiction and authority to do something, in counterpoint, to private. *Publicus.* That which belongs to all people or citizens etc., like public ministers. s.m. The town or city common. *Populus.* In public, mod. adv. Pub-
licly, in sight of everyone. *Coram omnibus, publicè, palàm.* To enter in
public. fr. To make the first entrance of the king, sovereign, ambassador,
etc. Manifesting himself with solemnity and pomp to the people.
*Solemniter ingredi.* SACAR AL PÚBLICO. Fr. SACAR A LA PLAZA.[8]

The 1869 edition of the dictionary contained a virtually identical definition,
but with one notable addition: "The totality of persons who share the same
interests or who choose to gather in a specific place. So they say that every
writer or every theater has its PUBLIC."[9] In other words, by the 1860s the
sense of the public as a group of individuals gathered together to promote
a common interest or concern had decisively entered the language.

The proliferation of public institutions and the new inflection of the
term *public* marked important transformations in both Madrilenean and
Spanish political and intellectual life that had a crucial impact on the nature
of colonial politics. Indeed, the most compelling explanations for the rise of
Spanish abolitionism point to the changes in Madrid's public life at
midcentury as the source of antislavery sentiment, especially the changes
wrought by the struggles over one of the most heated issues of the day, free
trade.

Speaking soon after the final abolition of slavery in Cuba in 1886,
Gabriel Rodríguez, a civil engineer, political economist, and one of Spain's
leading abolitionists, looked back on the origins of the Abolitionist Society,
founded in 1865. He noted that Madrid's Free Society of Political Economy
(Sociedad Libre de Economía Política) had held debates on Antillean sla-
very before the Abolitionist Society was organized. Many of the original
members of the Abolitionist Society came from the earlier group—political
economists such as Laureano Figuerola, Segismundo Moret y Prendergast,
Félix de Bona, and Luis María Pastor, among others. Also among the early
Spanish members were Democrats like José María Orense and Emilio
Castelar. The democratic newspaper *La Discusión,* edited by Francisco Pi y
Margall, was one of the first forums for abolitionism in Madrid.[10]

Alberto Gil Novales follows Rodríguez's interpretation of the origins of
the society, arguing that Spaniards and Antilleans founded the Abolitionist
Society in Madrid during an "age of societies."[11] Those included the Free
Society of Political Economy (founded in 1857), the Association for Tariff
Reform (Asociación para la Reforma de los Aranceles de Aduanas, 1859),

and the Association for Women's Education (Asociación de la Educación de la Mujer, 1869). One might also point to a range of institutions that were reinvigorated during the fifties and sixties, such as the Madrid Ateneo, the University of Madrid, and the Fomento de las Artes, an association for adult education. For Gil Novales, the key organizations in the formation of the Abolitionist Society were the Free Society of Political Economy and the Association for Tariff Reform, bastions of free-trade ideology.[12]

Why was free trade such a decisive issue? As in other western European countries in the mid-nineteenth century, debates over the relationship of domestic markets to the expanding British economy mobilized and unified regional economic interests on a national level. In Spain, the free-trade challenge consolidated a national public sphere in which local interests organized to pressure the state through the press, public meetings, books, and petition drives for or against free trade.[13]

The publics that formed and mobilized over the free-trade question later squared off over colonial slavery. The free-trade debates of the 1850s and 1860s in Spain not only laid the organizational and ideological foundations of the Abolitionist Society, as Rodríguez and Gil Novales argue, but also those of the opponents of abolition. Before the abolition campaigns, many groups had mobilized to resist free-trade legislation and to defend Spain's protectionist trade policies—one of the fault lines of colonial politics. Maintaining colonial slavery and protecting colonial markets were cornerstones of the political economy of Spanish liberalism that was consolidated in the revolutionary process of the 1830s. Commercial, agricultural, and manufacturing interests from throughout Spain that defended a protected metropolitan market also defended colonial slavery in the name of the "national economy."

As Rodríguez and Gil Novales point out, free-trade associations existed within a broader constellation of middle-class associations, parties, and institutions in Madrid in the fifties and sixties. Political economists were active regarding the question of free trade at the national level, but they were also engaged, along with other groups, with the "social question"—that is, the conflict between capital and labor—in Madrid. That experience produced a particular vision of the relationship between capital and labor that informed the political goals of metropolitan abolitionists. It also solidified the capital's middle-class associational culture. The fight over free trade, the subject of this chapter, consolidated the metropolitan public sphere and exposed one of the major fault lines of the Spanish colonial empire. Middle-class reformers' engagement with the "social question" in Madrid, dis-

**Richard Cobden, British industrialist and publicist admired by the Economists for his active campaining for free trade in Great Britain and abroad.** *Asociácion por la Reforma de los Aranceles de Aduanas, Ricardo Cobden.*

cussed in the following chapter, mobilized a local public that provided crucial ideological and organizational support for abolition.

## Free Trade and Protectionism in Spain, 1854–1868

During his 1846 tour of Spain in favor of free trade, Richard Cobden reminded an enthusiastic public in Cádiz of the benefits of commercial liberty:

> You all remember that for a year Cadiz enjoyed an extraordinary prosperity. You remember the fleet of vessels which crowded your bay, the vast traffic which filled your streets, and your warehouses charged with the productions of every clime? What was it that occasioned such a magical change in Cadiz? The climate, its harbour, its productions, everything was the same as they had been before—there was but one alteration which accounted for all the prosperity—*for one year Cadiz was a FREE port.*

That golden moment of prosperity was, however, long past. At present, Cádiz was suffering the stagnating consequences of a protectionist trade policy. Cobden left no doubt as to the origin of that policy: "In every country there is some particular interest which is afraid of freedom. . . . In Spain, you have the Catalonians, who are terrified at the mere name of Free Trade."[14]

Most Spanish free traders also blamed the strong protectionist policies of the Spanish state on the "industrial" party—that is, Catalan textile manufacturers. However, the lukewarm reception given to Cobden in Seville, Granada, Málaga, Valencia, and Barcelona demonstrated that agricultural, mining, and industrial sectors throughout the Peninsula agreed that the Spanish government should protect the domestic market for national producers. Significantly, Cobden received a warm welcome only in Madrid and the Andalusian cities of Cádiz and Jerez. In Madrid, civil servants and professionals advocated free trade as a fiscal device that would increase public revenues by cutting down on contraband and as a means of opening Spain to foreign capital. Cádiz and Jerez, meanwhile, already had strong commercial links with Britain.[15]

Strong protectionist sentiment from throughout the Peninsula was well in keeping with the cautious nature of the Spanish revolution of the 1830s. As Jesús Cruz demonstrates, the revolutions of the early nineteenth century had preserved the political and social ascendancy of the old-regime elite and protected prerevolutionary business practices.[16] Spain was no exception

within nineteenth-century Europe. Although the bourgeoisie has tradition-
ally been represented as a revolutionary class that erected a liberal market
society in place of feudalism, more recent historians emphasize the persistence of the old regime and the political and cultural conservatism of the
bourgeoisie (that is, owners of the means of production). Geoff Eley, for
instance, argues that the European bourgeoisie's liberalism was generally
limited to securing the conditions for the reproduction of capital. Its commitment to political liberalism, especially in its most radical democratic
form, and to standard beliefs of economic liberalism, such as free trade and
competition, was weak. In nineteenth-century Europe, Spain included, the
rise of democracy, expansion of civil rights, and liberalization of the
economy were generally carried out by the middle and popular classes in
conflict with the bourgeoisie.[17]

The 1850s and the 1860s were just such a period of struggle over the
political economy of Spanish liberalism. Was Spain to be a democracy? An
oligarchy? Was the economy to be based on a free market or on state intervention on behalf of domestic producers? What were the rights of labor?
These profound questions logically extended to the colonies, not only because Antilleans were fighting over the same issues, but because of the in-
timate links between the colonial and metropolitan political and economic
orders. Free trade was an issue that cut across the imperial political spectrum in complex ways. As we shall see, Spain's most ardent champions of
free trade were also abolitionists—a position that alienated them from the
colonial sectors that stood to benefit most from free trade: the slaveowning
planter class. While colonial slaveowners advocated free trade, metropolitan producers and defenders of colonial slavery categorically opposed free
trade because protected Spanish and Antillean markets were essential to
their prosperity. Nonetheless, while imperial hegemony was precarious and
complex, the lines of conflict and solidarity generally crystallized on the
question of slavery.[18]

Between 1854 and 1868, Spanish liberals sought to balance the centralizing tendencies of the liberal state with demands for a more robust and
less regulated form of capitalism. The dominant parties formed in the revolutionary era of the 1830s, the Moderates (Moderados) and the Progressives
(Progresistas), were relatively homogeneous in their representation of the
bourgeoisie and the professional classes, although they struggled over the
nature of the state and capital accumulation. The Moderates tended to favor the interests of the monarchy, the traditional aristrocracy, and the agrarian elite, while the Progressives had firm links with the urban popular
classes.[19]

For a decade (1843–1854), the Moderates ruled in close collaboration with the Bourbon monarch Isabel II, who refused to summon the opposition Progressive Party to form a government. Besides refusing to relinquish power, the Moderates oversaw a rapprochement with the Catholic Church, anathema to the anticlerical Progressives, and established one of the pillars of the centralized Spanish state: the Civil Guard (Guardia Civil), a rural gendarmerie stationed throughout the Peninsula and eventually the colonies. Though the Moderates defended the land reforms of the 1830s, they greatly distrusted an unshackled capitalist economy; the spectacle of revolutionary Europe in 1848 led them to restrict severely the creation of joint stock companies in Spain.[20]

The Progressives envisioned a more aggressive form of liberalism. They opposed the church, distrusted the Bourbon monarchy, sought to extend the franchise, and militated for a more expanisve capitalist economy. The intransigence of the Moderates and the monarchy, however, kept them out of power until they successfully allied with factions of the military and with discontented members of the Moderate Party to stage a *pronunciamiento* in 1854. Such military-civilian alliances were the medium of regime changes for much of the nineteenth century. Though the Progressives themselves were overthrown in 1856 by the Liberal Union (Unión Liberal, a new political party that embraced members of the Moderates and Progressives), the revolution of 1854 inaugurated a period of enthusiastic economic expansion. The Liberal Union's formula for rule was to combine the Moderates' style of centralism with the Progressives' desire for economic growth.[21]

In Spain, the polemic between free traders and protectionists became more intense after the revolution inaugurated an economic boom in the 1850s. The boom was stimulated by the expansion of railroad building and speculation, the mushrooming joint stock companies, the growth of the Catalan textile industry, and new land disentailments legislated in 1855. The period between 1854 and 1868, known as the Liberal Union era, was one of intense debate over the relationship of the Spanish economy to the expanding European economy in the so-called age of capital.[22] Similar conflicts over free trade erupted in most European countries in the fifties and sixties, as Great Britain sought to extend its continental markets. While intellectuals and civil servants pressed for free trade in newly formed associations like Spain's Association for Tariff Reform or the Belgian Free-Trade Association (Association Belge pour la Liberté Commerciale), developing manufacturing and agricultural sectors fought to protect their local markets against foreign competition.[23]

In Spain, free traders argued that the unrestricted entry of European goods, capital, and technology would benefit the Spanish economy and that the government would gain more revenue by imposing limited customs on these increased imports. Such revenue would help to repay Spain's significant foreign debt and free domestic capital for investment. Protectionists claimed that the government had to foster its national industries by maintaining the tariff schedule of 1849 that prohibited the entry of many items that competed with domestic producers and also penalized goods brought by non-Spanish carriers.[24]

Some export-oriented economic sectors supported free trade, such as the new railway companies that relied on the importation of foreign capital goods, Andalusian sherry producers, Valencian fruit growers, and, briefly during the Crimean War, Castilian wheat growers.[25] The greatest push for free trade, however, came from a group of Madrid-based political economists, many of whom had close connections to government agencies and the railway companies.[26] This group argued that the government's protectionist policies impeded economic growth, encouraged contraband, and enslaved the Spanish consumer to uncompetitive manufacturing and agricultural interests. Madrid's political economists were better poised in the 1850s to carry out an effective propaganda campaign than they had been at the time of Cobden's visit in 1846. Borrowing from the English publicist, previously isolated civil servants, university professors, engineers, and lawyers organized themselves into the Free Society of Political Economy and the Association for Tariff Reform, both founded in the fifties. These associations gave the political economists a powerful esprit de corps, a forum in which to develop a coherent critique of the Spanish state and economy, and the opportunity to publicize their doctrine through the periodical press. From this moment on, they were known in Spain as the Economists.[27]

The young civil engineers José Echegaray and Gabriel Rodríguez renewed the public debate over protectionism by founding the periodical *El Economista* in 1856. Echegaray and Rodríguez argued that political economy was a science of wealth that explained the natural functioning of the market. Absolute individual liberty to pursue wealth was the foundation of a natural market economy, and any impediment to the pursuit of individual wealth caused unseen but grave damage to a nation's economic well-being. Though protectionism appeared to stimulate national industry and agriculture, in reality it impeded the natural development of the Spanish economy. Furthermore, in an odd twist to classical theory, Echegaray and Rodríguez held that *production* was not the source of national wealth, as their protectionist adversaries argued. Rather, wealth was measured by *consumption*. A truly wealthy nation was one that was open to free trade to the benefit of the consumer. The consumer, not the producer, provided the measure of national wealth.[28]

Echegaray and Rodríguez stated their theory clearly in their criticism of a petition defending high tariffs sent by Catalan manufacturers to the Spanish constituent assembly: "We give more importance to the vote of the consumers because we believe, with the leave of the Catalan commission, that wealth is not *work* but the objects that satisfy our needs."[29] They concluded that the disappearance of Catalan industry was irrelevant to Spain's national wealth:

> Based as it is upon such an erroneous principle, the commission's memorial is a pure sophism. The textile industry will die! they exclaim with horror. What does it matter to us, as long as we have more textiles that are just as good? The textile industry will die! Who cares, if we have other textiles?[30]

Admittedly, Echegaray and Rodríguez represented the most extreme position within the free-trade camp. The acknowledged leader of the Economists, Laureano Figuerola, was himself a Catalan who before coming to the University of Madrid in the 1850s was an ardent defender of Catalan protectionist policies. He also represented Barcelona in the Spanish Parliament throughout the fifties and sixties.[31] Even at the height of the debate between free trade and protectionism, when he was one of the most vilified men in Spain, Figuerola insisted that he was a champion of Catalan industry.[32] He believed that lowering protective tariffs would make the Catalan textile industry more efficent and profitable. According to one historian, Figuerola's conversion from protectionism to economic liberalism occurred during a visit to the Crystal Palace in London. The displays of technology there convinced him that the Catalan textile sector would benefit from competition, which would force manufacturers to invest in the latest production processes in an effort to drive down costs.[33]

### The Catalan Protectionists

The Catalan industrialists, nonetheless, refused any compromise on the tariff issue, even with the views of moderate political economists like Figuerola. E. J. Hobsbawm observes that in the mid-nineteenth century, national and regional bourgeoisies that faced severe economic competition from Great Britain generally rejected economic liberalism and defended their interests in the name of the nation. For them, "Nation implied national economy and its systematic fostering by the state, which in the nineteenth century meant protectionism."[34] Such was the case in Catalonia and indeed throughout Spain. Here I focus on the Catalan response to free-trade initiatives, which was both unique and representative of other regions, because the Catalans were the most articulate and aggressive defenders of economic protectionism and because the link between Catalan protectionism and the Spanish colonial project was especially strong.

Production costs in the Catalan textile industry were high because of the lack of raw materials and the high cost of transport. Only protective tariffs allowed Catalan textiles to occupy a share of the domestic market.[35] Like producers in other less-developed European countries, such as the German states in the same period, Catalan manufacturers argued that the Spanish state ought to protect national industries against the mature British economy until they were sufficently developed to control the national market without assistance. For them, free trade in the age of capital represented total subjection to British economic interests.[36]

The main outlet for Catalan protectionist ideology during the renewal of the free-trade campaign was the *Revista Industrial,* founded in 1855 in Barcelona and edited by Adolfo Blanch y Cortada, a characteristic protectionist intellectual of the period. Whereas in Madrid the majority of the Economists hailed from the civil service or the professions, in Barcelona protectionist intellectuals were linked to the industrial and commercial bourgeoisie. One can make a rough distinction between two types of protectionists. On the one hand were "organic" intellectuals, themselves industrialists, landowners, merchants, or shippers who actively participated in public debate over the free-trade question. That group included Juan Güell y Ferrer,[37] an industrialist and landowner who had made his first fortune as a merchant in Cuba in the 1830s. Güell y Ferrer was perhaps the most prominent spokesman for protectionism in nineteenth-century Spain. Pedro Bosch y Labrús and José Puig Llagostera were manufacturers and landowners who were instrumental in founding the most influential Catalan economic association in the late nineteenth century, the Fomento del Trabajo Nacional.[38] These "organic" intellectuals were fierce nationalists, but they were Spanish, not Catalan nationalists. Throughout the nineteenth century, the bourgeoisie of Catalonia, and especially of Barcelona, generally identified themselves with the Spanish nation.[39]

Other protectionist intellectuals were at the same time poets, historians, linguists, and economists. They shared the nationalistic loyalties of the industrial bourgeoisie, but they were also Catalan nationalists, defending the conception of a Catalan nation within the larger Spanish nation. They were intimately involved in the revival of Catalan poetry and literature known as the Renaixença and in defending the political and economic interests of the

Catalan bourgeoisie. An important figure in this group was Buenaventura Carlos Aribau, personal secretary to the Catalan banker Gaspar de Remisa. Aribau's "Oda a la Patria," written in 1833, is generally considered the initiation of modern Catalan literature. (He also wrote an "Ode to Political Economy" in 1822.) Víctor Balaguer, the leading man of letters in nineteenth-century Catalonia, was also one of Spain's leading statesmen; José Leopoldo Feu was an essayist, social reformer, and lobbyist for Catalan interests in Madrid.[40] The shared idea of a Spain rejuvenated by a strong national economy whose leading sector would be Catalan industry united the two groups of protectionist intellectuals, despite their divergent cultural orientations.[41]

Blanch y Cortada's position illustrates this relationship. He was a poet, novelist, historian, coauthor of the first modern Catalan grammar, and contributor to *La Renaixença,* a Catalan literary journal that was one of the ideological fountainheads of the conservative political catalanism that emerged in the 1890s. He also edited Juan Güell y Ferrer's collected economic writings and was involved in protectionist politics throughout his career, generally as a journalist. He was the editor of the *Revista Industrial* and later *El Fomento de la Producción Nacional,* a periodical published by the Fomento del Trabajo Nacional.

The Catalan protectionists argued that the nation was the basic unit of economic activity and analysis, in opposition to the "individualism" of the Economists. According to the protectionists, Spain was currently only a series of unconnected regional markets with stronger links to foreign countries than to one another. The Spanish state should take the lead in forging a unified and harmonious national economy that would convert Spain into an economic power. Free trade, reliance on more developed foreign economies, and defense of the individual interests of the consumer were not the "science" of political economy: they were the products of English ideology. True political economy, which arose from practice, not theory, taught that free trade was valuable only for developed and wealthy nations. The weak had to protect themselves until their industries became truly competitive.[42]

The Catalans argued that they had already pointed the way toward the integration of the Spanish market by encouraging other sectors of the Spanish economy. They sacrificed their own profits by relying on more expensive Castilian grains rather than on cheaper foreign grains for the cause of national economy:

> The Spanish industrialists . . . are not and have never been egoists. The
> protection they ask for themselves they ask for every class of national

production, even to their own detriment. Even though cheap subsistence goods are of the highest importance to industry, the Catalan industrialists eat Castilian bread with pleasure, even though it costs twice as much as foreign bread. They were the only ones in 1846 to protest the importation of foreign grain. The Catalan industrialists believe that their interests are linked to those of agriculture and thus will always lend their support.[43]

Such sacrifice in the name of the national economy was one of the keys to Spanish economic renewal. Cooperation, not competition, between labor and capital, industry and agriculture, promised the forging of a "strong phalanx *[falange]* of great interests . . . systematically linked."[44] Such a powerful, integrated economy should be the end of all national economic policy.

The Economists responded to this vision of an economic "phalanx," and its antimarket implications, by defending competition. For the Economists, a "national" economy would emerge from the free and natural functioning of the market. Each nation would develop its natural place within the international division of labor. Protected industries were thus profoundly *anti*national:

> National industry for us only exists without the *protection* of power; that which exists independently. If the Catalan manufacturers cannot continue production without protective customs duties, then they do not have the right to call their industry national. If it cannot live without protection, then it matters little to us if it should disappear from Spain.[45]

Protectionists and Economists also disagreed over the role of the state. For the protectionists, private sacrifice was not enough to forge the economic phalanx. The state had to play a leading role in creating a national economy because private interests had a limited sphere of activity. Only the state possessed the necessary power and scope to coordinate and develop a nation's resources:

> Private interests can accomplish many things, and in Spain until now they have done everything. But their efforts are insufficient. The Administration must give them an impulse by removing the obstacles that hinder every well-conceived project. It must lend generous support to those projects aimed at the general good and stamp every project with the progress that an enlightened director knows how to organize.[46]

During this period, the Catalan protectionists looked to northern Europe for models of an active state, finding them particularly in France and

Prussia. For instance, French industrialists, men with practical knowledge of industry and a strong interest in the question, composed the state council that decided upon tariffs for every branch of the French economy. They were aided not only by their own expertise but also by minute statistical information gathered by the state. "This organization, gentlemen, is rational, logical, and expedient," stated a petiton to the Cortes in 1855, whereas the Spanish equivalent of the French council was made up of professional civil servants and political appointees with no knowledge of or interest in industry, commerce, or agriculture.[47]

The same neglect or mismanagement was evident in education and technical training. Hitherto, private institutions carried out most technical training, while the impoverished Spanish government failed to create an adequate primary school system. The protectionists argued that the government must invest in education for two reasons: first, to nip socialism in the bud by teaching the working masses their place in Spanish society,[48] and second, to provide industry with the trained labor force it needed, as in France, Belgium, and Prussia.[49]

Again, the Economists rejected the "paternalism" of protectionist ideology and reaffirmed the priority of the market and the autonomous individual. If indeed the state were the "father" whose duty it was to educate and protect his "children," the nation, then certain specific features of the Spanish case had to be highlighted. First, the Spanish state was an impoverished father and only such "spoiled children" as the Catalans could expect financial support. Second, on a more general level, any government was an ignorant father that knew nothing about economic activity. Finally, the state was incapable of initiating economic activity because human beings already contained within their natures the impulse to work, trade, and the like. The government's sole responsibility in stimulating economic activity lay in protecting the liberty and property of natural economic agents: "Humanity is not an unformed mass that governments can mold to their taste. It is not an inert mass that needs a shove to put itself in motion; . . . within itself it contains the force of progress, just as a locomotive encloses within its entrails the steam that drives it."[50]

### Agricultural Protectionism

Despite the Economists' denunciations of the "industrial" party, Catalan industrialists were not the only defenders of protectionism in Spain. Agricultural interests throughout the peninsula also opposed free trade. Although the 1850s inaugurated a period of sustained agricultural expansion in Spain, the landowning class that emerged from the disentailment of ecclesiastical lands in the 1830s and communal lands in 1855 sought to preserve the national market for its products.[51] Despite the increase in cultivated land throughout the Peninsula and the consolidation of capitalist relations of production based on cheap wage labor, Spanish agricultural products—especially cereals—remained uncompetitive in the world market because of low yields caused by the undercapitalization of production.[52] The second half of the nineteenth century saw an unprecedented increase in cereal production in Castile and Andalusia and continuous growth until the 1890s. But because production processes continued to be primitive, Spanish cereals were more expensive for Spanish consumers than imported cereals.[53]

Thus, the Economists' desire to emulate Cobden's most notable triumph in England, free trade in grains, provoked considerable reaction from threatened producers. The Economists' vision of a free market threatened Spanish agriculturalists just as much as it did Catalan manufacturers. Echegaray and Rodríguez concluded that the Catalan textile sector should disappear if it could not withstand foreign competition. Similarly, Laureano Figuerola argued that Spanish growers would have to switch to new crops if their grains were not competitive. Cheap bread for Spanish consumers was more important than profits for "egoistic" landowners.[54]

One of the most dogged critics of the Economists was the Andalusian agronomist Genaro Morquecho y Palma. Morquecho was the spokesman for the Farmers' Circle of Seville (Círculo de Labradores de Sevilla), an association that united the leading landowners in the region.[55] Seville's main source of wealth was agriculture, with wheat and barley being far and away the leading crops, followed by wines and olives.[56] Like his Catalan counterparts, Morquecho argued that the modernization of the Spanish economy lay in a plan of national economy whose bases were the protection of national producers and state investment in the economy. On the latter point, Morquecho called for increased investment in the agricultural infrastructure—canals, irrigation, rural banks—and technical education.[57]

Morquecho explicitly compared the vision of the state presented by the Farmers' Circle to that of Catalonia's Junta de Fábricas. He favored an alliance of Spanish agriculture and industry, on the one hand to combat the propaganda of the Economists, that "tyrannical sect,"[58] and on the other hand to lobby for an effective national economic plan.[59] As a precedent for such an alliance, Morquecho invoked the example set by the Catalan industrialists in favoring Spanish over foreign grains.[60]

Morquecho followed his call for a national alliance by touring Catalonia in the fall of 1859. In reports sent back to Seville, he appeared to be particularly impressed by the Catalan analogue to the Farmers' Circle, the

Catalan Agricultural Institute of San Isidro (Instituto Agrícola Catalan de San Isidro, IACSI), founded in Barcelona in 1851.[61] By the end of the 1850s, there were more than thirty subdelegations throughout Catalonia. The objectives of the IACSI were to disseminate modern agricultural techniques and to protect the interests of property holders. Later in the nineteenth century, the IACSI also ventured to form interclass alliances through Catholic labor unions.[62] Morquecho lauded the IACSI for its energy and initiative. He placed its origin and activities within the context of a general reaction against the government's vacillation on free trade, noting the organization of similar agricultural institutions in the Aragonese capital, Zaragoza, and in Valladolid, at the heart of Spain's greatest cereal-producing region, Castile.[63]

### *The Spanish Economic Circle: Industry and Agriculture United*

The projected union of agricultural and industrial interests became a reality in 1861 with the founding of the Spanish Economic Circle (Círculo Económico Español) in Madrid. The organization's purpose was to present a united front against the active propaganda campaign carried out in Madrid by the Association for Tariff Reform, founded two years earlier. The Economists established this association to organize a specific campaign for reforming tariffs apart from the general activities of the Free Society of Political Economy. Under its auspices, they gave public speeches on free trade in the Madrid stock exchange and the Madrid Ateneo, held public meetings in Madrid's theaters, petitioned the Parliament, and published pamphlets and a newspaper, the *Gaceta Economista,* to disseminate their message.[64]

Protectionist parties from throughout Spain formed a grand alliance to defend their interests against the Economists' propaganda campaign. Among the members of the Spanish Economic Circle were Catalan industrialists and landowners such as Juan Güell y Ferrer and Andalusian latifundists like Ignacio Vázquez. Vázquez was mayor of Seville, president of Seville's Farmers' Circle, and the second wealthiest man in the province after the duke of Osuna. Others included new and old aristocrats like the the marquis of Remisa (a Catalan banker) and the Extremaduran land magnate, the marquis de la Conquista (a title descended from Francisco Pizarro), and influential politicians, both conservative and liberal, like Claudio Moyano, Pascual Madoz, and José Canga Argüelles. The most prominent protectionist intellectuals directed and wrote for the Economic Circle's publication, *La Verdad Económica*. These included Buenaventura Carlos Aribau, Güell y Ferrer, and Morquecho y Palma, who was also secretary of the Economic Circle. Economic associations from throughout Spain were allied to the Spanish Economic Circle: the Council of Agriculture, Industry, and Commerce of Santander; the Industrial Institute of Barcelona; La Edenta of Valencia; the Madrid Iron Industry Commission; and Seville's Farmers' Circle and the IACSI.[65]

The Spanish Economic Circle imitated the activities of its rival association. Morquecho y Palma, José Román Leal, and other protectionist intellectuals met the Economists on their own ground by taking part in the public debates held by the Free Society of Political Economy and by publishing books and pamphlets refuting the free-trade doctrine.[66] The executive committee of the Spanish Economic Circle petitioned the Parliament, while agricultural and industrial protectionists explained their doctrine in *La Verdad Económica*.

The protectionists continued to preach that practice, not theory, was the basis of political economy. Practical experience taught that the national economy should take priority over the world market. Production and producers, not consumers, were the bases of national wealth. And, finally, the state stimulated economic growth more effectively than the market. In short, the protectionists favored the sort of economic "phalanx" articulated earlier by the *Revista Industrial*. Spain's different economic sectors should be linked. Spanish industry should be fueled by Spanish raw materials, Spanish workers fed by Spanish agriculture, and the Spanish national market supplied by Spanish consumer goods. The state should have the central role in organizing the phalanx by constructing infrastructure to connect isolated regions, protecting the national market for producers, and training the nation's workers.

For instance, in the introduction to *La Verdad Económica*, Buenaventura Carlos Aribau argued that the Economists' gravest error was their universalism: "They think of the world as a single State whose interests are identical everywhere. They reject all difference. They refuse to recognize the outstanding fact of the nationalities."[67] Another writer concluded that the existence of separate nationalities made political economy a practical science because its proper object of study was particular, historical entities, not the timeless, ahistorical economic agent that the Economists defended:

> Political economy is an eminently practical science which when put into practice can either protect or harm acquired rights. It therefore must be adapted to the essential conditions of time and place. Thus the Germans have quite rightly called political economy *national economy*.[68]

And if national economy were the proper form of economic organization, then the Spanish government had to continue its protectionist policies.

According to the Spanish Economic Circle in a petition sent to the Parliament in March 1861, the bases of Spain's national economy were the developing but still weak industrial and agricultural sectors that needed protection to flourish.[69] Juan Güell y Ferrer further emphasized the duty of the government to protect the national economy by arguing that the productive classes worked for the benefit of the whole nation:

> The protectionists repeat that a good, wise, and enlightened Government should concern itself only with the producers. It should ensure their happiness because it will thus ensure the happiness of the entire nation. All of the useful classes are producers. They are workers, some laboring with their arms, others with their intelligences. Together they contribute to the production of useful, necessary, and agreeable things.

As for the unproductive members of society, Güell considered them "vagrants horrified by work, swindlers, and thieves." Instead of protecting their interests, the government should "persecute, extirpate, or reduce their number, as one pursues and destroys the weeds that harm the sown field."[70]

The role assigned to the state in protectionist ideology, as seen in Güell's comments, was twofold. On the one hand, the state should protect national producers through high tariffs. On the other, it should intervene more directly in the national economy, whether by "extirpating" vagrancy or, more important, by using its power and wealth to coordinate dispersed private interests and stimulate economic growth:

> We . . . proclaim the principle of the just and rational intervention of the State as the basis of the protectionist system. The State's responsibility is to initiate major improvements by developing the major branches of national wealth through the means at its disposal. Without the support of the social power, individual efforts are sterile because they lack stimulus. This stimulus comes from competition, but only from galvanizing competition, not from ruinous competition.[71]

José Román Leal reinforced the argument that the state should provide the stimulus for growth while also regulating competition. Basing his arguments on the works of the German philosophers Krause and Schlegel, Leal held that the state arose from the natural human tendency to associate. Within the sphere of human associations, the state played the important role of managing civil society, and balancing individual interest and initiative with the common good.[72] For Leal, the national economy represented a third path to economic modernization, one that combined the useful insights of socialism and liberalism. On the one hand, like socialism, national economy or protectionism recognized production as a social process; on the other hand, like liberalism, it also acknowledged the importance of individual liberty and initiative in the production process. Leal condemned the other systems because socialism, by ignoring the individual, became "tyranny, force," while liberalism, because it did not recognize the complex set of relationships in which the individual existed, led to "decomposition, death."[73]

Güell's and Leal's protectionist ideology indicated the cautiousness of Spain's revolutionary settlement of the 1830s. Historians of nineteenth-century Europe now observe that the bourgeoisie had only a tenuous commitment to political liberty and the Smithian vision of the free market, preferring instead to limit political rights and economic competition.[74] Spain's debate over free trade and protectionism was thus typical of debates throughout continental Europe in the mid-nineteenth century. Whereas intellectuals and civil servants proposed adhering to liberal economic principles in the hope of modernizing Spanish productive capacity and reducing the state's foreign debt, agricultural producers and manufacturers relied heavily upon state intervention for protection against foreign competition and supremacy in the domestic market. The general triumph of the Spanish Economic Circle over the Economists was thus not surprising. Though the Economists continued to skirmish with protectionist groups throughout the Liberal Union period, the latter successfully pressured the Spanish state into maintaining the prohibitionist tariff schedule established in the 1840s.[75] As Pierre Vilar argues, Madrid politicians were often free traders by conviction but protectionists by political necessity, given the powerful resistance that free-trade initiatives generated.[76]

## National Economy and Empire

Understanding the interests of the Spanish Economic Circle is important not only because of what it tells us about the nature of Spain's "bourgeois revolution." It is also important because the Economic Circle's precedent of forming a national alliance of Spain's productive sectors remained part of the Spanish political landscape. In the next major confrontation between protectionists and Economists, the question of free trade was important but secondary. Spain's protectionist classes now mobilized to oppose the radical abolitionist movement that had emerged from the associations established by the Economists. Once again, Economists and protectionists locked in combat, this time to determine the fate of colonial slavery.

The productive sectors that mobilized to protect the national market for their goods and services saw the Antilles as an extension of that protected market. Indeed, the Spanish bourgeoisie's strategies for capital accumulation extended far beyond the Peninsula's physical (though not necessarily imagined) boundaries. An analysis of Spain's bourgeois revolution and the struggles over the nature of Spanish liberalism must reckon with the centrality of the colonial project. The Spanish government and Spanish producers used the protected Antillean market as a reserve for uncompetitive Spanish goods and a solution to Spain's chronic trade imbalance. (See table 4.) Because of the dominance of export agriculture—especially sugar, but also tobacco and coffee—the Antilles relied heavily upon foreign foodstuffs and consumer goods. High customs that penalized non-Spanish goods and carriers served to protect the predominance of Spanish foods, especially flour and wine, manufactures, and shipping.[77]

In contrast, Antillean exports, with the exception of Puerto Rican coffee in the 1880s and 1890s,[78] received no preferential treatment in the weak Spanish consumer market. For example, the leading consumers of Cuban sugar were Great Britain and the United States, while Spain protected its infant cane sugar industry in Málaga against competition from Cuban sugar.[79] (See table 5.)

Furthermore, after the loss of the other American colonies in the 1820s and the concurrent boom of sugar production in Cuba and Puerto Rico, the Antilles became one of the most important sources of Spanish wealth. Some of the greatest fortunes amassed during the nineteenth century were made under the Cuban slave economy: the slave trade, sugar cultivation, railroad construction, and shipping—or, in the case of the most spectacular fortunes, such as those of the Zulueta family, the vertical integration of all activities related to the colonial sugar economy.[80]

At a lower level, though politically no less important, the Antilles were an important source of capital for Spanish merchants. In the nineteenth century, Spanish merchants had a stranglehold on Antillean commercial networks in both imports and exports. For instance, in Santiago in eastern Cuba, 86 percent of all registered merchants in 1833 were Spanish. Between 1841 and 1862, the percentage remained at 80 percent. In the great western sugar regions of Havana and Matanzas, about 75 percent of registered merchants in the 1830s were Spanish. In Puerto Rico, approximately 80 percent of merchants were Spanish.[81]

Regional origin was also extremely significant. By far the largest percentage of merchants were from the Catalan littoral. Of the Spanish merchants in Santiago in 1833, 86 percent—or 71.4 percent of all merchants in the region—were from Catalonia.[82] The proportion of Catalans was less overwhelming though still significant among merchants in western Cuba—approximately 35–40 percent. In the west, a number of merchants came from Spain's northern maritime provinces: Cantabria, Galicia, Asturias, and the Basque country. Canarian and Castilian merchants were also numerous.[83] In Puerto Rico, merchants from Mallorca (one of the Balearic Islands) formed the dominant group,[84] though Catalan merchants from the coastal city of Villanueva y Geltrú were also significant.[85]

Colonial merchant capital played an important role in the development of the Spanish economy, notably in the Catalan industrial sector.[86] Juan Güell y Ferrer was one such example of an *indiano* (a former immigrant to the Antilles) who returned to Catalonia and turned to industry and agriculture. Antonio López y López, later the marquis of Comillas, converted his initial colonial earnings into Spain's largest shipping firm, the Compañía Trasatlántica.[87]

More typically, however, temporary migration to the Antilles to work in the mercantile trades served as a source of upward mobility for poor Spaniards or, especially in the case of Catalans, as a traditional career that was a part of entrenched and sophisticated immigration and business networks.[88] Jordi Maluquer de Motes observes that in some towns on the Catalan coast, such as Sitges, Villanueva y Geltru, San Feliu de Guixols, or Sant Pere de Ribas, landowners at times complained of having to import labor from the Catalan interior because so many young men temporarily migrated to the Antilles to make their living.[89]

Peninsular economic interests in the Antilles were thus profound and complex. The revolutionary settlement of the 1830s had not only consolidated a protectionist political economy in the Peninsula, but rested upon the strengthening of repressive institutions in the colonies as well. If we take Geoff Eley's insight into the conservatism of the nineteenth-century bourgeoisie and extend it to Europe's overseas empires, we find in Cuba and Puerto Rico the most striking manifestation of that conservatism; Spanish and Antillean landowners and merchants built their fortunes on chattel slavery, the most glaring symbol of the old regime.[90] Spanish industrial and agricultural producers who had fought for the protection of the national market in the fifties and sixties considered the Antilles an extension of that market. The preservation of the Antillean market was a policy that resonated deeply among the Spanish population, especially in the Spanish periphery, from the mightiest *hacendado* and slave trader to the humblest Basque or Galician employee in a relative's merchant house in Havana or Ponce. Any threat to the colonial status quo, of which slavery was the anchor, therefore provoked powerful opposition.

The Economists, in contrast, rejected both slavery and the protection of the Antillean market for Spanish producers as archaic institutions that retarded not only colonial but also metropolitan prosperity. Just as the protectionists were to mobilize along the lines of the Spanish Economic Circle after 1868, the Economists utilized their associations and political networks as vehicles for abolitionist politics. The free-trade campaign, however, was not the only precedent for abolitionism. The Economists were part of a group of Madrid-based liberals who were mounting a critique of the Spanish revolution and its limitations. The nexus of that critique was the social question, the relationship between capital and labor in Spain. That critique eventually produced major attacks not only on the political and economic conservatism of the Spanish revolution, but logically on the hidden yet integral facet of the revolution, colonial slavery.

# 4

# Family, Association, and Free Wage Labor

## SOCIAL REFORM IN LIBERAL
## MADRID, 1854–1868

In 1870, Spain's overseas minister, the young political economist Segismundo Moret y Prendergast, spoke before the Spanish Parliament in favor of the gradual abolition of slavery in Cuba and Puerto Rico. He asked his listeners to imagine the idyllic society that would emerge from slave emancipation:

> Imagine in a picturesque landscape a modest house lit by the rays of the setting sun. Inside, a black mother embraces her child. As he returns from work, the father lovingly greets his son. The planter, the former master, passes by on horseback through the beautiful farm where hordes of slaves once lived; . . . the planter waves in friendship to the former slave, who affectionately returns the greeting.[1]

Moret envisioned peaceful relations between former masters and their slaves, now landowners and free laborers, and a peaceful domestic family life for the new free laborers, with men at work in the field and women at home with the family. What enabled Moret to describe this scene? What ideological assumptions provided the details of this vision, particularly the divisions between capital and labor, and work and family?

Metropolitan abolitionist ideology originated in critiques of the "social question," the conflict between labor and capital, articulated by Madrid social reformers between 1854 and 1868. Whereas religious thought and organizations were crucial to the development of antislavery ideology and political mobilization in Great Britain and the United States, religion played

73

only a minor role in Spain. Rather, political and economic ideologies and forms of political action that had been developed in the protectionist campaigns and in middle-class social activism in Madrid lay the foundations for Spanish abolitionist thought and mobilization.[2]

A generation of Madrid liberals that came of age between the Spanish revolutions of 1854 and 1868 challenged the revolutionary settlement of the 1830s by fighting for greater economic liberalization and political democratization—struggles common throughout Europe in this period.[3] To carry out these reforms, the new generation founded or revitalized a network of educational, cultural, and political associations, on the one hand to militate for specific reforms, on the other to promote and publicize their doctrines so as to "improve" or harmonize Spanish society.

Between 1854 and 1868, liberals in Madrid established or transformed the Free Society of Political Economy (1857), the Association for Tariff Reform (1859), the Fomento de las Artes, the Madrid Ateneo, the University of Madrid, the Association for Women's Education (Asociación para la Educación de la Mujer, 1869), and the Spanish Abolitionist Society (1865). This generation also founded in 1876 the Instituto Libre de Enseñanza, the premier educational institution in Spain until the civil war of 1936–1939; the Social Reform Commission (Comisión de Reformas Sociales, 1883), the forerunner of the Ministry of Labor; the Madrid Geographical Society (Sociedad Geográfica de Madrid, 1876); the Society of Africanists and Colonialists (Sociedad de Africanistas y Colonialistas, 1883); and a series of institutions dedicated to women's education, including the Instructors' School (Escuela de Instruices, 1869), the Ladies' Commercial School (Escuela de Comercio para Señoras, 1878), and the Postal and Telegraph School (Escuela de Correos y Telégrafos, 1882).[4] I focus here on the forms of political action and the often contradictory political and economic ideologies that characterized Madrid liberalism. If the debate over trade policies consolidated a national public sphere that was to shape the struggle over colonial slavery, associational life in Madrid created the organizational and ideological precedents for the Spanish Abolitionist Society.

## Ideological Change and Criticism of the Spanish Revolution, 1854–1868

The Economists were one of three concurrent and overlapping movements that rose to prominence in Madrid during the Liberal Union era that advanced the cause of abolition. The other two groups were the Krausists (who took their name from a German philosopher) and the Democratic

Party. Each group sought to extend and refine what they called the middle-class revolution— or, in other words, to challenge the limitations of Spanish liberalism. Both their critiques of Spanish liberalism and their actions were largely centered on what they called the "social question" and its remedies.

As we have seen, political economists argued that the Spanish government still practiced "feudal" or "mercantilist" economic policies, especially protectionism, that curtailed the full functioning of the market. In championing the market, the Economists—whose members were chiefly lawyers, civil servants, engineers, and professors—defended free wage labor categorically, while conceding that a market economy created an atomized society. The Economists opposed any state intervention in the social question or any claim against the rights of capital to exercise full economic freedom. Their solution to the social question was to allow labor to organize peacefully in mutual-aid societies and cross-class educational associations that would assist workers in times of unemployment and raise their moral level by teaching them the virtues of hard work and resignation. They also advocated strengthening the working-class family by keeping working-class women in the home so as to provide a stable environment for male workers and children.[5]

While the Economists were interested in furthering the freedom of the market, the Krausists, followers of the philosopher Karl Christian Krause (1781–1832), were far more concerned with assuaging the social and political conflicts created by the middle-class revolution. Krause's Spanish popularizer was Julián Sanz del Río, who had studied with Krause's students in Heidelberg in the 1840s. In 1854, Sanz del Río was named professor of the history of philosophy at the University of Madrid, where he soon gained an enthusiastic following.[6]

The Krausists believed it was necessary to reestablish the social bonds that the middle-class revolution had severed. They defended the political and economic freedom supposedly created by the middle-class revolution, but they believed that Spanish society must be harmoniously ordered through corporate and natural associations to countervail the potential chaos of absolute freedom. The Krausists advocated the creation of a national educational system that would enlighten all Spanish subjects regarding their proper position within Spanish society. This society was necessarily hierarchical because not all people were born with equal or equivalent intellectual or economic capacities. To incorporate all strata of Spanish society into the state, the Krausists advocated the formation of professional associations representing doctors, printers, construction workers, and so on. A comprehensive national educational system would teach the members of each profession their place within the social and political hierarchy, while the associations would guarantee all members of society political and economic representation and a form of social organization that countered the atomization caused by the market. The family was one of the forms of "natural" human association most vigorously championed by the Krausists. A properly ordered family prevented alienation, provided early education for children, and reflected the ideal of harmony between the sexes.[7]

Like the Krausists, the Democrats sought to incorporate all members of Spanish society into a harmonious state, though unlike the Krausists they believed in the political equality of all "citizens." The Democratic Party, founded in 1849, joined Spain's disparate republicans and the left wing of the monarchist Progressive Party, which sought to ensure the sovereign power of the Cortes over the monarchy. The division between republicans and monarchists was not the party's only quarrel, however. Despite their consensus on political democracy, the Democrats were deeply split over the question of state intervention in the economy to guarantee equality.[8]

"Individualist" Democrats like Emilio Castelar argued that the free laboring individual was the basis of any modern social order. They denounced state intervention in the economy as a return to "absolutism." The individualists believed that the resolution of the social question would come through a political, not an economic, settlement. They characterized the conflicts within middle-class society as being between the "people" and "parasites," who exercised unjust economic power through their monopoly of political power. In a democratic state, oligarchic political and economic power would be broken, and all individual citizens would be free to pursue wealth on an equal footing. One of the most important consequences of political equality for workers would be full freedom of association. The Democrats, both "individualists" and "socialists," held a far more conflictual view of the relationship between capital and labor than did the Economists or the Krausists. Thus Castelar, for instance, defended labor's right to associate in trade unions and mutual-aid societies to combat capital's attempts to depress wages.[9]

The "socialist" Democrats, such as Fernando Garrido and Francisco Pi y Margall, sought to empower labor even further. They argued that the logical extension of the middle-class revolution was the redistribution of the disentailed lands that had been unfairly appropriated by a small oligarchy in the thirties and forties. Pi, for instance, believed that the propertyless individual was defenseless because he was subjected to the marketplace. The political solution advanced by the individualists was futile because members of the proletariat lacked the material resources to be equal citizens. Therefore, to attain the promise of economic and political freedom held out by the middle-class revolution, Pi and the socialists advocated on the one hand distributing the bounty of the revolution, and on the other empowering labor in the marketplace through associations similar to guilds.[10]

Despite their differences over political and economic rights, both individualist and socialist Democrats shared a similar conception of the function of the family in a market society—a conception underpinned by a shared ideology of gender. Citizens and workers were men. Women were wives and mothers, performing crucial roles in a market society. Like the Krausists and the Economists, the Democrats saw the family, with the woman in the home, as an essential complement to liberal political and economic institutions because of its stabilizing influence. Thus, the private association of the family would complement the public association of male workers in resolving the social question.

## Association

The right of association was one of the most controversial political issues in the aftermath of the revolution of 1854. In this phase of the struggle over the political economy of Spanish liberalism, certain forms of association were immediately sanctioned, such as capital's right to form joint stock companies.[11] On the other hand, the government limited the right of workers to form associations, specifically to demand higher wages and to influence the labor process. This decision was aimed particularly at the textile workers of Barcelona, who during the Progressive Biennium had mobilized to protest the introduction of self-acting looms, had mounted a petition campaign to demand full freedom of association, and had organized a general strike in 1855. During the 1854–1868 period, the right of association for workers was generally limited to mutual-aid societies and cooperatives. Trade unions and political parties were officially banned.[12]

The different definitions of *association* for Spanish liberals between 1854 and 1868 reflected its contested meaning. In liberal discourse, the definition ranged from the association of capital to create savings institutions for unemployed workers, to the association of trade unions to pressure employers for better salaries and working conditions, to the reorganization of labor into associations that regulated trades in a manner similar to guilds. All agreed on the importance of educational associations for "improving" the worker.

The Economists generally agreed with limited forms of association.

They were above all interested in furthering the flow of European capital into Spain, hence their militant campaign against the government's protectionist policies and their defense of capital against the "socialist" or "communist" demands of labor. For instance, in 1862 the Economists criticized a petition signed by 15,000 Catalan workers in favor of the right of association because the workers spoke of "the need to *combat* capital." The Economists chastized the workers for their failure to realize that "in a completely free economic regime, the relation between labor and capital is not a struggle, but a perfect harmony."[13]

The Economists argued that capital and labor were essentially harmonious partners in production. Resolving the social question could not come at the cost of capital, the animating spirit of production, but through the betterment of the workers. Since workers were free individuals, they should be permitted to exercise their natural right to associate. Segismundo Moret y Prendergast stated this position in a lecture before a group of artisans in the Fomento de las Artes, a school for adult technical education: "The greatest necessity of the working class . . . is free labor in its full extension, and as its first consequence, freedom of association."[14]

By *free labor* and *freedom of association,* the Economists understood the forms of association officially permitted during the 1854–1868 period: mutual-aid societies, savings institutions *(cajas de ahorros),* schools such as the Fomento de las Artes, and reading rooms *(gabinetes de lectura).* In other words, they advocated forms of association that in theory improved the "moral" condition of the worker or that provided professional training to make him more competitive in the labor market without making any claims against the rights of capital.[15]

The Fomento de las Artes in particular was an important example of the sort of workers' association favored by Madrid-based liberals. In 1847 a group of Madrid artisans had founded the Velada de Artistas, an artisans' social club. Middle-class reformers soon transformed it into an association for workers' education.[16] The Economists hoped that in the Fomento de las Artes workers would hear the teachings of political economy and come to appreciate the harmonious relationship between capital and labor. They would thus understand that "all of their interests are on the side of economic liberty!"[17] The institute offered training in various trades and courses in mathematics, political economy, and languages; it sponsored trade fairs, a choral society, and public speeches by distinguished intellectuals. In the 1860s, its professors and speakers included such future abolitionists as the political economist Moret, the Democrats Emilio Castelar and Manuel

Becerra, and the Krausist philosopher Fernando de Castro, who in 1863 delivered a speech at the Fomento de las Artes entitled "The Worker's Morality." Although the speech emphasized respect for private property, it was much admired by a worker-student, Anselmo Lorenzo, one of the founders of the Spanish anarchist movement.[18] In the 1880s and 1890s, the dominant figure in the institute was Spain's most famous abolitionist, Rafael María de Labra.[19]

Reformers valued associations like the Fomento de las Artes not only for their didactic function, but also because they served as bases for political support. Such support was especially important for the Democrats and their successors, the splintered republican parties of the Restoration (1875–1923). During the Restoration, as the suffrage gradually expanded, republicans established social clubs to attract supporters and to woo voters away from other republican factions and the Socialist Party (PSOE) and to encourage them to vote. (Abstention was common among anarchists.) The Republican associations offered a range of educational and cultural services that might include classes with a heavy emphasis on anticlerical "social science," choral societies, reading rooms, and cafes.[20]

Rafael María de Labra's attempts to establish his party in Barcelona during the Restoration illustrates the importance that republicans assigned to popular associations in coordinating political support. In the 1890s, with universal male suffrage restored, the rival republican parties jockeyed for position in Barcelona, an important republican stronghold because of its organized working class.[21] A letter to Labra from one of his Barcelona organizers reported the weakness of Labra's and Nicolás Salmerón's Centralist Republican Party by pointing to the party's inability to run a club:

> Since last August we don't even have a club *[Casino]*. We had to move out of our last flat because we couldn't pay the rent or the gas. We have collected enough funds to set up another club, but we haven't been able to do so yet because the landlords refuse to allow their flats to be used as clubs. This state of affairs has caused desperation among our friends.[22]

During the Liberal Union period, however, given the restrictions on political organizations, the Democrats placed more emphasis on educational and cultural associations like the Fomento de las Artes. The future abolitionists in the Democratic Party had broader notions of association than those advocated by the Economists. Some emphasized the "improvement" of the worker, while others defended the workers' right to play a more active role in managing the production process. This divergence over the rights of labor divided the Democratic Party into the so-called individualists and socialists.

Emilio Castelar, the best-known individualist, often found himself in agreement with the Economists' campaigns for economic liberty. For instance, he argued that free trade was one of the crucial steps in the achievement of universal freedom.[23] His participation in the free-trade campaigns gave Castelar an opportunity to carry out his own political propaganda. How, Castelar asked in a public speech organized by the Association for Tariff Reform, could the Economists defend economic liberty while denying political liberty to the mass of the Spanish nation? Only those who enjoyed political liberty were truly free to pursue and defend their economic interests. In particular, workers could not defend themselves adequately in the market without politcal rights.[24]

In Castelar's view, the individual's rights should be enshrined in a secular state that recognized and protected each citizen's freedom and equality of opportunity. The individual's rights were not simply limited to the marketplace, as the Economists held.[25] Castelar envisioned a democratic state of equal citizens who freely associated and competed in the market economy. Democracy would ensure the resolution of the social question because it would provide workers with the civil and political rights they needed to defend themselves against capital:

> The isolated worker succumbs. Alone, he cannot resist the demands of capital. It is in the capitalist's interest to decrease wages. But once the worker has associated with his brothers, he will alleviate his hard luck and difficult condition. He will be able to set the price of his labor; he will determine his hours; he will have savings that will support him in his old age.[26]

Though Castelar disagreed with the Economists concerning the limits of association and the inherently antagonistic nature of the relationship between labor and capital, he agreed with their defense of economic individualism and the free market. He defended the workers' political rights and their right to struggle with capital for higher wages and better working conditions, but he relegated this struggle to the marketplace. The state established the rules of the game by protecting the right of association and private property, but it allowed free individuals to carry on this conflict among themselves. Castelar argued vehemently that the state had no role in the production process, as advocated by various schools of European socialism. Castelar likened socialism to Oriental despotism or the absolutism of the old regime because it sought to eradicate the cornerstone of modern Western civilization: freedom for the laboring individual. Searching for European examples to support his position, Castelar defended the English trade unions against the French social workshops of the 1848 revolution. According to Castelar, the latter

> fomented laziness, compromised individual labor, produced expensively and badly, disturbed the natural economic laws, subverted society, and tired the workers themselves who eventually came to prefer an insecure tomorrow and uncertain bread to the forced labor and bitter bread of socialism. . . . Regulate associations through state power and you will have another absolutist association: the . . . abolished guilds in which there were not workers but slaves.[27]

Castelar aimed his condemnation of socialism for reenslaving labor at the "socialist" wing of his own party. The Democratic Party united political leaders engaged in distinct local political struggles. Not surprisingly, the most prominent of the so-called socialist Democrats hailed from Barcelona, the city with Spain's most advanced industrial sector and the most militant working-class organizations.

As in the rest of Spain, association had various meanings for Barcelona Democrats.[28] For instance, Ceferino Tressera, a Republican who had fought with Garibaldi in Italy, put together a sort of workers' catechism in 1862 entitled *El libro del obrero* in which he brought together republicans like himself and José Anselmo Clavé with prominent neo-Catholic conservatives such as Joan Mañé y Flaquer, Manuel Duran i Bas, and José Leopoldo Feu. The message of *El libro del obrero* was clear, despite the range of political attitudes it represented: workers should associate to improve themselves— for instance, in Clavé's famous choral societies ("a school for dignified citizens," as Tressera called them)—and they should accept their subordinate position in an industrial society.[29]

On the other side were figures such as Francisco Pi y Margall and Ramón Simó y Badia, who during the Progressive Biennium (1854–1856) were deeply involved in the Barcelona workers' struggle to achieve full freedom of association. Pi and Simó formed part of a workers' front established in Madrid during that period as the directors of the newspaper *El Eco de la Clase Obrera*. They joined with the two "worker" deputies in the Constituent Assembly, Joaquim Molar and Juan Alsina, to coordinate an active campaign in favor of the right to associate.

Within this front, however, there existed a disjuncture between the radical discourse of the newspaper and the moderate demands for association

voiced in the 1855 petition to the Cortes that was signed by 33,000 workers.[30] For Pi, association went far beyond the right to resist capital. Association was the right of workers to control and administer their own labor
through various institutions. For instance, he advocated the creation of a
workers' bank and trade schools supported by the government. More radi-
cally, he argued that workers in all trades must serve apprenticeships and
meet regulations established by workers themselves before entering the
labor market. He also argued that labor should be organized in labor ex-
changes at the regional and national level and distributed according to
fluctuations in the economy. Workers would be dispatched to areas where
labor was needed and transferred from economically depressed regions. In
short, workers' associations ought to administer work and production
rather than trust to the anarchy of the market.[31] To those who denounced
him as a socialist or absolutist and who defended the priority of the rights
of capital, Pi responded: "It is labor that has created capital, not capital labor."[32]

The workers' petition to the Cortes, in contrast, demanded the political
right to associate without any mention of labor's right to organize production—a concept far too radical for a Cortes dominated by the mainstream
liberal parties, the Progressives, the Moderates, and the new fusion of elements from both parties, the Liberal Union. The position articulated in the
petition more closely resembled the idea of association put forward by the
Economists or individualist Democrats like Castelar than that of the socialists. The petition defended free wage labor and the market as natural, but it
also claimed the right of association as a further natural right that accompanied the rise of individual freedom: "We only [ask for] the universalization
of a right, or better said, the recognition of an inherent liberty."[33] The workers argued that only the right of association guaranteed them subsistence-
level wages and the conditions in which to form mutual-aid societies to
protect themselves during industrial crises. Furthermore, according to the
petition, association was the only way to address the improvement of the
worker through education and stengthening the family.

The disjuncture between Pi's and Simó's radicalism and the moderate
demands of the workers indicated the restrictions on association during the
Liberal Union period. In general, Spanish liberals understood association
as the coming together of free individuals dedicated to the improvement of
the workers through education and mutual aid. This view stressed the essentially harmonious nature of capital and labor. The answer to the social
question lay in reinforcing the workers' moral and economic position, not
in checking the rights of capital. Free wage labor and the market were sac-

rosanct. Pi's call for the reorganization of production by workers was an iso-lated, politically marginalized position.

### The First International and the September Revolution (1868–1874)

The limits of the liberal view of association and the middle-class nature of Spanish antislavery became clearer after the democratic revolution of 1868. With freedom of speech and association established as guaranteed rights, socialist critiques of liberalism appeared. The most radical critique came from the First International. The Italian anarchist Giuseppe Fanelli, a dis-ciple of Bakunin, came to Spain in 1868 to establish a branch of the Inter-national (founded in 1864). In Madrid, he discovered his most eager con-verts in the heart of the liberal association par excellence: the Fomento de las Artes. The initial Madrid nucleus of the International was made up of workers from preindustrial trades: a ropemaker, a carpenter, a goldsmith, a journalist, a lithographer, two tailors, two shoemakers, two engravers, four printers, and five painters.[34]

One of Fanelli's first converts was the printer and prizewinning student of the Fomento de las Artes, Anselmo Lorenzo.[35] In his memoirs, Lorenzo spoke warmly of the institute during the 1860s. Despite the dominance of liberal ideologues such as Moret, it served the crucial function of uniting Madrid's progressive elements, both middle-class and proletarian. Lorenzo claimed that at the institute workers learned the science of political economy and were weaned away from the tavern. Fanelli and the Interna-tional, however, provided the worker-students with a critique of political economy as taught at the institute and indicated the limits of middle-class associationism.

One of Lorenzo's first acts in 1869, after the encounter with Fanelli, was to enter another of Madrid's preeminent liberal societies, the Association for Tariff Reform, to debate political economy and propagate the International's position on the social question.[36] Lorenzo made his debut at a public meeting of the association held at the Madrid stock exchange. When the floor was opened to the public, Lorenzo delivered a speech on the need of the newly triumphant revolution to go beyond guaranteeing political rights and address the social question. He placed special emphasis on the importance of education in creating true social and political equal-ity. Despite Lorenzo's trepidation, the Economists, who dominated the As-sociation for Tariff Reform, enthusiastically applauded his speech and in-sisted that he be seated next to the president for the remainder of the meet-ing. Lorenzo's emphasis on the role of education in resolving the social question, his endorsement of political economy, had temporarily gained him and the International the approval of such prominent Economists as Laureano Figuerola, José Echegaray, and Gabriel Rodríguez, all of whom were ministers or deputies in the new government. Moret, who had recognized Lorenzo as a student from the Fomento de las Artes, was especially pleased.[37]

The membership was less tolerant of Lorenzo's intervention in the next public meeting of the association. This time, Lorenzo spoke of the "importance of human reason's independence from all religious dogma." His listeners now responded with shouts of "Get out!" ("¡Fuera!"). When Lorenzo and his companions defended their freedom of speech in a public forum, the formerly benevolent Economists turned on them their full oratorical contempt, conceding the Internationalists' right to speak while cursing their ignorance.[38]

Liberals' frustration with the workers' use of their freedoms of speech and association reappeared more dramatically in October 1871 in the aftermath of the Paris Commune, as the Cortes debated a government proposal to outlaw the International in Spain.[39] The debates over the ban also demonstrated the rifts within the liberal parties that composed the Spanish Abolitionist Society concerning the limits of association. Although the Economists, Krausists, and Republicans who animated the antislavery movement categorically opposed the government's ban, they disagreed among themselves over the "errors" or righteousness of the International.

The Economists took the most conservative stance within the antislavery movement. Gabriel Rodríguez, for instance, argued that although force would not eradicate the International, it still must be fought. Members of the International should be allowed the right of association and speech, but their opponents should unwaveringly combat the movement through the same means:

> We cannot place our confidence in the State or the government. Instead, where there is an Internationalist idea, form an anti-International association; where there is an article, write an opposing one; and if it uses the sword, then use the sword, but always within the law.[40]

Thus, while opposing the government's proposed ban on the International, Economists such as Rodríguez and Moret were members of the association opposed to the International, the Defense of Society (Defensa de la Sociedad), which united political, military, and intellectual figures from across the political spectrum. The association billed itself as an alliance of "permanent and fundamental interests against the doctrines and tendencies of the International." Its motto was "Religion—Family—Country—Work and Property."[41]

Republicans and Krausists, in contrast, took a far more conciliatory stance toward the International. Both saw its appearance as a legitimate expression of the "fourth estate's" claim and right to forge new social bonds after the destruction of the old regime. The Krausist philosopher and soon-to-be president of the First Republic (1873), Nicolás Salmerón, argued that the dissolution of feudal society's corporate bonds had created an atomized society. The International was symptomatic of the new social order in which individuals experimented with new forms of association to overcome the pure egoism of middle-class society.[42] He and his fellow Krausist Eugenio Montero Ríos, at the time minister of governance (that is, minister of the interior), defended the International's existence because of their belief in the inviolability of individual rights such as the right of free speech and association. They also advocated forging new organic bonds among the various classes of Spanish society by invigorating public education and religious institutions. Through secular education and religious instruction, the fourth estate would learn the principle of "duty" *(deber)* and renounce the International's mistaken belief in the inevitability of class conflict in the new middle-class regime.[43]

The "socialist" wing of the newly formed Federal Republican Party (which supplanted the Democratic Party after 1868) sympathized even further with the International, emphasizing workers' rights rather than duties. Like the Krausists, Pi y Margall saw the International as the fourth estate's entrance into public life. Like the Internationalists, he also saw class conflict as an essential feature of middle-class society. This conflict would be resolved by the distribution of property to all members of society. Spain's middle-class revolution had not gone far enough in destroying feudal privilege because it had created a class of proletarians, now stripped of the paternalistic relations of the old regime, antagonistic to the new order. According to Pi, the "universalization" of the middle-class revolution was the answer to the International:

> Do you not constantly repeat that property is the complement of the human personality? That it is the sine qua non of the family's independence, the bond between future and past generations? If so, then it is natural for the proletarian class to say: if property is the complement of the human personality, then I, who sense in myself a personality as eminent as that of the men of the middle class, need property to complement it.[44]

Thus, in direct response to the Economists' individualism, Pi argued that the individual was incomplete without the redistribution of property.

The Federal Republican and Fourierist Fernando Garrido echoed Pi's argument. He held, indeed, that not only must the middle-class revolution be universalized so as to reconcile the antagonisms within middle-class society, but further, that the laboring classes were the only legitimate heirs of the shattered old regime. Their labor was the source of society's wealth:

> The advent of the middle class to power is justified by its destruction of the aristocratic and clerical classes' privileges. What cannot be justified is the appropriation of the property of the dispossessed classes that was destroyed in the name of great social interests, in the name of progress and liberty.
>
> The property of the dispossessed classes belongs to the nation. And it belongs most of all to those who had nothing, because the possessing classes had acquired their property improperly, because they had not worked for it. This property should have been given to the working classes because they had been dispossessed by the aristocracy.
>
> To avoid the repetition of these evils is why the International Workingman's Association has been founded.[45]

Garrido also denounced the hypocrisy of middle-class attacks on the rights of workers to associate. While seeking to ban the International, the same middle-class politicians permitted the existence of ultramontane religious associations, namely the Catholic Church, within Spanish borders. According to Garrido, Spanish workers joined the International to claim their rights as Spanish citizens. The Catholic Church, in contrast, was both a feudal relic and a threat to the Spanish nation because Catholics were subordinated to a foreigner: the pope. For Garrido, the International represented the extension of the middle-class revolution. Middle-class politicians' attacks on the International represented their own subordination to the feudal past.[46]

Where the "socialist" wing of Spanish republicanism broke with the International was not in their critiques of middle-class society, but in their attitudes toward political participation and the locus and agents of social change. Garrido's confrontation with the International during the September Revolution brought these differences into sharp relief. According to Anselmo Lorenzo, Garrido had enjoyed tremendous popularity among Spanish workers prior to the September Revolution. Garrido and other Federal Republicans, however, opposed the antipolitical strategies of the Internationalists. They believed that social change could be enacted only by a democratic state that represented the people as a whole.⁴⁷ Garrido denounced the abstention of the Internationalists, arguing that they were being secretly manipulated by the Jesuits so as to undermine the new democratic regime.⁴⁸

The Internationalists took umbrage at Garrido's condescension. They believed, particularly the Bakuninists, that the redistribution of property would come only through spontaneous and violent revolution that would destroy not only private property but also the state. Workers did not need the middle-class parties and the state to better their social condition because they were the agents of historical change. Change took place not through the mediation of the state but in direct confrontations between workers and capitalists in "society."⁴⁹ The triumph of the workers presupposed the destruction of the state and the return to the organic and harmonious functioning of society, now free from the violence and conflict produced by private property and coercive political institutions.⁵⁰

The split between workers and middle-class reformers over political action and participation had implications for the antislavery movement. Like Garrido and the republicans, Spanish abolitionists believed that they defended the rights of workers, all workers. They argued that Spanish workers had a natural interest in abolitionism and that they should support the Abolitionist Society's actions and policies. Although Internationalists occasionally expressed an abstract sympathy for colonial slaves, they felt more strongly a visceral distaste for the condescension (as expressed by Garrido or the Economists) and reformism of middle-class associations like the Abolitionist Society.

In January 1873, the Abolitionist Society held a triumphant mass demonstration in Madrid in favor of the abolition of Puerto Rican slavery. The society's newspaper, *El Abolicionista Español,* reported that more than 10,000 people took part. Only the absence of workers in the crowd dimmed the enthusiasm of the event. The abolitionist public was decidedly middle-class:

> The attendance was extraordinary. Estimates ranged from 10,000 to 16,000 people. Missing was the working mass that usually attends other demonstrations, especially republican demonstrations. On the other hand, the number of well-to-do people and of those active in politics was so great that we can roundly claim that we do not know of another public act attended by so many persons of that class.⁵¹

Spanish workers, or at least the organized Internationalists, responded to such criticisms by claiming that they were more concerned with the "white slaves"⁵² that the middle-class exploited in the metropolis. According to one Barcelona Internationalist newspaper, the true abolition of slavery in the colonies would be guaranteed only if the abolitionists transformed the slaves into independent producers with their own land and means of production. Otherwise, "emancipation" would merely reproduce the slavery that already existed in Spain:

> The slavery of the [blacks] is the usurpation of their physical and intellectual powers to the benefit of their masters. The salary of [Spanish workers] is the usurpation of their physical and intellectual power to the benefit of the wealthy. What is the difference?[53]

That separation between middle-class reformers and the organized working class was due not to the dynamics of colonial politics but to the separation between middle and working-class activists concerning the "social question" in the metropolis.[54] The majority of the abolitionists opposed radical working-class politics and sought to resolve the social question by incorporating Spanish workers into a harmonious yet hierarchical capitalist social order. Workers would learn their "duties" in such a reformed society through education and peaceful mutual-aid associations. Even radical "socialist" republicans like Garrido and Pi, both members of the Abolitionist Society, while they criticized the limits of the middle-class revolution, alienated organized workers by emphasizing the top-down nature of social change. The Internationalists, in contrast, sought direct worker participation in the process of social change and more far-reaching changes than those envisioned by middle-class reformers. They sought to overcome hierarchy and stratification both in the process of social change and in the end result of that change. Internationalists might have had some interest in antislavery politics, but they had none in the patrician associationism which the Abolitionist Society represented.

## The Family

The family occupied an important and ambiguous position within liberal economic ideologies. As Lynn Hunt argues concerning liberal discourse on the family during the French Revolution: "The individual was always imagined as embedded in family relationships and . . . these relationships were always potentially unstable."[55] On the one hand, Spanish liberals sanctified the family, celebrating it as an inviolable sanctuary from public life that had a stabilizing and moralizing effect on Spanish society. On the other, they distrusted the family, seeing it as a private institution that mediated between the individual and natural political and economic institutions. It was thus a possible site of subversion and reaction. The problem for Spanish liberals was to strengthen the family while also asserting some control over it and its members.

In either case, a gender ideology that divided men and women into public and private spaces underpinned liberal conceptions of the family. Men and women had distinct but complementary roles within society. Men played out their roles in politics and the market, while women created a peaceful haven in the home. Liberals believed that this division of men and women into public and private spaces stabilized men, protected the honor of women, and provided children with a loving environment in which to grow and learn.

The darker side of the family was its private nature. Within the family, women might hold inordinate power. Liberals distrusted the supposed power of women because they believed women to be pawns of the Catholic Church. Liberals sought to counteract this potentially harmful influence by altering the sharp division between public and private and imposing some sort of moral or intellectual control over women. Thus, especially in the case of middle-class women, they advocated education and explored making limited public sites available to women. The entrance of women into public life would both "civilize" the harsh public sphere and "civilize" ignorant women who exerted too much authority in private.[56]

### The Family and the Social Question

In discussing solutions to the social question, Spanish liberals placed great emphasis on the revitalization of the working-class family. Moret's description of the happy postemancipation household was an echo of an earlier description of a Spanish worker's home after the triumph of free trade.[57] According to the interpretation of Spanish society made by the new generation of Spanish liberals, the working-class family felt most keenly the atomizing effects of the middle-class revolution. The capitalist's demand for cheap labor, steadily declining wages, and the risk of unemployment in times of industrial crisis drove every member of the working-class family—men, women, and children—into the workplace to earn subsistence wages. The dissolution of the family led to further immiseration and immorality: women could not learn to be mothers because they were away from home and in the workplace, where their honor was constantly at risk, children were uneducated and unloved, men lost their authority and their self-respect because they could not support their families.

The perception of the worker family in crisis and dissolution clearly contradicted the notion of the harmonious relationship between capital and labor. How could capital and labor be in harmony if that division were tearing apart the family? Spanish liberals resolved that contradiction by arguing that association and the family formed a symbiotic solution to the social question. Association provided workers with higher wages and relief in times of unemployment, thus allowing men to earn sufficent wages to preserve the "natural" family order: men at work, women and children at home. The strengthened family stabilized the male worker, protected the honor of women, and provided children with a loving environment and opportunity for education, all of which ensured the reproduction of healthy and industrious workers. In short, the family, like the various forms of association, improved the condition of the worker and complemented, rather than antagonized, capital.

The Economists addressed the relationships linking the working-class family, the individual, and the market in their debates in the Free Society of Political Economy.[58] The most dogmatic Economists fully defended the effects of market forces on the family and insisted that "nature demands the woman's participation in industrial functions."[59] But the majority of the Economists argued for the importance of protecting the family against the market. Though they staunchly defended the natural functioning of economic laws, they also defended what they considered the natural roles of men and women in society: men were public workers, and women were also workers, but they worked as mothers and wives.

Moret, for instance, stated quite clearly, "The female worker is no longer a woman."[60] The woman's separation from her natural place in the home had demoralizing and denaturalizing consequences both for her as an individual and for the working population in general:

Instead of the mysterious and pure life of the domestic hearth, . . . so necessary for her as well as for us, [the female worker] lives under the direction of a foreman, surrounded by companions of dubious repute, in constant contact with men, separated from her husband and from her children. In the worker's home, the father and mother are absent fourteen hours a day. Thus, the family does not exist. . . . The results are a horrifying mortality rate, sickly temperaments in the surviving children, increasing racial degeneration, and a total lack of moral education.

Women thus must remain in the home, sheltered from the immoral workplace, and provide the proper care and education of their children. "The woman must work," wrote Moret, "but that work is in the home."[61]

Luis María Pastor based his advocacy of a gendered division of public and private spheres on the "natural" physical, intellectual, and emotional differences between men and women. According to Pastor, men were ambitious, hardworking, and individualistic. Women were essentially emotional beings who achieved their full potential only through their relationships with other persons:

> Observe the woman in any of life's situations: daughter, wife or mother, she never has a completely independent existence. She is a planet that reflects light, not a fixed star that shines on its own. . . . Weakness and timidity are the essential condition of women. And in the very character of this weakness, one finds proof of the idea that the woman is always united to another existence. If she is cowardly and fearful when she herself is directly attacked, she becomes a lion when her parents, her husband, or the child of her womb are threatened.[62]

Pastor's discussion of women's dependent nature was a particularly clear example of the gendered nature of the liberals' economic ideology. The Economists were staunch economic individualists and argued that the free individual was society's basic economic unit. But that individual was clearly a man possessed of certain male characteristics: ambition, virility, assertiveness, and so on.[63] Women were not free economic agents but dependent beings who in contrast to men were emotional, timid, and pliant. They were daughters, wives, and mothers instead of capitalists, politicians, or lawyers because their nature suited them for nurturing humanity's emotional capacities and rendered them ineffective in the public world. Their responsibility in a liberal market society was to secure the peaceful haven of the home where they cared for their parents, husbands, or children. According to the Economists, in the case of the working class, women carried out the crucial function of providing a safe and loving environment for their worker husbands and their children, who themselves were future workers or homemakers.

### Women in Public

Though liberals considered women to be dependent, they did not believe them to be powerless. Pastor's image of the lion protecting her kin reflected the liberals' distrust of the emotional power of familial bonds. Liberals feared a private sphere dominated by beings outside the economy, women, because it could produce loyalties or behavior that contradicted the harmonious functioning of the market or the polis. Classic examples of the behavior criticized by liberals were bread or draft riots, commonly incited by women. In these cases, familial bonds superseded natural economic or political laws. Another potential danger was the influence of the Catholic Church, especially among middle-class women.[64]

To countervail what they saw as the seclusion of the family, liberals sought to open the public sphere to women and thus exert some influence over them. They hoped that the presence of women would also civilize the harsh male public world. This endeavor was, however, generally limited to middle-class women. For working-class women, liberals favored the strict division of public and private because of its supposedly beneficial effects on the social question.

The venue for the discussion of middle-class women's incorporation into public life was the Association for Women's Education (Asociación para la Educación de la Mujer), founded in 1869. The spectacle of men lecturing to a female audience on women's education demonstrated not only the nature and content of education for women at the time, but also what were considered appropriate public spaces for women and the gender hierarchies within them. Women were properly expected to belong to associations or attend meetings dedicated to social reform, whether the cause was women's education or the abolition of slavery, because women's emotional and compassionate natures predisposed them to aid the less fortunate. Men, however, clearly took the lead in these associations and instructed women in their proper roles.

The organizer of the lectures, held at the University of Madrid, was the university's rector, Fernando de Castro, a Krausist, who at the time was also the president of the Abolitionist Society. Castro brought together Krausists, political economists such as Moret and Joaquin María Sanromá, and Federal Republicans like Pi y Margall to lecture to middle-class women on their role within Spanish society.

In his inaugural lecture, Castro argued that modern philosophy recognized the unity of humanity, despite its apparent divisions. Those differences were complementary and harmonious, not antagonistic.[65] One of the fundamental human divisions was that between men and women. Castro described that division in a geometric metaphor:

> The man is a staight line whose unity, inflexibility and always constant direction signal his severe and progressive character. The symbol of the woman is the curved line whose . . . undulations signify her flexibility, her inconstancy and lack of progressive initiative, her conservative spirit, and that amiable sweetness and exquisite dexterity that soften the tensest and most difficult relations in both Society and the family.[66]

Given these distinct yet harmonious natures, Castro explained, men were best suited for a public life of politics and business, while women were made for the home and the care of their families, where they provided a gentle refuge from the harsh and inflexible male public world. While that division was natural, Castro argued that women required instruction in their roles as homemakers. Women could not remain in ignorance as they once had, but rather must be enlightened as to their true nature and responsibilities. According to Castro, education was especially important because of the domestic power that women wielded:

> One of the capital questions that the progress of civilization has raised for debate in modern societies is the education of the woman. [She is] man's companion, life and soul of the family, teacher of customs, the gentlest and most intimate influence. For that reason she is perhaps the most powerful influence among all those that shape life's pattern and direct the providential fulfillment of human destiny.[67]

Because women possessed such power, men must teach them to use it wisely and productively. Castro stated that women ought to be instructed in the fields that directly concerned them: religion, home and family, pedagogy, and so on. Education would aid the woman in running her household and educating her children. It would also improve the relationship between the sexes by raising women's cultural level to one closer to that of men.[68]

Castro warned, however, that exalting the woman as educator of her children and making her an emotional and intellectual companion to her husband did not empower her to overstep her auxiliary position within the natural gender hierarchy of the family and society. Men remained dominant partners in the relation between the sexes, and Castro advised his public to respect the ultimate preeminence of the male:

> Your destiny as wives and mothers is to council and influence. You must not impose. The moment you decide to coerce the man, taking advantage of the ascendancy and empire that your weakness and your tears give you, you commit the gravest and most unpardonable error.[69]

Like Castro, other male speakers addressed women's education in terms of the woman's role within the family and the home. Castro and other abolitionists such as the Economist Moret or the Federal Republican Pi y Margall, even while speaking of the need to raise the intellectual and cultural level of women, enforced a strict division between the public male world and the private female world. Women were chiefly educators of their children and companions to their husbands.[70]

Other speakers, however, argued that relegating women to the home was unnatural and unjust, both for women and Spanish society as a whole. Women could play useful roles within society, and their presence as public actors would have a civilizing and beneficial effect on Spanish manners and culture. The Economist and abolitionist Joaquín María Sanromá, for instance, stated: "I do not vacillate in avowing that the development of civilizations always is measured by the degree of influence that the woman exercises in all aspects of social life."[71] Sanromá argued that women's natures made them perfectly suited for certain public activities that were easily reconciled with their primary responsibilities as wives, mothers, and daughters:

> Why can the woman not be a mother, daughter, or wife at the same time that she is an artist, industrialist, traveler, writer, teacher, and above all, citizen? Why can religious sentiment, love, and friendship, the only affections that certain schools ascribe to women, not be harmonized perfectly with the artistic sentiment, with some inclination for business, with the passion for abundant reading, . . . and with the instinct for the great political and social reforms.[72]

While acknowledging women's aptitude for politics, business, and the arts, Sanromá held that women would act differently from men and that their actions would have different consequences. Women would soften the harsh public sphere, making social interaction more harmonious and cordial. Regarding social reform—the public vocation for women par excellence in male liberal discourse—women breathed compassion and spirit into the arid male world. In this dichotomy, men were intellectual and formal, women emotional and compassionate: "You are the great lever, the great moral force brought into the political world. Your mission is to light the fire of sentiment in those icy atmospheres. Oh! for too long politics have been a snowy region!"[73]

Like Sanromá, Rafael María de Labra, the most radical metropolitan abolitionist, affirmed the importance of women's participation in social and political reform movements. Labra, however, spoke of women's need to act to overcome their own subjugation within Spanish society instead of emphasizing their potential civilizing effect on male society. In contrast to other speakers, Labra addressed the legal system that effectively contradicted the cultural affirmation of marriage and motherhood by suppressing women's individual rights. Under Castilian law, women had virtually no rights: spinsters (*solteras*) were minors until their fathers died; widows could lose their children if they remarried; and the married woman, according to Labra, "by the mere fact of her marriage loses her personality almost

Rafael María de Labra (1841–1918).
Photo: Robert Paquette.

absolutely. She owes her husband fidelity and companionship; she owes him, more than obedience, submission."[74] Thus, while many claimed that the role of "wife and mother is august," the current legal system worked to undermine the dignity of women: "Our customs exalt the mission of the married woman, but our laws weaken and debase that mission, and in this relation, the laws have greater force and efficacy."[75]

To counteract this pernicious process and achieve the "emancipation of the woman," Labra advocated three crucial reforms: recognition of women's juridical personality; civil marriage based on free contract; and a "family council" that would address conflicts between mothers and fathers, treating them as equals.[76] According to Labra, Spanish women could reach these goals only gradually through persistent public and private propaganda. He dismissed the campaigns and ideas of "Yankee" and English women or the French St. Simonians as too radical for a conservative country like Spain. However, he concluded, in a century that saw the abolition of slavery and experiments with universal male suffrage, and even female suffrage in Australia, the emancipation of Spanish women would eventually arrive. Even though it would require a gradual yet constant propaganda campaign, Labra told the women of his audience, "I assure you that you will be invincible."[77]

The female members of the Association for Women's Education apparently held similar views about men and women, public life and the home, using liberal discourse on the sexes to legitimate circumscribed public roles for themselves.[78] One of the association's offshoots was the short-lived Women's Athenaeum (Ateneo de Señoras), also founded in 1869, directed by the novelist Faustina Saez de Melgar. The Athenaeum offered free instruction to working-class and middle-class women in several subjects—calligraphy, drawing, painting, music, arithmetic, religion and morality, English, French, Italian—to prepare them for the care and education of their families or, Saez de Melgar claimed, in the case of the most destitute, for work.[79] The directors of the Women's Athenaeum upheld the same principles concerning association and the family as those propagated by associations like the Fomento de las Artes. All hoped to improve the condition of the workers through education and, in this particular case, to prepare women for their work as wives and mothers. Whereas in the Fomento de las Artes professors lectured on political economy or the trades, in the Women's Athenaeum courses on religion and the formal arts dominated, reflecting Fernando de Castro's invocation that women's education should be guided by "*morality, religiosity,* and *beauty.*"[80]

The belief in a separate domain created by and for women also figured into abolitionist ideology and political strategy. In 1873, Concepción Arenal, the most famous female reformer in nineteenth-century Spain, sought to instruct women as to how they could serve the abolitionist cause. Her advice echoed the image of women as compassionate reformers described by Sanromá, as well as the vision of women exercising power and influence through their position within the family. Arenal argued that women found slavery noxious because it denied human love and natural familial bonds:

> The poor black suffers all of humanity's pains. He is the man without a companion, without a home, without a family; the woman without legitimate love; the old man without shelter; the child without support; the invalid without assistance; the child without a mother; the mother without a child.[81]

How could women help abolish slavery and allow slaves to regain their natural rights? Men could discuss and make speeches in the Cortes or in their clubs, but women must work within their private world, through prayer and the access to public life they enjoyed through men:

> Are we not more than half the human race . . . ? Do we not have fathers, sons, husbands, brothers who cannot remain deaf to our voice, who have never been deaf when that voice is the voice of heartfelt justice, of the justice that resounds in the conscience?[82]

Though Arenal posited the division of men and women into public and private spheres, her advice concerning female abolitionism pointed to why male liberals feared that division as only tenuous. In this scenario, many male reformers believed that women, although private, irrational, and religious beings, could exercise considerable power over public politics through their position within the family and the nature of their relationships with male politicians.

## Toward Abolitionism

The question of colonial slavery erupted into Spanish public life in the midst of this process of ideological transformation within Madrid liberalism and national mobilization over free trade. The U.S. Civil War, British pressure on the Cuban slave trade, the brief reincorporation of Santo Domingo into the Spanish Empire (1861–1865), and the metropolitan government's decision to act on the slave trade all joined to kindle wide public debate in Madrid among Spanish and Antillean politicians and intellectuals over colonial reform.[83]

I have argued that metropolitan abolitionist ideology originated in the critique of Spanish liberalism made by Madrid's active middle-class social reformers during the Liberal Union era. The liberals who animated the Abolitionist Society defended free wage labor in the metropolis while seeking to harmonize capital and labor through various forms of association and by strengthening the family so as to foster economic growth within a stable political and social order.

The attack made by Economists, Krausists, and Democrats on Spanish liberalism and capitalism dovetailed with Antillean attacks on Spanish rule in the colonies. Like Antillean reformers, Madrid's liberals criticized the centralizing tendencies of the Spanish state and its repressive economic measures. Thus, the metropolitan initiatives against protectionism and oligarchy easily meshed with the colonial attacks on the slave trade and nonrepresentative rule, facilitating the alliance of Spaniards and Antilleans. Differences within local interests, however, produced important divergences among Spaniards, Cubans, and Puerto Ricans, especially concerning the central issue of slavery, as will be shown in chapter 5.

Important differences also existed within Madrid's reformist public. The tension inherent in the attempt to harmonize the rights of capital and labor divided the antislavery movement after the Abolitionist Society's initial consensus on gradualism broke down. The gradualists generally found themselves in agreement with Cuban liberals, who feared the consequences of emancipation, while the advocates of immediate abolition aligned themselves with the Puerto Rican liberals who pursued the same goal, at first for Puerto Rico, but later for Cuba as well. Many abolitionists defended a gradualist policy so as to respect the rights of property, that is, the slaveowners' right to own slaves, and to avoid the disruption of production that slave emancipation might entail. Moret's vision of a peaceful postemancipation society epitomized this tack.

Those who condemned gradualism, such as the Economist Sanromá, the Republican Castelar, or the Krausist-Republican Labra, demanded immediate and unindemnified abolition. Labra was an admirer of the radical phase of U.S. Reconstruction and in 1873 advocated state intervention on behalf of the freedmen's political and economic rights.[84] Again, his was a lone voice. The majority of radical abolitionists argued that abolition and the defense of free labor was a sufficent policy. Guaranteed the right to sell their labor freely, the freed slaves would care for themselves through their families and their innate industriousness.

New political forms and strategies developed in the Liberal Union period were just as crucial as ideological changes. The associations and institutions that flourished between 1854 and 1868 served as the vehicles for abolitionist propaganda and political mobilization:[85] the Free Society of Political Economy, the Fomento de las Artes, the University of Madrid, and the various political parties provided the bases for the abolitionist organization and its personnel. The growth in Madrid of specialized journals and newspapers such as *El Economista,* the *Gaceta Economista,* the *Fomento de las Artes,* and the *Revista Ibérica* was also crucial. They provided the models for abolitionist publications like the *Revista Hispano-Americana,* the *Voz del Siglo,* and *El Abolicionista Español.*

Finally, the public debates in Madrid's associations and in the specialized press had created in the capital a "reformist" public that attended public meetings and speeches promoting free trade or workers' education at the Madrid stock exchange, the Madrid Ateneo, and the University of Madrid. The abolitionists addressed this public through similar venues and tactics: the press, and parades, speeches, and rallies held in Madrid's theaters and the Ateneo. Chapter 5 explores the formation of this colonial and abolitionist public sphere and the ideologies and forms of political action that emerged from it.

# 5

# The Colonial Public Sphere

## THE MAKING OF THE SPANISH
## ABOLITIONIST SOCIETY,
## 1861–1868

Seymour Drescher writes: "The rise of antislavery has to be imagined less as a correlate of expanding new class domination than as one of the new modes of social mobilization."[1] This observation is particularly relevant for the study of antislavery in Spain and the Antilles. The first serious challenges to colonial slavery in the 1860s arose in the context of new forms of political mobilization, on the one hand by metropolitan and colonial liberals active in Madrid, and on the other by planters, slaves, and freedmen in eastern Cuba.

The nexus between abolitionism and capitalism was also crucial. Scholars on British antislavery such as David Brion Davis link the rise of antislavery sentiment to the development of capitalist social relations in the metropolis. The ideology of free wage labor espoused by Anglo-American abolitionists helped to legitimate new forms of labor discipline and political domination in industrializing economies.[2] In Spain and the Antilles, however, capitalism produced a counterhegemonic abolitionist movement. Abolitionism arose among groups seeking to transform the nature of Hispano-Antillean liberalism and capitalism.

By analyzing the origins of the Spanish Abolitionist Society (founded in 1865), this chapter will show how Madrid became a site from which creoles and Spaniards could attack Antillean slavery. Spanish and Antillean reformers founded the Abolitionist Society during a period of state-sponsored reform between 1861 and 1868. The United States' Civil War and renewed British and North American pressure on the slave trade to Cuba had

led the Spanish state and Antillean slaveowners to seek political and economic reforms in the colonies, abolition of the slave trade, and some form
of gradual emancipation controlled by the slaveowners.[3]

However, the metropolitan government did not monopolize discussion
or political action during this period. For the first time since the 1830s,
Cuba and Puerto Rico sent elected representatives to Spain to discuss reforms. The Spanish goverment permitted the formation of a tenuous colonial public sphere in which members of the creole elite could organize
themselves to pressure the state. That public sphere was not spatially
confined to the colonies. In fact, creoles found great possibilities for organization and expression in Madrid. Creole critics of the colonial order
sought to forge alliances with their Spanish counterparts to pressure the
government and influence what they called "public opinion" independently
of the state.[4]

Reformers in Madrid acted in relation to a series of other publics mobilized around the questions of slavery and colonialism throughout the empire and the broader Atlantic world. For example, Joan Casanovas demonstrates the vibrancy of political activity in Havana during these years, when
workers and property owners formed cross-class alliances to militate for
greater political autonomy.[5] Moreover, reformism, whether in Europe or the
Caribbean, existed alongside growing movements for Antillean independence. Puerto Rican and Cuban patriots throughout the Atlantic world—in
Florida, New York, and Paris, for instance—organized to fight for separation
from Spain. Though these publics were often separated by wide distances,
the political and ideological boundaries between them were quite porous,
especially as some reformers turned to separatism and exile.[6]

This chapter concentrates on the Madrid public sphere and the initiatives forged within it. The first part of the discussion concerns the response
of the Spanish state and Antillean slaveowners to the crisis of the 1860s,
revealed in the informal contacts between slaveowners and powerful Spanish political figures, as well as in the forum (the Junta de Información) convened by the government to discuss colonial reforms. The official reformism of this period, most notably the abolition of the slave trade to Cuba in
1867, eventually brought about important changes in the colonial order.
Just as significant, however, were the unofficial aspects of the reformism of
the 1860s that took place in Madrid's lecture halls, newspapers, and theaters, to which the discussion turns. These included the establishment of
the Abolitionist Society, a hybrid association that fused colonial and metropolitan ideologies and political strategies. While Spanish and Antillean reformers initially joined in seeking a colonial bond strengthened by greater

liberty and racial unity, divergent attitudes toward race and its implications for slave emancipation eventually drove apart Cuban, Puerto Rican, and Spanish activists. Finally, the chapter concludes with a comparison of the Abolitionist Society with other Atlantic antislavery movements.

## Official Reformism: Slaveowners and the State

Puerto Rican and Cuban slaveowners found themselves in different positions by the 1860s. There were vastly more slaves in Cuba than in Puerto Rico: there were 370,553 in Cuba in 1862, against only 41,736 slaves in Puerto Rico in 1860.[7] Though Puerto Rican sugar planters clung tenaciously to their slave labor force and constantly pressured the colonial administration for greater coercion of the free rural population, José Curet notes that by the 1860s many Puerto Rican planters were willing to consider some sort of abolition process with indemnity in the hope that fresh infusions of capital would enable them to modernize their production processes. That strategy was most vigorously championed by intellectuals like José Julián Acosta in Puerto Rico and, beginning in the 1860s, in Spain as well.[8]

Cuban planters, on the other hand, still benefited from a successful labor system. The search for ways to bring Cuban slavery to an end, no matter how gradual, arose primarily from political causes. Cuban slavery was still booming in the 1860s, and slaves continued to form the core of the Cuban labor force even during the gradual abolition of slavery in the 1870s and 1880s.[9] Important changes in the geopolitics of Atlantic slavery, however, forced the Spanish state and Cuban planters to begin to search for alternative forms of labor. The most crucial events were the outbreak of civil war and emancipation of the slaves in the United States. Great Britain took advantage of those changes to form an alliance with the United States to place greater pressure for curbing the Cuban slave trade, which was finally banned by the Spanish government in 1867. Spaniards and Cubans now recognized the urgent need for some kind of reform to appease Great Britain and the United States, and they saw that with the end of the trade, abolition of slavery itself would have to be considered. However, Cuban slaveowners made it clear to the Spanish government that they would vigorously resist any decision regarding slavery made without their consent.[10]

The activites of José Luis Alfonso and Carlos Drake Nuñez del Castillo, the count of Vega-Mar, in Madrid illustrate the concerns and interests of Cuban slaveowners. Alfonso wrote to Saco from Madrid: "Carlos Drake and I have taken the initiative. We . . . are negotiating with the government for *political rights* and the administrative reforms that the country demands.

However, we are doing this in a friendly and private manner."[11] Alfonso was following in the footsteps of his brother-in-law, Domingo del Monte, who in the 1850s had sought political reforms through private discussions in Madrid. For instance, in the early 1860s he established the Cuban Committee (Comité Cubano) in Madrid, a group composed of major Cuban slaveowners with important political and economic links with the Peninsula. Members included Vega-Mar and the marquis of O'Gavan, Spanish deputies in the Cortes, and Spanish functionaries familiar with Cuba such as Jacobo de la Pezuela.[12]

Alfonso reported to Saco about his meetings with Salustiano de Olózaga, leader of the Progressive Party, and with key members of the Liberal Union government. These included the president of the cabinet of ministers, Alejandro Mon; the current overseas minister, López Ballesteros; and two former and future overseas ministers, Augusto Ulloa and Antonio Cánovas del Castillo.[13] The Spanish government apparently encouraged Alfonso and his brand of political action. In 1864, Alfonso wrote to Saco that the government had just bestowed upon him the title of marquis of Montelo and that several former captain generals of Cuba—Leopoldo O'Donnell, now president of the government, and the senators Francisco Serrano y Domínguez and José Gutiérrez de la Concha—expected him to become a senator.[14]

Vega-Mar was a senator, a slaveowner, and a landowner and entrepreneur in Spain. In a report written for the Spanish government, Vega-Mar recognized that slave emancipation was inevitable. He argued, however, that the rights of Cuba's slaveowners should be preeminent in any consideration of abolition, that they should be guaranteed indemnity and the continued labor of their freed slaves through lengthy apprenticeships.[15] After the September Revolution in Spain and the Grito de Yara in Cuba in October 1868 (marking the onset of the Ten Years' War), Vega-Mar reiterated this position in a series of unpublished reports. In the increasingly polarized political atmosphere of post-1868 Madrid, Vega-Mar urged the Spanish government to protect the property of Cuba's slaveowners by resisting radical abolition and by blocking the introduction into Cuba of universal manhood suffrage, enacted in Spain in 1868. If Spain failed to respect the rights and wishes of the slaveowners, Vega-Mar threatened to reactivate the annexationist alternative they had pursued in the 1850s when Spain hesitantly challenged the slave trade.[16]

Alfonso spelled out the dilemmas facing Cuban slaveowners like himself and Vega-Mar in a series of letters to Saco. He noted that slaveowners, both Cuban and Spanish, were already scrambling to find alternative sources of labor, given the inevitable abolition of the slave trade and the eventual abolition of slavery itself. He emphasized that the slaveowners themselves had to manage the emancipation process, since they had the practical knowledge of running plantations and the most immediate interest in preserving labor and production. To that end, he outlined the reforms that he hoped Saco would advocate at the government's Junta de Información.[17]

Alfonso, like Arango before him, favored strengthening the slave family and working toward a greater balance of the sexes on the plantations. The latter problem, he argued, would be self-correcting after the abolition of the slave trade. Regarding the family, he said that slaveowners should respect slave marriages and resist separating family members. Slaveowners could not force slaves to marry, however. He described his use of the following measures to encourage marriages on his sugar plantation, "San Cayetano": "I adopted two measures. The first was to persude them to live in a Christian manner and in families. The second was to make the young unmarried black women sleep together *enclosed* in a big room." Alfonso argued that the second measure discouraged concubinage and extramarital unions.

Besides respecting and encouraging the slave family and a "Christian" way of life, Alfonso advocated a series of measures that he believed would lessen the physical toil of slavery and ease Cuba's transition to free labor. He favored limiting the workday to twelve hours during the off season and fourteen during the harvest *(zafra)*. He also favored providing slaves with better food, which would necessitate lowering the customs on imported foodstuffs: "I would give them *bread* twice a day if it were not so expensive," he wrote. On the other hand, he defended the continuation of physical punishment: "Where there is forced labor, there must be corporal punishment." Slaveowners could take a step toward free labor, however, by using more contract laborers. Alfonso favored importing Indians from Yucatan because he believed them to be Christianized and docile, while their proximity to Cuba allowed for the introduction of entire families rather than single males. The use of Chinese contract laborers he considered an absolute failure. According to him, they were sodomizers and heathens, smoked opium, and were prone to suicide and attempts to escape: "In short, I am not for the Chinese."[18]

### Spanish Generals and Creole Reformers

The regime that came to power in Spain in 1868 was potentially attractive to Vega-Mar, Alfonso, and other Cuban slaveowners. Two of the prime movers in the revolutionary coalition were the former captain generals of Cuba,

Francisco Serrano y Domínguez, duke of la Torre (1859–1862), and Domingo Dulce y Garay (1862–1866). Serrano in particular was one of the new regime's strong men, serving as regent until the Constituent Assembly elected a new monarch to replace the deposed Bourbons.

Serrano and Dulce represented a complete change in policy and style from their *ayacucho* predecessors such as Tacón and Valdés. Their colonial credentials were impressive. Besides serving as captain general, both Serrano and Dulce had married into the Havana sugar aristocracy.[19] During their tenure they had adopted the cause of Cuban reformism, advocating colonial constitutionalism, abolition of the slave trade, and strengthening the slave system.[20] One of the clearest indications of their rapprochement toward creole reformers was their patronage of *El Siglo*, a reformist newspaper published in Havana by a knot of former annexationists that included Miguel de Aldama, the count of Pozos Dulces, José Morales Lemus, and José Antonio Echeverría.[21]

The limits of the reformism embraced by Serrano, Dulce, and their creole partners were indicated by the bans placed by both captain generals on the public discussion of slavery. Serrano, for instance, while urging the metropolitan government to tighten pressure on the slave trade, issued a circular in Cuba forbidding any discussion of the abolition of slavery itself.[22] Dulce went even farther, requesting a ban on the discussion of slavery and abolition in Spain because of the difficulty of blocking the introduction of Spanish newspapers into Cuba. A central fear of both Serrano and Dulce was that Cuban slaves would catch wind of abolitionist discourse, a particular risk after slave emancipation in the United States, and act to end their servitude.[23]

Serrano and Dulce were sympathetic to long-time Cuban proposals for reforming colonial society such as abolishing the slave trade and encouraging European immigration. As Arango y Parreño had done in the 1830s, Dulce argued that to preserve slavery and thus Cuban prosperity and tranquility, it was vital to ban the slave trade and encourage the "moralization of the slaves through the means of matrimony and the family."[24] When the Spanish government formed a commission in 1866–1867 to deliberate on colonial reforms, Dulce proposed, concerning slavery, that the government should "promote and favor white immigration" and "encourage the amalgamation of races, or better said, the absorption of the African by the European."[25] Dulce's recommendation was reminiscent of Saco's strategy for ending slavery, stressing the need to "whiten" the slave population before emancipation could begin. Regarding the "amalgamation of races," Dulce pointed out: "Fortunately, the Latin race has always demonstrated its privileged aptitude for such fusion or absorption," unlike the Anglo-Saxon race, which usually eradicated or segregated other peoples.[26]

Serrano sounded a similar note in his report. He proposed a ban on the slave trade and a free womb (granting freedom to slaves' children) so that no more slaves would be born in Cuba. Slaveowners would serve as the patron *(patrono)* of freeborn children until they reached the age of twenty-one. Furthermore, Serrano advocated a ban on corporal punishment and the continuation of a traditional Spanish form of emancipation, *coartación,* whereby slaves could purchase their freedom from their owners. Finally, he favored European, especially Spanish, immigration and a ban on the trade in Chinese and Yucatecan indentured laborers—which, he argued, only worsened Cuba's confusion of races. (This was a critique frequently voiced by Cuban liberals.)[27]

In short, in the early 1860s, Cuban slaveowners and powerful members of the Spanish political and military leadership were in agreement about the need for gradual changes. However, more radical visions of slavery and emancipation within the empire would ultimately disrupt the plans of the Hispano-Cuban elite.

### The Junta de Información (1866–1867)

Divergences over the slavery issue became apparent even in official forums. The culmination of the official reformism of the 1861–1868 period was the Junta de Información sobre Ultramar, a council to discuss overseas affairs assembled by the Spanish government in 1865. It was composed of Cuban, Puerto Rican, and Spanish representatives chosen to deliberate on political, economic, and social reforms in the Antilles. Cuba and Puerto Rico elected their own representatives, while the Spanish government appointed an equal number of qualified Spaniards to the Junta.[28]

The election of Antillean representatives did not proceed as smoothly as the government and colonial conservatives had hoped. To their dismay, the majority of Cuban and Puerto Rican representatives were creole reformers who advocated significant political and economic liberalization. For instance, two of the contributors to *El Siglo,* José Antonio Echeverría and the count of Pozos Dulces, were elected in Cuba, as was José Antonio Saco—significantly elected by Santiago de Cuba, the city he had represented in the 1830s when he was expelled from the Cortes. Three of the four Puerto Rican deputies, including José Julián Acosta, were abolitionists.[29]

Cubans and Puerto Ricans, while agreeing on the need for political and economic reform and abolition of the slave trade, were seriously divided on the question of slavery—a split prefiguring the conflicts and divergences that would emerge after the outbreak of revolution in Spain and Cuba in 1868. The abolitionist representatives from Puerto Rico—Acosta, Segundo Ruiz Belvis, and Francisco Mariano Quiñones—took the initiative on the question of "social" reforms by proposing the immediate abolition of slavery in Puerto Rico with or without indemnity.[30] Their proposal also required that freed slaves sign three-year contracts with their former masters.[31]

A proposal for immediate abolition, and without indemnity at that (even though it was only for Puerto Rico and made in the closed sessions of the Junta) threw the Cuban representatives into a panic. The leader of the Cuban delegation, José Morales Lemus, wrote to the creole slaveowner Miguel de Aldama:

> The Puerto Ricans' motion has put us in a compromised situation. If we remain silent, some will interpret it as acquiesence to immediate abolition which in Cuba would be more than absurd and cruel; it would be a direct attack on civilization and the homeland *[patria]*. On the other hand, some might suppose that Cuba is indifferent to the dangers that surround it and has given little thought to the question, or insanely aspires to perpetuate in its core the cancer that corrodes it and poisons its existence.[32]

To counteract the motion, the Cuban delegation proposed a plan for the gradual abolition of slavery in Cuba. The Cubans advocated the abolition of the slave trade, a free womb, freedom for slaves over the age of sixty, *coartación,* and a lottery that would free a certain number of slaves each year. They also demanded indemnification, a much more costly and unlikely process in Cuba, where there were more than 350,000 slaves, than in Puerto Rico, with little more than 40,000.[33]

Not only did the Cubans find themselves in disagreement with their Puerto Rican counterparts, they also clashed with the Spanish state. Despite the patronage of Serrano and Dulce, and even though the government had formed the Junta to discuss reforms, most creoles distrusted the intentions of the Spanish state, given its history of intransigence in colonial affairs. The Puerto Rican abolitionist representatives to the commission experienced the government's wrath most acutely. Their proposal for immediate abolition had not only threatened the Cuban delegation but also set off a stormy reaction among conservatives, especially peninsular merchants and bureaucrats, in Puerto Rico.[34]

Creoles' distrust was further borne out as the government ignored the proposals made in the Junta and those made by Serrano in the Senate. In response to concurrent economic and political crises—the financial crash of 1866 and subsistence crisis in Spain and the series of aborted Progressive *pronunciamentos* led by General Juan Prim—the Moderate government became increasingly reactionary in its domestic and colonial policies as it sought to maintain control.[35]

In any event, even before that period of reaction, creoles had hedged their bets by seeking alliances and political support independent of the government and the Hispano-Cuban military and political elite. In 1850, Saco had written that the Cubans could gain significant reforms by establishing newspapers in the Court and working with the Spanish opposition.[36] Such was not the case in 1850, but the free-trade debates and the transformation of public life in Madrid during the Liberal Union era created new opportunities.

## Reinventing Empire: New Visions of Spanish Rule in the Caribbean

In the 1860s, Cuban and Puerto Rican reformers moved within the reformist milieu of liberal Madrid, forging ideological and political alliances strengthened by their common criticisms of the political economy of the Spanish empire. Important differences between Cuban and Puerto Rican reformers, however, led them to advocate different strategies for remaking colonial rule. Cubans eagerly denounced the slave trade, protectionism, and nonrepresentative rule, but they remained relatively silent on the question of slavery, as they sought not only to control slave labor but also to maintain white hegemony. In contrast, Puerto Ricans attacked slavery head-on and figured prominently in the founding of the Abolitionist Society.

The alliances forged between Spaniards and Antilleans involved not only criticisms of the dominant structures of the Spanish colonial empire, but also the articulation of alternative visions of Spanish rule in the Caribbean. If for reformers slavery, the slave trade, and a strong Spanish military presence were no longer sufficent legitimation for the colonial bond, what did justify it? I will argue that Spanish and Antillean reformers articulated a vision of Spanish colonial rule based not only on political and economic liberalization, but also on racial identification between white colonists and the metropolis. In other words, the reformism of the 1860s represented an attempt not only to remake the political economy of empire, but also to reaffirm the ideological legitimacy of Spanish rule in the Antilles.[37]

The 1860s were a time of some imperial ferment in Spain. While the Antillean question was clearly central, it was still one among several recent

*La Ilustración Español y Americana*, Madrid, 10 May 1870.
The illustration depicts the monument to the Second of May,
commemorating the Madrid uprising against French troops in 1808 and
the bombardment of the Peruvian fortress at Callao in 1866.
A slave cuts sugar cane under an overseer's gaze in
the lower left-hand corner of the masthead.

colonial entanglements. Spanish military and political leaders had fanta-sized about reasserting Spain's role in the Americas since the wars of decolonization in the 1820s. The 1860s saw some timid gestures in that di-rection. For instance, in 1866, Spain found itself embroiled in the short-lived War of the Pacific with Peru, which saw little more than the Spanish bombardment of the Peruvian fortress of Callao but was heralded in Madrid as a glorious victory. Spain had joined England and France in a punitive expedition against Mexico, but the Spanish commander, Juan Prim, had quickly withdrawn his forces.[38] Spain was also active in Africa and Asia. It joined France in an expedition to Indochina and in 1859 fought a war in Morocco that provoked tremendous popular support throughout the coun-try.[39]

The most significant adventure, however, was the reincorporation of Santo Domingo into the Spanish Empire between 1861 and 1865. Spain was never able to assert effective control of its former colony in four years of fighting, although the occupation did have profound effects on the other Caribbean colonies. Spain used the Cuban treasury to pay for the occupa-tion, and its move to raise taxes to cover the deficits incurred in Santo Domingo helped trigger the decision of planters in eastern Cuba to rebel against Spain in October 1868.[40]

The presence of colonial delegates in the capital and the recent colonial actions inspired Madrid's liberals to extend their critique of the Spanish revolution to the colonies. As in their engagement with the free-trade cam-paigns and social reform, they denounced the limitations of the revolution-ary settlement of the 1830s. Along with Cuban and Puerto Rican reformers, they conceived of a new colonial regime that would benefit not only Cuba and Puerto Rico, but Spain as well.

A representative view from the period is found in Félix de Bona's study of the differences between English and Spanish colonialism. Bona was an Economist and was thoroughly attracted to what he saw as the laissez-faire style of English rule in the Americas based on free labor, free trade, and self-government.[41] He argued that colonialism in the early modern period—of which Spanish colonialism was the prototype—was based on force and domination. The last hundred years of colonial history and England's rise to world dominance had demonstrated, however, that liberty and com-merce were more effective and productive bonds between the metropolis and its colonies. In particular, the continued economic ties between En-gland and the United States, even after their political separation, proved that political domination was obsolete. Bona writes:

[The old international politics] were based on the belief that nations became powerful and prosperous only when they dominated and impoverished their neighbors. The practice of commercial liberty has shown that nations are much more powerful and wealthy when the nations that surround them are powerful and wealthy, enriching each other through trade.

Similarly, the colony that comes to be sufficently enlightened, powerful, and wealthy to proclaim its autonomy is more productive when emancipated than when subjected to its old metropolis.[42]

In the particular case of Spanish rule in the Antilles, Spain could not afford the costly colonial administration based on a standing military government and economic protectionism.[43] Rather, Bona believed, Spain should create a minimal administration that guaranteed property, trade, and order, thus stimulating the Antillean economies and therefore the Spanish one as well: "Spain's strength and power will languish with domination, but they will grow with a system of cosmopolitan and liberal government."[44]

In debates held at the Free Society of Political Economy, the Economists envisioned a new Spanish colonialism based on economic liberty. Laureano Figuerola argued that economic interest was the foundation of modern colonialism, and that such interest flourished only in absolute liberty: "It is necessary to acknowledge liberties. There is no danger that emancipation will follow. The colony can emancipate itself from the State, but it will not emancipate itself from the *interests* of the metropolis."[45]

The denunciations of the repressive features of Spanish rule in the Antilles and the liberal principles expressed by the Economists were music to the ears of Antillean reformers, Cuban and Puerto Rican alike. Since the 1830s, they had hoped for inclusion within the Spanish liberal regime and for easier access to foreign markets. But while the Economists and other Madrid liberals did not have to convince an Antillean public about the benefits of economic and political liberty, they did have to worry about the Spanish political and economic elites who depended on protected markets and generally feared the loss of the Antillean colonies should political control be loosened.[46] To those who feared the loss of markets or the colonies themselves, both Antillean and Spanish reformers responded that more than material interests linked Spain and the Antilles. The final guarantee of Spanish rule in Cuba and Puerto Rico was not the Spanish military and customs officers, but the profound racial identification between Spain and the white population of its last American colonies.

José Antonio Saco was an early advocate of a colonial bond legitimated by racial identification. In the 1840s and 1850s, he and Domingo del Monte had tactically articulated Cuba's Spanish origins for a Spanish public, a form of "strategic essentialism" adopted by Cuban reformers active in Madrid in the 1860s.[47] Saco's biographer Pedro de Agüero in 1858 presented him as the champion of reformed Spanish rule in Cuba, comparing him to Daniel O'Connell, the Irish nationalist hero:

> Saco is today the *silent O'Connell* of the island of Cuba, that is to say, the hushed champion of the *legal revolution,* the mute representative of the *pact of justice* that should be made between the colony and the metropolis so as to end the complaints of the former and the suspicions of the latter. Our opinion is that by raising our voice and unfurling the banner of legality "SPANISH CUBA, BUT CUBA WELL GOVERNED" will quickly win as many supporters in Cuba and Spain as the great Irish patriot had.[48]

Only a few years later, the "hushed champion" of "Spanish Cuba" received his opportunity to speak, both for himself and through other Cuban reformers who adopted his strategies. When the young Cuban intellectual Antonio Angulo y Heredia assumed the editorship of the Krausist *Revista Ibérica* in 1863, he set out to accomplish the reformist tasks dictated by Saco: to create a forum dedicated to the Cuban question and to forge alliances between Cuban and Spanish reformers, in part by celebrating Cuba's Spanish origins. In his presentation, Angulo echoed Saco's discussion of the profoundly Spanish origins of the Cuban nation:

> Oh! it is absolutely impossible for us to renounce our sentiments, our ideas, our religion, our customs, our language. Thus, we can by no means renounce our Spanish nationality. No, we can neither make nor desire that impossible renunciation of our own being, our own soul, our own civilization, our own history.[49]

By the 1860s, Cuban reformers like Saco and Angulo spoke to an enthusiastic Spanish public, one that wholeheartedly embraced the idea of racial and cultural unity between Spain and Cuba. The unity of "Spaniards" on both sides of the Atlantic had been the basis of liberal colonial policy in the first third of the nineteenth century when the American colonies sent representatives to the Cortes (1810–1814, 1820–1823, 1834–1837). That understanding of "Spaniards" was highly racialized. The law required that representatives must be able to prove European descent on both sides of the family. People of African origin were explicitly excluded. Thirty years later, the Spanish reformers who created the Abolitionist Society in 1865 sought to recast Spanish colonialism on commercial grounds and on the basis of racial and cultural identity with Cuba and Puerto Rico. However, as I will demonstrate, the question of racial inclusion versus exclusion was complicated by abolitionism.[50]

The conjunction of the Antillean question with Spain's renewed imperial interventions moved many Spaniards to hope that successful reforms in the Antilles would serve as a model for the rest of the Americas. The visions of Spain in America articulated by the diplomat and journalist Eduardo Asquerino and the Democrat Emilio Castelar were typical of opinions voiced in Madrid's liberal circles. For them, the racial identity between Spain and its colonies would be an important element of Spain's new American presence.

Asquerino, for example, in his influential panhispanist newspaper, *La América,* listed three international goals for Spain: an Iberian union, reform of Spain's current colonial administration, and creation of a "Latin" league in the Americas to protect the Latin race against the rising dominance of the great Anglo-Saxon power, the United States. In his words: "Two rival races are disputing the dominion of the New World; the Latin race and the Anglo-Saxon race. The latter is more vigorous, more active, and since the end of the last century, more civilizing and powerful than the former."[51] Asquerino saw continued Spanish rule in Cuba as the linchpin of a league that would check the ascendancy of the Anglo-Saxons:

> Alas! if [the United States] were to possess Cuba, everything will change. Her soldiers, acclimatized in Havana's barracks, will no longer be decimated by the heat; the means of transport will be infinite and very fast. . . . Triumph will be swift in coming. We repeat again, oh! for the Spanish American Republics the day that Cuba ceases to be Spanish! Oh! for the Latin race in the New World if our advanced sentinal in the Atlantic falls wounded through treachery.[52]

Emilio Castelar, an early contributor to *La América,* also embraced the idea of a reconstituted Latin unity in Europe and the Americas. Like Asquerino, Castelar saw the Americas wracked by conflict between the Anglo-Saxon and Latin races. He proposed Latin unity because the Latin race had a more profoundly civilizing mission than the Anglo-Saxon:

> The Latin race can exercise an apostleship in the New World superior to that of the Anglo-Saxon race. . . . The Anglo-Saxon does not work for an idea, he works for commerce. The Anglo-Saxon is enclosed in his own

individualism. He lacks the lively sympathy for other peoples and humanity which is the glory of the Latin race.[53]

Whereas Castelar opposed the "commercial" sensibility of the Anglo-Saxons to the universalism and idealism of the Latins, other Madrid reformers sought to combine elements of Spanish and English colonialism to recast the colonial bond with the Antilles and revitalize Spain's mission in the Americas. Not surprisingly, the Economists, admirers of Cobden, believed that Spain could draw valuable lessons from the history of English colonialism. Nonetheless, the Economists also saw racial identification as a crucial aspect of colonialism.

For instance, echoing the panhispanism of Asquerino and Castelar, Félix de Bona argued that Spanish military adventurism in Santo Domingo would only serve to alienate the Spanish American republics from Spain by reinforcing the traditional image of Spanish colonial rule and Spanish attitudes toward the Americas. By ruling Santo Domingo, Cuba, and Puerto Rico through a liberal regime, Spain could win the sympathies of its former colonies and serve as the leader in a league of Spanish nations in the Americas that would oppose the United States' hegemony and militarism, epitomized for Bona by the annexation of Texas and William Walker's expedition in Nicaragua.[54]

At a meeting of the Free Society of Political Economy in 1862, Luis María Pastor addressed the traditional Spanish mistrust of creoles when he argued that granting political and economic liberty to Cuba would not lead to Cuba's annexation to the United States. Though the United States was increasingly becoming Cuba's economic metropolis, Pastor claimed (using an argument similar to those made by Saco in the annexationist debates) that the racial and cultural differences between Cubans and North Americans were too great, while the identity between Spain and Cuba was permanent and profound:

> Regarding a union with the United States, it is highly unlikely. Everyone who knows that country knows that the sweet, soft, generous, indolent character of our islanders contrasts notably with the severe, tenacious, enterprising character of the Yankees. Language, habits, customs, religion, relationships, and sympathies all link our islanders to Spain and separate them from the North Americans.[55]

Thus, Madrid reformism in the fifties and sixties placed a strong emphasis on Spain's Latin racial identity and on the "mission" of the Latin race in Europe, the Americas, and the Antilles—a mission to which creoles like Saco and Angulo could appeal. As in the early nineteenth century, Spaniards hoped to cement colonial hegemony by including creoles within the liberal regime and within the Spanish nation.[56]

The reformist vision of a new Spanish colonialism was most clearly elaborated in the *Revista Hispano-Americana*, founded in 1864 by Bona, an Economist; Antonio Angulo y Heredia, Saco's Cuban disciple; and Julio de Vizcarrondo, the Puerto Rican abolitionist. During this period of official reformism, the range of discussion in the *Revista Hispano-Americana* was limited. Writers focused on the slave trade, political and economic reforms, immigration, and (occasionally) the gradual abolition of slavery. The proposals made for immediate abolition advanced by the Puerto Rican representatives in the Junta de Información were nowhere to be found. Abolishing the slave trade and increasing white immigration dominated the debate, reflecting the weight of Cuban concerns. The *Revista* published petitions sent by Cuban "planters with slaves" to the Spanish Senate that favored abolishing the trade and urged harsher measures to ban the trade effectively.[57]

For Cuban reformers, ending the slave trade did not imply the abolition of slavery. For instance, the Cuban Francisco Armas de Céspedes, author of the most important gradualist tract of the period,[58] argued that the slave trade was doomed and that slaveowners must learn how to reproduce and civilize their slave populations both to guarantee a supply of labor and to prepare for gradual abolition. In other words, he expounded the vision of a reformed slavery being abolished at some time in a hazy future, a view directly descended from the tepid abolitionism of Arango.[59] Calixto Bernal, a Cuban member of the Spanish Democratic Party, favored European immigration as a correlate to abolishing the slave trade. In this manner, Bernal wrote, Cuba would increase its labor force and strengthen white hegemony: "The transformation [to free labor] cannot take place without the accumulation of free laborers *[brazos]*; that future will never be assured unless those laborers are numerous and of the white race."[60] One strategy to increase the white population and settle Cuba's vast lands proposed by Bernal was to grant land to Spanish conscripts serving in Cuba.[61]

Creating the "special laws" for the Antilles promised by the Spanish constitutions of 1837 and 1845 was a central concern of the reformism of the 1860s. Between 1861 and 1868, reformers considered constitutional rule and the dismantling of the captain general's centralized command as the first steps in strengthening the colonial relationship. Angulo, for instance, stated that Cuba would remain part of Spain only if Cubans were granted the rights of Spaniards:

Most urgent for our compatriots is TO SEE THEMSELVES REINTE-
GRATED INTO THE POLITICAL LAW OF SPAIN; TO BE SPANIARDS
IN THE PLENTITUDE OF THE LAW, NOT JUST IN NAME. Thus it is
indispensable to give PREFERENCE TO POLITICAL RIGHTS AS THE
ORIGIN, SUM, AND GUARANTEE OF ALL OTHER LIBERTIES.[62]

The *Revista Hispano-Americana* represented an important step in the formation of Spanish and Antillean alliances independent of the Madrid-Ha-
vana power elite. In the unofficial reformism of the 1860s, Spaniards and
Antilleans articulated a critique of the imperial system that synthesized criticisms made in both the colonies and in the metropolis. Spaniards and
Antilleans condemned the repressive features of the imperial system and
envisioned a reformed Spanish rule based on political and economic liberty, a plan that flew in the face of the actual political economy of colonialism. In seeking to explain the continuity of empire after reform, Spanish
and Antillean liberals responded that the racial identification between colonizer and colonized would cement Spain to Cuba and Puerto Rico. While
in retrospect their visions of empire might seem utopian and impracticable,
they are important to reconstruct and understand because for a brief moment during the revolutionary period called the September Revolution
(1868–1874), Madrid's liberals held the reins of power and their colonial
policies were informed by the reformism of the 1860s.

### The Spanish Abolitionist Society: Labor, Race, and the Contradictions of Liberalism

But the reformers of the *Revista Hispano-Americana,* the Free Society of Political Economy, and the Ateneo faced obstacles other than metropolitan
and colonial conservatives. They faced division within their own ranks. And
the wedges that forced that division were slavery and race.

In their forays into the public sphere of Madrid liberalism, Cuban
creoles emphasized the importance of political reforms; they limited their
discussion of slavery to the private realm of Spanish officialdom. Puerto
Ricans, in contrast, took advantage of the political associations in Madrid to
take public action against slavery. They were willing to mobilize all resources available to them—short of armed violence or the mobilization of
slaves themselves—to achieve this goal. One of their moves was to found the
Abolitionist Society.

The crisis of Puerto Rican slavery and the articulation, by a faction of
colonial society, of an abolitionist strategy as a way out of that crisis were

**Julio de Vizcarrondo**
(1829–1889).
García, *Fotografías.*

the primary forces behind the formation of the Abolitionist Society. Nonetheless, the society's form and tactics derived from Madrid liberalism, making it truly hybrid—or, in other words, an amalgam of colonial and metropolitan political forms, interests, strategies, and ideologies.[63]

The society's initial membership included the most illustrious figures
from the capital's reformist circles, including older established figures like
the Progressive leader Salustiano de Olózaga and the Democratic head José
María Orense (the marquis of Albaida), and Senator Luis María Pastor, an
Economist. Also among the founders were younger liberals like the Economists Segismundo Moret y Prendergast, Gabriel Rodríguez, and Félix de
Bona; the Democrats Manuel Becerra, Cristóbal Sorní, and Emilio Castelar;
and the Krausists Nicolás Salmerón and Rafael María de Labra, soon to
become Spain's leading abolitionist. From the beginning, the membership
of the Abolitionist Society illustrated the continuity between domestic reformism and abolitionism, particularly between abolitionism and the program of the Economists. Especially after the free-trade campaigns of the
mid-1850s through the early 1860s, the Economists were the most highly
organized and militant group in Madrid intellectual and political life.[64]

Prominent men were not the only ones mobilized for abolitionist politics. Julio de Vizcarrondo's wife, Harriet Brewster de Vizcarrondo, a North
American, organized a women's chapter of the Sociedad.[65] Though ephem-
eral—I have not found any mention of the women's chapter after 1865—the

women's chapter further reveals the continuity between reformist politics and discourse in Spain and the colonies. The organization of separate chapters for men and women, and the different roles prescribed to each, reflected the belief among Madrid reformers that males and females had distinct tasks to perform. While men engaged in the harsh, competitive world of politics—in this case through the press, demonstrations, and the Cortes—women animated the moral imperative of abolitionism through their compassionate natures and their private influence over men. While men criticized slavery for its stagnating, destabilizing effects on society as a whole, women empathized with the slave, especially the slave woman, who was deprived of natural familial bonds.[66]

In 1865, *El Abolicionista Española* published a series of letters from women's antislavery societies in Britain addressed to the "ladies *[señoras]* of Madrid" urging them to use their positions within Madrid society to help the abolitionist cause. In introducing the letters, the Spanish commentator explained specificaly how abolitionist sentiments arose in women:

> The woman's heart, supremely sensitive and compassionate, could contemplate slavery with indifference as long as it did not know the odious reality or was unaware of the depth of its horrible consequences. But today, now that it perceives with pain the bitterness and sufferings that further weigh the chains of the unhappy slave, it energetically protests against such injustice and its voice will not be lost in the void.[67]

A letter from Birmingham asked Spanish women to imagine the sufferings that slaves endured because of slavery's disregard for human emotional bonds. To overcome this outrage, the women of Birmingham advised their Madrid counterparts to exercise their influence over their male relations, a suggestion well in keeping with the gender ideology of Madrid liberalism.[68]

The Abolitionist Society's initial demands were more moderate than those made by Puerto Rican representatives in the Junta de Información. It proposed the abolition of the slave trade—a proposal supported by a wide range of interests for different reasons—and the gradual abolition of slavery in Cuba and Puerto Rico. In a petition sent to the Cortes concerning the slave trade, the Abolitionist Society advocated "studying the means by which to enact [abolition] without threatening public order or causing social disruptions and with the least possible prejudice to interests created under the protection of legislation."[69] Luis María Pastor, a Moderate senator, an Economist, and a member of the Abolitionist Society, proposed a bill in the Senate for a free womb law as well as apprenticeships for children born to slave mothers. Pastor also advocated indemnification and creating a more comprehensive abolition law based on the reports to the Junta de Información.[70]

Puerto Rican abolitionists and their Spanish allies argued that Puerto Rico was especially well suited for abolition. Julio de Vizcarrondo, for instance, at a session of the Free Society of Political Economy, argued that Puerto Rico was in a better position than Cuba to enact abolition. The fundamental difference was the racial division of labor in each island: "Cuba and Puerto Rico find themselves in different conditions regarding slavery. In Cuba there are black workers; in Puerto Rico white and black workers." In Puerto Rico, free labor—a term practically synonymous with white labor, for Vizcarrondo—in the sugar sector was on the rise, stimulating greater productivity: "Previously in Puerto Rico, there were 70,000 slaves and they produced 50,000 hogsheads [of sugar]. Today, fewer than 8,000 cultivate cane and they produce 200,000 hogsheads. Thus, production is not dependent on the work of blacks." In Cuba, slaves provided most of the labor on the sugar plantations, which not only was a less productive system but also had the effect of racially marking and segregating labor: "In Cuba, work is degraded and the white will not work at the side of the black who is subjected to the whip."[71]

For Vizcarrondo, the coexistence of white and black workers in Puerto Rico facilitated the transformation to free labor, first because it was a sign that the change was already well under way, second because work was not racially stigmatized. Cuba, in contrast, suffered from the degradation of work that characterized premodern societies. That degradation arose from the enslaved condition of most laborers and the racial stigma attached to work. In other words, work in Puerto Rico was based on "true" economic relations or interests, while in Cuba, racial and social preoccupations blurred the economic bases of work and made the transition to free labor even more difficult.[72]

While Cubans and Puerto Ricans agreed on the need to "whiten" the Antillean labor force through both miscegenation and immigration, though disagreeing on the timing of abolition, Spaniards argued that economic verities cut across racial differences, a position that eventually alienated them from Cuban reformers. The Spanish abolitionists posited the essential equality of all races before the impetus of the market.[73] When conservatives argued that blacks were brutal and lazy by nature and thus must be enslaved both to civilize them and to extort hard work from them, abolitionists responded that the artificial condition of slavery *created* the putative faults of African laborers.[74]

For example, the journalist José Ferrer de Couto, a paid agent of the

Spanish government assigned to New York, where he sought to counter Antillean separatist propaganda, weighed into the reformist debate of the 1860s with one of the most recalcitrant defenses of slavery. He argued that that the "civilized" nations had the right and duty to enslave "backward" races.[75] The Economists, most of whom were members of the Abolitionist Society, refuted Ferrer de Couto's arguments in the Free Society of Political Economy. Laureano Figuerola countered that blacks, when free, had to work to survive, like all human beings. Thus, they could work just as hard and productively as whites. Slavery, however, deprived them of the necessary stimulus to do so.[76] Another political economist made a similar point; slavery contradicted the universal motivations of all workers, thus giving blacks the appearance of indolence:

> Slave labor lacks the two conditions that labor requires to be useful; the internal and external conditions, morality and interest. The slave lacks the latter becasue he does not enjoy the product of his labor. The master's interest does not fill this breach. The master fights the [slave's] indolence, an indolence that is not inherent to the black race, as some suppose, but the unavoidable consequence of the slave regime.[77]

Moreover, to those who pointed to the recent uprising in Jamaica at Morant Bay as proof that Caribbean blacks, slave or free, were savages who refused to work, the abolitionists responded that in the case of Jamaica, limitations placed on the full exercise of freedom had moved the free population to violence. Indeed, in appraising other emancipation processes, especially in British colonies and North America, the Spanish abolitionists consistently held that the historical record demonstrated the superiority of immediate, rather than gradual, emancipation. Gradualism, they argued, bred resentment, whereas immediate abolition produced gratitude and industriousness. This position was in stark opposition to the interpretation of postemancipation society by British liberals in the 1860s.[78]

Thus, metropolitan abolitionist discourse apparently effaced racial difference, treating Antillean slaves as "universal" economic agents who, like all human beings, responded productively to natural economic stimuli and reluctantly or violently to "artificial" labor regimes such as slavery. For them, Antillean slavery was a feature of the Spanish Empire that, like protectionism, retarded growth and bred unrest. For most Spanish abolitionists, the market was the panacea not only for Antillean labor, but for the imperial order as a whole.

Their position stood in stark contrast to that of Cuban reformers. While Cubans such as Saco and Arango y Parreño had mounted strong critiques of slavery as violent, unproductive, and destabilizing, they had also defended it as a necessary evil for the foreseeable future. In their eyes, slaves would undermine white hegemony through race war or miscegenation. Even the Puerto Rican abolitionists shared this racial thinking, in spite of their willingness to attack slavery head-on. One reason they were willing to do so was their belief that Puerto Rico had overcome the racial barriers that still prevailed in Cuban society, because Puerto Rican labor was desegregated and because of the putatively high incidence of racial mixing.

Did the belief in the universal effects of the market lead Madrid's liberals to envision racial equality in postemancipation societies? The answer is no. While they affirmed Spain's racial unity with the Antillean white elite, they simultaneously implied their racial difference from Antillean slaves, as Spanish liberals had done throughout the nineteenth century. Indeed, their belief in the universal stimulus of the market was shot through with assumptions of racial difference and hierarchy.[79]

Abolitionists envisioned freed slaves as partners in a new Spanish colonial system, but decidedly subordinate ones. They typically represented whites and blacks as living in peaceful harmony, a displacement of their ideal vision of metropolitan class relations onto the colonies—a vision also shaped by their conception of putative racial characteristics. They believed that as a *race*, Africans were best suited to be a free working *class*.[80]

The Democrat Fernando Garrido, for instance, in his description of postemancipation society in the Antilles, argued that only blacks could carry out agricultural labor in tropical climes: "In those hot regions, the white man cannot withstand the most important jobs, like the cultivation and harvesting of cane and the making of sugar. The black has the physical conditions needed to work freely and to multiply in a climate similar to Africa's."[81]

Abolitionists believed that Africans' emotional and psychological characteristics reinforced those physical qualities. Rafael María de Labra argued that even under the brutal conditions of slavery, African slaves demonstrated their docility and humanity through their dedication to family life, education, and music.[82] He further emphasized the slaves' benign nature by showing that crime rates in the Antilles were far lower than those in Spain or other European countries.[83] The violence or sloth that conservatives attributed to blacks were the results of slavery, argued Labra. Once free, slaves would become hard, dependable workers. When conservatives pointed to the Haitian revolution, Labra and other abolitionists responded that Napoleon, not Toussaint L'Ouverture and the slaves of St. Domingue, precipitated the bloodshed. Napoleon had misjudged the slaves' temperament and made the fatal error of attempting to rule them through coercion rather than accommodation: "The black is cheerful and good-natured (in fact, he is much more cheerful than intelligent), but that same quality joined with his robustness makes him terrible when accosted. He loses his moral faculties and becomes a wild beast."[84] In other words, the continuation of slavery only bred violence and insubordination among the slave population. If Spain abolished slavery, Antillean slaves would fulfill their "natural" role as docile free laborers.

The question of racial difference had vexed Spanish liberals in formulating colonial policy throughout the nineteenth century. In the 1810s and 1820s, revolutionaries had explicitly excluded people of color from the liberal regime and the Spanish nation. In the 1830s, the liberal Cortes had legitimated the expulsion of colonial deputies in part by claiming that the question of representing a racially heterogeneous population required "special laws." By the 1860s, abolitionists had apparently come to overlook race as a qualification for liberty and nationality. A closer inspection of abolitionist ideology, however, reveals that Spaniards, like the Cuban and Puerto Rican elite, still saw "whiteness" as the basis of the Spanish nation on both sides of the Atlantic. Nonetheless, that view did not absolutely determine the abolitionists' attitudes toward freedom and citizenship; changing political circumstances after 1868 would lead to new visions of freedom and nationality in both Spain and the Antilles.[85]

## Conclusion: The Abolitionist Society in Comparative Perspective

A crucial development in the interaction between colonial and metropolitan reformers in the 1860s was the establishment of the Abolitionist Society. How did it compare with other Atlantic antislavery movements? At first, the society resembled what Seymour Drescher characterizes as the "continental" model of antislavery movements: an association of metropolitan elites that worked in cooperation with the state and with slaveowners to ensure a smooth emancipation process; it was not a broadly based popular movement that sought a "political" solution to slavery by challenging entrenched slaveowning and official interests, as in the British and North American cases.[86]

However, Spain's Abolitionist Society more closely approximated the Brazilian abolitionist movement, which, as Drescher argues, combined elements of both models. It existed within a political and ideological network that provided the basis for more radical action under shifting political conditions. During the uncertain and censored final years of the Liberal Union era, the Abolitionist Society enjoyed only a limited range of political expression and activity. After the revolution of 1868, however, it resorted to extraparliamentary mobilization and overtly challenged the powerful metropolitan and colonial classes interested in protecting Antillean slavery. Indeed, within the political economy of the Spanish Empire, which relied heavily on slave labor, abolitionism was a potentially subversive and counterhegemonic movement.[87]

Moreover, if we consider the dynamics of politics and social change within an imperial framework, the impulse of Puerto Rican abolitionism resembled the regional dynamic of the Brazilian antislavery movement. Slavery was stagnant in Puerto Rico, but planters, slaves, abolitionists, and the colonial state still struggled over the institution's fate.[88] By the 1860s, some planters were willing to consider abolition with indemnity for slaveowners, and abolitionists like Acosta argued that Puerto Rico's population density made a transition to free labor feasible. The stagnation of Puerto Rican slavery and the rise of abolitionism bore similarities to the forces shaping abolitionism in northeastern Brazil, an economically depressed sugar-producing region. In both cases, while sugar planters clung tenaciously to their slaves, a faction of the regional elite advocated abolition as the solution to labor shortages and economic stagnation. Those strategies to hasten the end of slavery and the transition to free labor had important consequences for slavery on a broader level. In Brazil, abolitionists eventually overcame the still energetic sectors of the slave economy, while in Puerto Rico, as we shall see, abolitionists not only successfully abolished slavery there, but also threatened powerful interests in Cuba and Spain.[89]

Drescher's discussion of the central role of popular mobilization in the rise of antislavery movements is also useful for analyzing the dynamic of abolitionism in the Spanish Empire. Changes in Madrid's middle-class associational culture during the Liberal Union era facilitated the formation of the Abolitionist Society. However, whereas Drescher's analysis concentrates on metropolitan forms of political action, I see the Abolitionist Society as an essentially hybrid form of political organization. The society's origins are not to be found simply in Spain or the colonies but in the interaction of transatlantic forces and publics. Madrid, as noted earlier, was only one center of discussion of slavery and colonialism. The possibilities for action against slavery, therefore, arose in many contexts: local, imperial, and transatlantic.[90]

The nexus between capitalism and antislavery is also crucial.[91] In the Spanish Empire, however, the antislavery campaign was not a legitimation of the developing capitalist order, as in Great Britain or the United States, but a critique of the dominant structures of Hispano-Antillean capitalism and liberalism. Abolitionists mobilized against the revolutionary settlement of the 1830s, which was based on maintaining slavery, the slave trade, protected markets, and limited access to political representation, and instead championed free markets, free labor, and greater (and in some cases univeral) political rights. Thus, Hispano-Antillean antislavery, while clearly liberal and procapitalist, sought to subvert and transform the reigning structures of imperial power. In this sense, capitalism and liberalism in the Spanish Empire helped shape a profoundly counterhegemonic project.[92]

As an alternative to the imperial system consolidated between 1833 and 1868, Spanish and Antillean reformers envisioned a model of colonialism that they believed resembled the British example in the Americas. Canada, in particular, was a much admired example; the colony enjoyed political and economic autonomy while still indentifying closely with the metropolis, in no small part due to racial homogeneity between the two.[93]

Though white Antilleans and Spaniards agreed on the need to reform repressive political and economic structures and on their own racial unity, they disagreed over the strategies for ending slavery, and those divisions arose largely from the question of race. Antilleans, especially Cubans, sought both to ensure an adequate supply of plantation labor and to preserve white hegemony by prolonging slavery and "whitening" the slave population; however, Spanish abolitionists believed that only immediate abolition would bring class and racial harmony. That belief arose not only from their own experience as social reformers in Madrid, but also from their understanding, as latecomers to abolitionism, of the consequences of slave emancipation in the Americas. Almost all Spanish abolitionists denounced slavery, gradualism, and apprenticeships, and most argued for the social, political, and economic superiority of immediate abolition and free wage labor. This position diverged from the responses to abolition by "emancipators" in other slave societies in the 1860s. Hardly an accurate interpretation of the historical experience of other postemancipation societies, it reflected the Spanish abolitionists' goals as reformers within the Spanish Empire, their commitment to the market as the panacea to colonial and metropolitan ills, and their displacement of metropolitan class ideologies onto the colonies.[94]

Finally, one other point of comparison leads to the next section of this work: the intersection between revolution and slavery. Robin Blackburn argues in compelling fashion that the Atlantic world's "age of revolution" revolved around the fate of colonial slavery. Colonial revolutions were often led by slaveowners seeking to assert more effective control over the lo-

cal society, while metropolitan revolutionary regimes attacked colonial slavery so as to bolster their own ideological legitimacy. As we have seen, the
Spanish revolutions of the nineteenth century, generally caused by elite
struggles over the nature of capital accumulation and political representation, had important consequences for colonial slavery. The revolutions of
the 1830s consolidated Antillean slavery, while the revolution of 1854
opened up the possibility for a new style of colonial politics and for abolitionism that came to fruition in the 1860s.[95]

Spain in the 1860s was again on the verge of revolution, as the
Progressives, the Liberal Union, and the Democrats responded to the economic collapse of 1866 and sought to combat the increasingly authoritarian
rule of the Bourbon monarch Isabel II and her Moderate Party ministers,
who had returned to power. This time, the colonial question was explicitly
part of the struggle over the political economy of the empire.[96]

Colonial and metropolitan reformers had conflicting expectations of the
revolution. In 1866, a year in which General Juan Prim launched an aborted
*pronunciamiento,* Antonio Angulo y Heredia wrote to Saco:

> I still hope that the not too distant triumph of the liberal parties in
> Spain will improve the luck of our poor country. The day in which I lose
> that hope and the hope that Spain will regenerate itself through liberty,
> that day I will move to a free, foreign country where I can educate my
> children under the moral influence that only the customs and institu-
> tions of a free people produce.[97]

Spain's liberal parties did triumph two years later. By that time, however,
some Cubans had decided that their freedom could come only if they were
independent of Spain. The concurrent and interrelated revolutions in Spain
and Cuba opened up new political opportunities for previously constrained
actors, transformed the nature of abolitionist politics, and led to major challenges to Antillean slavery that threatened the gradualist measures favored
by the Spanish state and the colonial planter class.

# 6

# Revolution and Slavery

The simmering regional, colonial, class, and ethnic tensions in the Spanish Empire exploded in the autumn of 1868. The ensuing years witnessed shifting alliances among various factions of metropolitan and colonial society as they struggled to defend or to abolish slavery. Local initiatives in Spain and the Antilles sent shock waves through the rest of the empire, provoking distant yet energetic responses. Some colonial opponents of slavery fought for independence, while metropolitan abolitionists sought to reconstruct Spanish colonial hegemony on the basis of free labor. Colonial and metropolitan conservatives resisted antislavery initiatives on the local level before organizing a transatlantic coalition of the Antillean and Spanish right to reassert the status quo.[1]

In Spain, the military-civilian coalition headed by General Juan Prim y Prats triumphed in September 1868, deposing the Bourbon dynasty and installing as regent Francisco Serrano y Domínguez, a central figure within the Hispano-Cuban elite, until the election of Amadeus of Savoy in 1870 to the Spanish throne. Serrano and his protegé, Abelardo López de Ayala, the provisional government's first overseas minister, were comforting figures for metropolitan and colonial conservatives. However, other members of the government and other parties within Prim's coalition, especially abolitionists and free-traders, were troubling for the right. The civilian parties that supported Prim included the Progressives and the Liberal Union, who had chafed at the increasingly intransigent rule of the Moderates. One leader of the Progressives was Laureano Figuerola, an Economist and an abolitionist. Prim's appointment of Figuerola as his first minister of the treasury *(hacienda)* dismayed Spain's protectionist classes.

Moreover, the Democrats (who after 1868 split into the monarchist Radical Party and the Federal Republican Party) had supported Prim, and members of that party soon joined the government, including Manuel Becerra, a member of the Abolitionist Society who became overseas minister in 1869. The Spanish constitution of 1869 was one of the most liberal in Europe at the time, calling for universal male suffrage and extensive civil rights. Despite the prominence of conservative figures like Serrano, the new regime threatened the central structures of metropolitan and colonial hegemony: slavery, protectionism, and centralized oligarchic rule.[2]

Events in Cuba and Puerto Rico were even more threatening to the colonial status quo and polarized the revolution. The outbreak of a separatist rebellion, eventually known as the Ten Years' War, in eastern Cuba quickly ended the harmony between metropolitan revolutionaries and Antillean (especially Cuban) slaveowners.[3] Important figures in the east like the slaveowner Carlos Manuel de Céspedes rebelled against their continued subjugation to metropolitan and western slaveowning interests after the failure of the Junta de Información (1866–1867). Spanish liberalism had failed in their eyes, and they now turned to separatism as an alternative. Their mobilization encouraged the participation of slaves and free people of color in eastern Cuba, who eventually forced the colony's separatist leaders to declare the abolition of slavery and forced apprenticeships in December 1870. Slaves rebelling against slavery and an active abolitionist force terrified the planters of the west, even though the Spanish military was largely successful in preventing the rebel forces from entering the western provinces. Western planters openly resisted any abolitionist initiative, no matter how timid, from the Peninsula.[4]

Cuban slaveowners' resistance to abolition did not, however, sever the connection between abolitionism and revolution in Spain or in Puerto Rico. In Puerto Rico, too, marginalized creoles had rebelled against Spanish rule, but the colonial regime quickly suppressed their uprising.[5] Unlike their Cuban counterparts, some Puerto Rican slaveowners sought to negotiate abolition with indemnity through politicians and abolitionists like J. J. Acosta or Luis Padial Vizcarrondo. Though sugar planters still relied heavily on slave labor, because Puerto Rico's slave population was much smaller than Cuba's, Puerto Rican slaveowners could gamble on indemnification. Acosta and Padial continued to push for the immediate abolition of slavery in Puerto Rico through Parliament and the Abolitionist Society while also bargaining with slaveowners.[6]

Among metropolitan revolutionaries, abolitionism became a dividing and defining issue as the initial revolutionary coalition broke apart. As discussed in chapter 5, political and military leaders like Serrano were not the only Spaniards to mobilize around the question of abolition. The Abolitionist Society unified a series of representatives from Madrid's liberal circles who had a history of challenging entrenched political and economic interests, most clearly manifested in the free-trade campaigns of the fifties and sixties. Metropolitan and Puerto Rican abolitionists used the new freedoms of speech and association to maneuver among the parliamentary parties vying for control of the state during the revolution. Indeed, the revolutions in Cuba and Spain eventually transformed antislavery from a policy controlled by the political and military elite to a political rallying cry that resonated throughout Spain.

Chapters 6 and 7 discuss the mobilizations for and against slavery, concentrating on the strategies of the Abolitionist Society, whose demands for the immediate abolition of Antillean slavery were both counterhegemonic and hegemonic. On the one hand, abolitionists and their political allies called for immediate abolition to subvert the bases of conservative power in both Spain and the Antilles. On the other hand, they believed that immediate abolition would also reassert Spanish hegemony in the Antilles by winning the loyalty of discontented sectors of colonial society and by undercutting the appeal of the Cuban insurgency.[7]

This chapter surveys the metropolitan and colonial responses to revolution, especially those of Puerto Rican and Spanish abolitionists. Chapter 7 discusses the high point of counterhegemonic colonial politics in Spain and Puerto Rico during the First Republic. This was a time of severe crisis for the Spanish state, as it faced not only the Cuban insurgency but also a renewal of the Carlist conflict in northern Spain and regional uprisings along the Mediterranean littoral.

## Spain

The triumph of the revolutionary parties in Spain in September 1868 provoked an outpouring of opinions on Antillean slavery. The most prominent abolitionists in Madrid demanded immediate action, though only of a moderate nature. Rafael María de Labra convinced Madrid's revolutionary junta to include a free womb measure as one of its planks.[8] A group of Puerto Rican and Spanish abolitionists petitioned the Overseas Ministry, calling for the enactment of the political and economic reforms discussed in the Junta de Información and a free womb law.[9] Puerto Ricans "residing in this capital" followed with similar requests.[10] Spanish merchants, agriculturalists, and manufacturers from regions with strong ties to the Antillean market urged caution.[11] In a private communication, a Cuban slaveowner, the count of Vega-Mar, threatened a resurgence of annexationism if the Spanish government did not protect the interests of Cuban slaveowners.[12] The new regime displayed its commitment to gradual abolition and its sensitivity to slaveowning interests by first declaring that all children born to slaves after the triumph of the revolution would be free and then failing to publish the decree in the colonies.[13]

### The Breakdown of the Reformist Coalition

One of the casualties of the revolution was the reformist clique of Cubans, Puerto Ricans, and Spaniards who had gathered in the Madrid Ateneo, the Free Society of Political Economy, and the *Revista Hispano-Americana* prior to 1868. While Puerto Rico was able to send representatives to the Cortes (although the constitution of 1869 was not fully implemented in Puerto Rico until 1873), the Spanish government decided to suspend elections in Cuba until the insurrection had been quelled. Even more important, however, were the divisions among reformers concerning slavery. The timing of abolition ultimately separated Cuban reformers like Saco from Spaniards and Puerto Ricans, even though all agreed on the urgency of political and economic reforms.

The Abolitionist Society quickly mobilized to demand more radical action from the provisional government. In a public meeting held at a Madrid theater in December 1868, activists called for immediate abolition in the Antilles. The official text produced at the meeting served as the basis for the more than seventy petitions in favor of immediate abolition that soon poured into the Overseas Ministry from every part of the Peninsula. The society and the provincial petitioners denounced slavery as an archaic and inhuman institution that violated the principles of the democratic revolution.[14]

The petitions were apparently coordinated by the Progressive and Democratic parties, as a glance at Barcelona's revolutionary junta suggests. In October 1868, Barcelonans endorsed the Madrid junta's call for abolishing Antillean slavery.[15] The bulk of the junta was made up of Progressives, Democrats, and republicans, indicating the prominence of the left-liberal parties in spreading abolitionist sentiment from Madrid, where the party heads, such as Salustiano de Olózaga and José María Orense, were Abolitionist Society members.[16]

The prospect of abolition and its support, not only by the Abolitionist

Society but also by the revolutionary parties, horrified Cuban reformers. José Antonio Saco, for instance, writing from Paris, argued that the revolution had to respect not only the property of slaveowners, but also the safety and integrity of white creoles: "Many abolitionists err in considering [emancipation] only from the point of view of the slave's liberty, forgetting the interests of the masters and of the State. If there is a black race in Cuba, there is also a white one."[17] Nicolás Azcárate, who had been one of Cuba's representatives to the Junta de Información, echoed Saco's concern for the safety of white Cubans during slave emancipation. A few months before the triumph of the revolution in Spain, Azcárate wrote to a Cuban friend from Madrid telling him that he dreaded the consequences of the victory of the revolutionary parties: "Things are going very badly here. I greatly fear a serious change when we least expect it. I fear it because I fear the exaggerated impulses of a radical party that, without thinking of Cuba's white humanity *[humanidad]*, will care only for the violent redemption of its black humanity."[18]

In a pamphlet published in 1869 meant to dispel charges that he supported the Cuban separatist movement, Azcárate reiterated Cuba's Spanishness. He also, like Saco, spoke out against the dangers posed to white creoles:

> In number 12 of the *Voz del Siglo*, . . . it says: "We are sincere and ardent enemies of Cuba's emancipation. For us, Cuba's emancipation will lead either to a race war or to the loss of the nationality that we cherish with a familial love. . . . We honestly believe that those who work for Cuba's independence are denying to Cubans their rights as Spaniards."[19]

For Azcárate, the insurrection and the spontaneous abolition of slavery in the east, if they continued unabated, meant "the death of white Cuba, which is my homeland and the birth of a black Cuba which . . . could never be my home, but only the horrible tomb of my hopes and memories."[20]

Calixto Bernal, a charter member of Spain's Democratic Party and one of the Cuban representatives to the Junta de Información, defended the right of Cubans to rebel because of the tyranny of Spanish rule and the unjust privileges enjoyed by Spaniards in Cuba. He saw, however, a relatively simple solution to the insurrection, one that he had consistently articulated through the pages of the *Revista Hispano-Americana* in the 1860s: grant white creoles full political rights, end the unfair privileges extended to peninsular Spaniards, and the Cuban rebels would become good and loyal Spanish citizens.[21]

Typically, though, Bernal was quiet on the question of slave emancipa-

tion. In contrast, Spaniards who agreed with his position on colonial constitutionalism generally favored abolition. The separation that Cuban reformers like Bernal, Saco, and Azcárate had drawn between white liberty
and black slavery collapsed in the new political situation of post-1868 Spain
and Cuba. A letter from Bernal to the Cuban José Antonio Echeverría in
1874 captured the rupture between Spaniards and Cubans who in the 1860s
had worked together. Bernal wrote, "We cannot count on Labra. He is tal-
ented but he has become involved in radical politics. . . . He has abandoned
the Cubans and instead campaigns for the blacks and defends them in his
manner. . . . The same has happened with Castelar and the other so-called
liberals here. They flee from Cuba as though it burned them. In any case,
they prefer blacks to patriots. We cannot count on anyone."[22]

### Peninsular Conservatives: The Protectionist Background

While the immediatism of the Abolitionist Society and the insurrection in
eastern Cuba placed formerly prominent reformers like Bernal on the mar-
gins of colonial politics, there were more forceful responses to abolitionist
mobilization. Important economic groups had a significant interest in maintaining the status quo in the Antilles—an order threatened by the new regime.

The September Revolution and the Ten Years' War posed especially
powerful threats to the established order. In Spain, the revolution was
identified not only with abolitionism, even though of a moderate nature,
but also with free trade. The first treasury minister of the new government
was Laureano Figuerola, leader of the Economists. In a sense, the revolution had exposed the key lines of conflict between liberal and conservative
elites within the Spanish colonial system. Metropolitan and colonial conservatives clung to slavery and protectionism during a period in the Atlantic
world when wage labor and free trade were growing under British commercial hegemony, while liberals sought to establish a less regulated
economy based on free markets and free labor.[23] These lines were not clear-
cut and congruent. For instance, some Antillean sugar planters preferred
free trade because it would give them free access to the North American
sugar market and enable them to import cheaper foodstuffs and consumer
goods; however, others with access to Spanish commercial networks favored a protected market for Spanish carriers and goods. On the other
hand, most planters, whether free-traders or protectionists, submitted to
Spanish political and economic hegemony because Spain was unique
among European metropolises in defending slavery and the slave trade
until the late nineteenth century. Moreover, metropolitan free-traders also

opposed slavery, a position deeply antagonistic to all Antillean planters. In moments of political crisis like the September Revolution and the Ten Years' War, colonial slaveowners and metropolitan conservatives mobilized against the revolution, overcoming certain differences, especially concerning trade policies, to unify for the defense of colonial slavery.[24]

In Spain, the defense of slavery led through protectionism. Upon assuming power, Figuerola succeeded in pushing through the Constituent Cortes a moderate free-trade tariff that would reduce customs on foreign manufactures over a twelve-year period. He also lowered customs on foreign cereal grains. Figuerola hoped through these measures to increase public revenues by stimulating foreign trade. New revenues were to go toward the payment of Spain's large foreign debt. Coupled with the mobilization of the Abolitionist Society and the rebellion in eastern Cuba, this free-trade legislation provoked sharp, though initially isolated, responses from regions and classes with strong interests in maintaining both slavery and protectionist trade policies.[25]

After the success of the revolutionary parties in September 1868, several petitions arrived at the Overseas Ministry requesting that the provisional government delay submitting any legislation on slavery to the constituent assembly until colonial slaveholders had been consulted on how best to carry out the abolition process. Not surprisingly, these petitions came from groups from the Spanish periphery with strong protectionist and colonial interests. The petitions represented "merchants, shipowners, property owners, and citizens of Santander"; "merchants of Asturias, some of whom are shipowners from the coast, others *hacendados* and industrialists from the Antilles"; "merchants, shipowners and citizens of Vigo [Galicia]"; "merchants, shipowners, and manufacturers from Palma de Mallorca"; and ".merchants and shipowners" from Valencia, Villanueva y Geltrú [Catalonia], and Barcelona.[26]

The arguments put forward in the various petitions were virtually identical and appear to have been written in common. All stressed the importance of the Antillean market for the health of the Spanish economy and the necessity of preserving tranquility. The Barcelona petition, for instance, argued that "Cuba's and Puerto Rico's domestic institution . . . mistakenly called slavery" was founded on an acquired and legal right that had existed for more than three hundred years. It was ingrained in every aspect of Antillean life and could not be changed overnight, largely because the slaves would not know how to exercise their liberty properly. Slavery was such an integral part of the colonial economy that any drastic changes would disrupt production; freed slaves would refuse to work and indeed would perhaps seek vengeance against their former owners. Finally, the disruption of production and social disorder would "cause the ruin of the islands of Cuba and Puerto Rico, and with it, the commerce, industry, and agriculture of some of the Peninsula's cities and provinces."[27]

The defense of slavery because of its importance in preserving public order and maintaining productivity echoed protectionist denunciations of the new free-trade legislation. The congruence of protectionism and antiabolitonism was especially clear in Barcelona. With the triumph of the revolution, Catalan textile manufacturers had immediately formed a new association, the Fomento de la Producción Nacional in 1869 to combat the government's new free trade policies.[28] Guillermo Gräell, one of the most important protectionists of the late nineteenth and early twentieth centuries, claimed that he converted to the protectionist camp after witnessing a protectionist rally in Barcelona in 1869 of more than 40,000 people from every class—a massive demonstration in a city of approximately 150,000 inhabitants.[29]

Juan Güell y Ferrer, a leading manufacturer with strong colonial ties who had been active in the protectionist campaigns of the Liberal Union era, was one of the paladins of Catalan protectionism and antiabolitionism. In a response to a speech by the Economist Segismundo Moret y Prendergast (author of the 1870 gradual abolition law), Güell graphically described the ruin that the Economists' policies would bring down on Spain:

> When Mr. Moret sees the beautiful ideal of cheap foreign goods fulfilled
> . . . , he will see ships pass by the coasts of *verdant* Galicia, *the once
> industrious* Catalonia, *flowery* Valencia, and immortal, dead Cádiz, his
> own home. They will say: there is nothing here for us. This is a nation of
> pretentious scholars, of loudmouths and idiots. They did not under-
> stand that without producing exchangable goods that we would bring
> them cheap goods while they had the capital to pay for them, but that
> we would not give them gifts once their capital was spent.[30]

Güell foresaw the same ruin for Spain and Cuba if the government did not protect Cuban property and production by stamping out the rebellion and ensuring labor by defending the rights of slaveowners. According to Güell, Cuba would fall into ruin without the reassertion of Spanish might.[31] As for Spain, if it were to lose Cuba, it would sink to the lowest point in its history, the late seventeenth century:

> Our opinion is that . . . the loss of Cuba would reduce Spain's political

and economic importance by half. Such a loss would place Spain below the level it reached in the sad and melancholy times of Charles II, when politically we were almost wiped from the map of Europe, while economically we were such a nullity that even the monarch himself lacked the means for a decorous existence.[32]

Thus, protectionists and antiabolitonists foresaw ruin for Spain if they did not succeed in overturning the revolution's policies. Free trade would exclude their goods and shipping from the Antillean and national markets, while abolishing slavery would cause the irreversible decline of Antillean and Spanish prosperity and perhaps lead to the colonies' independence from Spain. Although these metropolitan protestors were at first marginalized after the revolution, access to political and ideological resources on a national level, first mobilized during the protectionist campaigns of the Liberal Union period, eventually enabled them to coordinate their efforts. Moreover, the protectionist defense of the "national economy" and of slavery coincided with conservative resistance to the revolution in the colonies. Even in the early days of the revolution, conservatives laid the basis for counterrevolution.

## Cuba

By the winter of 1868–1869, when the abolitionist petitions hit the Overseas Ministry, the question of abolition had become more complicated. In October 1868, the creole *hacendado* Carlos Manuel de Céspedes sounded the Grito de Yara, a call for Cuba's independence from Spain. The separatist campaign mobilized discontented groups from eastern Cuba across class and racial boundaries, including major landowners, small farmers, free laborers, and slaves. Though planters like Céspedes were inclined to maintain slavery and respect the rights of property owners, the internal pressure caused by rebellious slaves forced the insurgent leadership to pass various emancipation acts between 1869 and 1870, and finally to abolish slavery and other forms of bondage completely in December 1870.[33]

The west's response to the eastern rebellion was dramatic. Slavery still flourished on the western plantations, and slaveowners had no intention of freeing their slaves in the near future.[34] Led by Spanish slaveowners and traders like Julián Zulueta and the conservative Captain General Lersundi, western elites, particularly Spaniards, mobilized through the Volunteers, paramilitary units first established by José Gutiérrez de la Concha in the 1850s to defend Cuba against annexationist invasions.[35]

The radical and intransigent Spanish response to the insurgency cut off any chance for negotiation and forced creole reformers to choose between accommodation with the Spanish party and support for the rebels. For instance, a faction of the western elite, led by the slaveowner Miguel de Aldama, tried to manipulate the insurgency to coax from Spain the reforms discussed in the Junta de Información. They appeared to be succeeding when the metropolitan government dispatched General Domingo Dulce to Cuba to replace Lersundi.[36]

The Volunteers, however, brooked no reconciliation or moderation. In January 1869, Aldama wrote Dulce from his plantation, "Santa Rosa," to request guns and men to protect his family and property from hostile attacks. Already, a mob had sacked the Aldama palace in Havana.[37] Writing to his friend (and soon-to-be fellow emigré) José Morales Lemus, Aldama admitted that his and Dulce's cause was lost: "Dulce has to fight against the revolution of Yara and the Volunteers' position. How can he deal with such a terrible situation? How will our country save itself from the consequences of either?" In fact, it was the Volunteers, not the rebels of the east, that Aldama saw as the more serious problem: "I predict that our absence [from Cuba] will be lengthy. Even after the Government has easily overcome the revolution of Yara, it will not be able to do the same with the other. To me, the armed Volunteers are the incarnation of the slave-trading party *[partido negrero]*, and they are preparing for battle with the Spanish revolution because it seeks to abolish slavery."[38]

Aldama was mistaken about the defeat of the "revolution of Yara," but his diagnosis of the political situation in the west was shrewd. The period when creole and Spanish reformers like himself and Dulce had held sway in Havana was now over. The Spanish intransigence and anticreole sentiment of earlier periods, such as the Tacón administration (1834–1838) or the period of La Escalera (1843–1844), once again reigned. The Volunteers and the Spanish party soon forced Aldama, Morales Lemus, Dulce, and other reform-minded creoles and Spaniards from Cuba. And eventually, as Aldama predicted, they also turned against the September Revolution, not only by resisting envoys like Dulce, but also by organizing an array of conservative forces in Spain and the Antilles into a powerful counterrevolutionary movement.[39]

## Puerto Rico

Puerto Rican slaveowners were more subjected to the power of the revolutionary state than their Cuban counterparts. Whereas in Cuba many eastern slaveowners openly fought for independence and in the west slaveowners defied any policy that contradicted their interests, in Puerto Rico, the Spanish state stamped out any challenges to its sovereignty. The most significant challenge was the Grito de Lares, a separatist insurrection that broke out in October 1868 in one of Puerto Rico's interior coffee regions that was part of an islandwide plan. In Lares, landowners, laborers, and slaves rebelled against the colonial state, slavery, and the economic power of local peninsular merchants.[40] The uprising lasted only three days before the colonial government suppressed it. Local participants in the rebellion were imprisoned, as well as well-known liberal figures from throughout the island suspected of involvement with the separatist movement, including J. J. Acosta.[41]

Rebellion having failed, emancipation in Puerto Rico would have to come through the auspices of the Spanish state. While slave labor was still pivotal on the island's sugar plantations, Puerto Rican planters could hope for indemnity, unlike their Cuban counterparts.[42] Puerto Rican slaveowners realized their position, and some sought to bargain with abolitionists like Acosta. In November 1868, the Ponce slaveowner Gustavo Cabrera wrote to Acosta that many in Ponce had reconciled themselves to abolition, recognizing not only the new political currents of the September Revolution, but also the validity of the abolitionist alternative articulated by Acosta and others since the 1850s:

> Men who until recently opposed the abolitionist idea today contemplate abolition as the first step along the road of progress. . . .
>
> We want to elect you or Román [Baldorioty de Castro]; . . . you and Román should send me a letter outlining the reforms that you think will improve our situation; . . . concerning slavery, you should *sweeten* [*azucararan*] it a bit by making it gradual and giving us five to ten years.[43]

Acosta responded by defending his long-held belief in the viability of immediate abolition:

> We can and should discuss whether abolition should be simultaneous or gradual. We advocate simultaneous abolition and with indemnification paid immediately because we believe that it is best to end the old system and begin another, unburdened and aided by the ten million pesos that will enter the country.[44]

In other words, Acosta reiterated the urgency of Puerto Rico's transition to free labor. He and other abolitionists like Baldorioty de Castro and Julio de Vizcarrondo had argued since the 1850s that Puerto Rico had enough laborers of sufficently industrious habits to create a functioning labor market. Moreover, he believed that with indemnity, slaveowners would receive the injection of capital they needed for modernizing production. Only modernization of processing techniques would preserve for Puerto Rico a niche in the highly competitive world sugar market. By transferring investment from labor to technology, Acosta and other abolitionists hoped that Puerto Rican planters would be able to resuscitate their declining industry.[45]

Puerto Rican abolitionists pushed for their program in Madrid's new political climate. Julio de Vizcarrondo was one of the driving forces behind the Abolitionist Society's demands for an immediate end to slavery. His cousin, Luis Padial Vizcarrondo, raised the question of immediate abolition and constitutional rule in the colonies during the Constituent Cortes of 1869.[46] In 1869, the revolutionary government convened a revival of the Junta de Información to discuss reforms in Puerto Rico. The government conceded that Puerto Rico was in a more favorable position than Cuba to enjoy immediate concessions. The subcommittee on slavery decided to recommend gradual abolition, a move led by the Economist and abolitionist Luis María Pastor.[47]

There was, however, considerable dissent among members of the subcommittee. A group of Puerto Rican conservatives opposed any measure other than *coartación,* self-purchase by slaves, arguing that the Spanish state was too impoverished to indemnify slaveowners, even in Puerto Rico. At the other end of the spectrum, the young Spanish abolitionists Rafael María de Labra and Joaquín María Sanromá, together with Luis Padial, voted for Pastor's gradualism only after noting their preference for immediate abolition.[48] Besides the claims of justice and revolution, the minority found Puerto Rico's peculiar racial, social, and physical conditions to be propitious for immediate abolition: "The conditions of work in Puerto Rico, the culture and economy of that society, the proportions of the races and classes, the moral situation of the slaves, the character of the black race (most of whose individuals are creoles), and even the island's geographical and topographical disposition rule out any fear that radical measures concerning slavery will alter public order or disrupt economic life."[49]

## The Moret Law, 1870

Many feared, however, that abolition in Puerto Rico would not simply disrupt that island's productivity but lead to abolition and total economic collapse in Cuba as well. Though some Puerto Rican creoles and the Abolitionist Society supported immediate abolition, the revolutionary regime acted to assuage the fears of slaveowners and metropolitan merchants, planters, and manufacturers. The Moret Law of 1870, named for the overseas minister, Segismundo Moret y Prendergast, an abolitionist and an Economist, was a logical outcome of the moderate abolitionism favored by the government that came to power in 1868. By 1870, however, gradual emancipation pleased no one.

The law passed in June 1870 called for the freedom of all children born to slaves after September 1868, in honor of the September Revolution, and of all slaves over the age of sixty. Slaves who served in the Spanish military would gain their freedom, as would those not registered in the official census. Children of slaves had to serve their mothers' masters until the age of eighteen and then receive half wages until the age of twenty-two, when they would become fully free. The law prohibited the use of the whip and established *juntas protectoras* to enforce the rights of slaves. Finally, the Moret Law called for an indemnified emancipation plan once the Cuban insurrection had ended and Cuban representatives had taken their place in the Cortes.[50]

The 1870 Moret Law attracted immediate opposition, the most vehement from slaveowners in western Cuba. As Rebecca Scott shows, the Cuban slaveowners' strategy was to delay emancipation as long as possible while in the meantime seeking new sources of free labor. They resisted subordination to any external authority regarding their slaves and estates. They forced the captain general to delay publication of the new law for several months and made several changes, including revoking the ban on the use of the whip. They also made sure that the *juntas protectoras* would represent their interests. For instance, Julián Zulueta and Francisco Ibáñez, two of the most important Spanish slaveowners in Cuba, were prominent members of the central *junta*. Puerto Rican slaveowners were similarly defiant in the immedaite aftermath of the law's passage.[51]

Puerto Rican and Spanish abolitionists also opposed the gradual measure. The Republican Emilio Castelar said during the debates over the Moret Law in the Cortes: "I listened to [Moret] with immense sadness when he stood on the first day to say: 'I have satisfied the property owners.' I would have wished this satisfaction to be for the slaves, for such was the duty and obligation of the overseas minister."[52] Thus, as colonial slaveowners and metropolitan protectionists moved to stifle the Moret Law, abolitionists prepared to push it farther.

# 7

# "Today Victory Is Assured"

## ABOLITIONISM AND A NEW
## IMPERIAL ORDER,
## 1870–1874

Seeking to convince the newly formed Radical Party to support the Abolitionist Society's call for immediate abolition in the Antilles, Rafael María de Labra argued that emancipation would bring liberty not only to Antillean slaves but also to Spaniards in the Peninsula:

> Today victory is assured; to battle. . . . We are not fighting today for Cuba; we are not fighting for Puerto Rico. The question is more serious: it is *to be* or *not to be*; . . . against theocracy, monopoly, and dictatorship, what we are committed to is the liberty of Spain.[1]

How did Labra make the connection between emancipation of Antillean slaves and liberty in Spain?

After the disappointment of the Moret Law, the Abolitionist Society fought for immediate abolition by allying itself with the most diehard revolutionary parties, the Radicals and the Federal Republicans. This alliance with the revolutionary left was made easier by the polarization of the revolution caused by the colonial question, by conservative opposition to the monarchy of Amadeus of Savoy, and after 1872 by the renewal of the Carlist war in northern Spain. In the heated political atmosphere of the early 1870s, abolitionism became equated with support for the September Revolution, while opposition to abolition became a rallying point for the counterrevolutionary, pro-Bourbon right.[2]

One of the new groups that emerged from the conflicts of the revolution was the Radical Party, headed by Manuel Ruiz Zorrilla. The Radicals unified the left wing of the old Progressive Party (Praxades Mateo Sagasta's Constitutional Party represented the right wing) with the *cimbrios,* monarchist members of the Democratic Party, and their program represented a broad challenge to the revolutionary settlement of the 1830s. The Radicals defended the standard positions of the nineteenth-century Spanish left: separation of church and state, free municipal elections, free trade, suppression of indirect taxes *(consumos)* and the draft *(la quinta),* and universal manhood suffrage. Their democratic, antioligarchic, and anticlerical policies greatly resembled the positions of the Federal Republican Party, the inheritor of the Democratic Party of the Liberal Union. The two parties diverged, significantly during the September Revolution, over the form of government. The Radicals defended the monarchy and argued that Spain was not yet ready for a republic. The Republicans rejected not only monarchy but also the centralism of the liberal state. Indeed, in 1873, Federal Republicans staged uprisings in Valencia and Murcia in favor of a decentralized, federalist regime.[3]

The challenge to traditional Spanish liberalism had revolutionary implications for the colonies as well. Slavery and nonrepresentative rule in the colonies were part and parcel of the revolution of the 1830s. In the political cockpit of Spain and the Antilles between 1868 and 1874, the Radicals and the Federal Republicans turned to abolitionism as a concrete method for breaking the political and economic dominance of the Hispano-Antillean right and consolidating the democratic revolution. Moreover, the abolitionists and their political allies envisioned the remaking of empire as a hegemonic project. They believed that abolition and political reforms would halt the Cuban insurrection and win the loyalty of creoles and freed slaves for Spain.[4]

This chapter analyzes the abolitionist and revolutionary strategies after the Moret Law. It discusses the abolitionists' arguments for the urgency of immediate abolition in both Puerto Rico and Cuba. It then turns to the transatlantic mobilization of conservatives against abolitionism and the September Revolution during the battle over Puerto Rican slavery, tracing the alliances between colonial and metropolitan counterrevolutionaries to the struggles of the Liberal Union. The final section focuses on the First Republic (1873–1874), the most radical and traumatic moment of the September Revolution, and its short-lived efforts to remake Spanish rule in the Antilles.

## "Slavery Has Died in Our Antilles":
## Abolitionism and Colonial Hegemony

Abolitionists and revolutionaries attacked slavery in Puerto Rico and Cuba for different reasons: they saw abolition in Puerto Rico as politically practicable and abolition in Cuba as politically imperative. As we have seen, Puerto Rican reformers had urged immediate abolition since the 1860s. During the September Revolution, abolitionists like Acosta fought against conservatives in Puerto Rico, especially Spanish commercial interests, and the moderate colonial state. The political vehicle of Puerto Rican reformers was the Liberal Reformist Party (Partido Liberal Reformista), founded in 1870. Their conservative opponents, generally peninsular merchants, soon followed by establishing the Unconditional Spanish Party (Partido Español Incondicional) and organizing a Volunteer corps, as Spaniards in Cuba had done.[5]

In the first years following the September Revolution, the Spanish government blocked efforts to elect abolitionists like Labra or Baldorioty de Castro to Parliament. (Because districts could choose any representative regardless of residence, during the revolution Puerto Rico was represented by the Spaniards Rafael María de Labra, Joaquín María Sanromá, Gabriel Rodríguez—proponents of immediate abolition—and by José Laureano Sanz—twice captain general of Puerto Rico and a leader of the conservative counterrevolution.) In 1871, Captain General Gabriel Baldrich reported to the overseas minister in Madrid: "You can rest assured that Labra will not be elected. As I said in the last mail, I am the enemy of all extremes."[6]

Baldrich and the revolutionary regime saw peninsular conservatives as the other extreme in Puerto Rican politics. Spaniards in Puerto Rico opposed any reform in the colonial system, such as abolition or extending Spain's 1869 constitution to Puerto Rico. Moreover, the Volunteers violently harassed creole supporters of abolition and constitutional goverment.[7]

Despite official disapproval and conservative intransigence in the early years of the revolution, Acosta, Baldorioty de Castro, Pedro Gerónimo Goico, and other creole abolitionists and reformers kept up their campaigns both in Spain and Puerto Rico. In Puerto Rico, they sought to convince planters of the benefits of immediate abolition for the future of sugar production. Following Acosta's arguments, Puerto Rican abolitionists held that shifting investment from labor to technology would resuscitate sugar production. They especially favored a transition to the *central* system, whereby the work of harvesting and grinding sugar cane was divided between estates dedicated to each function. Such a system would create a more efficient division of labor and capital.[8]

They also praised the superiority of free laborers. Wages would encourage them to work harder, while the *central* system would provide unlimited work opportunities: "Wealth and well-being will rapidly spread through the entire region. The worker *[bracero]* will be powerfully stimulated by the wage to which previously he could not aspire."[9] Wage labor would encourage not only greater productivity among the work force but also frugality and discipline, as workers learned to save their wages to satisfy new material desires: "It is well known that the possession of a modest sum awakens the desire to increase it. This desire is a new promise of morality and a guarantee of order, circumstances that could be developed in the heat of the *central* to the benefit of the individual and society."[10]

To further ensure the morality and dependability of the free labor force, abolitionists advised planters to devise new methods for attracting and accommodating their workers. For instance, they advocated creating popular libraries, mutual-aid societies, and working-class social clubs.[11] One writer urged capitalists to build housing with each new *central* so that workers could rent and eventually own their own dwellings. Thus, workers too would become respectable property owners, and the employer would always have his work force close to hand—unlike the present system in which workers lived scattered through the countryside, out of the employer's reach.[12]

Puerto Rican abolitionists sought to convince not only their own slaveowners but the Spanish state as well. The latter effort was carried out in Madrid in alliance with metropolitan abolitionists and whatever revolutionary parties supported colonial reform. The reformer Manuel Fernández Juncos wrote to José Pablo Morales in 1873 that Puerto Ricans should take advantage of politics in Spain to further their goals without committing to a specific metropolitan political platform: "We should not choose between monarchists and Republicans. . . . Our politics right now should be local politics. We must reform our country's economic and administrative laws. Those who seek those reforms are reformists, those who oppose them antireformists."[13] Already during the state reformism of the 1860s, Puerto Ricans and Spaniards had argued that Puerto Rico was ready to abolish slavery. They believed that Puerto Rico had already made the transition to free labor and class society. Abolitionists represented Puerto Rico as a racial paradise, an ideal New World colony ready for liberal reforms, especially abolition. Spanish abolitionists championed the arguments, first made by Acosta in the 1850s, that racial antagonism had been overcome in Puerto Rico. Labra, for example, noted that "the mulatto is a major element of

[Puerto Rico's] population."[14] For Labra, the mulatto's prominence signified that "true" economic interests had supplanted the racial or caste preoccupations that marred most colonial societies: "In Puerto Rico, rather than *whites* and *blacks,* there are laborers and capitalists, agriculturalists and industrialists. That is, human interests, social interests, permanent economic, political, and moral interests are more important than the shades of skin color or the preoccupation with origin."[15] Moreover, abolitionists pointed to the predominance of free labor and the broad range of smallholdings, so different from the huge plantations of western Cuba, as indicators of Puerto Rico's modernity and social equilibrium.[16]

While abolitionists saw abolition in Puerto Rico as politically viable, they saw emancipation in Cuba as politically urgent, despite their reservations about Cuba's racial balance. Most Spanish abolitionists regarded the principles of the Cuban separatists legitimate. They believed that just as the revolution in Spain had overthrown unjust institutions, colonial insurgents were fighting to do the same in a Cuba still perverted by dictatorship, protectionism, and slavery. For them, the September Revolution had betrayed its ideals by supporting the old regime in the colonies. In 1870, Fernando Garrido, an abolitionist and a Federal Republican, proclaimed Cuban slaves' attack on slavery "a victory for progress" and "glorious and useful for Humanity."[17]

Nonetheless, the abolitionists opposed Cuban independence and sought to reassert Spanish colonial hegemony by abolishing slavery and regaining the loyalty of Cuban rebels. In his criticism of the gradualism of the Moret Law, Emilio Castelar argued that the government was aligning itself with the wrong party in Cuba:

> I said, if we give liberty to whites and blacks, the reactionaries and slave traders will rebel. If we do not give them liberty, if we delay reform, then those raised close to the United States, those who carry the idea of liberty in their conscience, the reformers, the revolutionaries will rebel.
>
> So much was certain: we had to choose between one or another rebellion. Why, September revolutionaries, have you chosen the catastrophe that separates us from Europe and America? Why have you chosen war, the war of the colonist who demands his rights, the war of the black who needs his liberty?[18]

Most Spanish abolitionists considered immediate abolition imperative after the Grito de Yara. In 1869, the mobilization of slaves as rebel fighters had prompted Rafael María de Labra to declare: "Slavery has died in our Antilles."[19] In 1872 Labra defended his advocacy of immediate abolition in a letter to the electors of his home district in Asturias: "Today the nerve of the insurrection is being fed by the colored race, by runaway slaves and escaped Chinese, by armed men who espouse abolitionist propaganda on the border of the western department, right at the foot of the great *ingenios* and within reach of the huge droves of slaves."[20] Labra and others argued that Spain's defense of slavery fired the rebellion because slaves saw an opportunity to end their bondage by joining the insurgent forces. If Spain abolished slavery, the rebellion would lose a vital source of manpower and legitimacy, while Spain would win for itself the loyalty of the former slave population. As Castelar said in the Cortes in 1870, Spain had the opportunity "to carry out the great act of calling to civil life, of calling to the rule of law, 400,000 men." The key was to do so under Spanish, not Cuban, auspices.[21]

The problem was to find the political opportunity to carry out this hegemonic project, one impeded by the government's appeasement of Cuba's Spanish party. The abolitionists denounced conservative intransigence and argued that only a complete overhaul of the colonial system would preserve Spanish sovereignty in Cuba.[22] It would also firmly establish the September Revolution in the Peninsula. In January 1873, Gabriel Rodríguez explicitly linked abolition and revolution, slavery and reaction, in a Radical Party meeting at which the Abolitionist Society and the Radicals reconfirmed their mutual commitment to immediate abolition in Puerto Rico. Rodríguez portrayed the Antilles as the cradle of Spanish reaction:

> Under the present regime and dominated by slavery, our overseas provinces are special schools, breeding grounds for reactionary elements; . . . the Spaniards who return from the Antilles are indifferent to the generous aspirations of the liberal parties and are blind and impassioned reactionaries. It is not in vain that they breathe the poisoned atmosphere of slavery.[23]

## Counterrevolution and Counterhegemony

January 1873 was a tense moment in Spain, as revolutionaries and counterrevolutionaries squarely faced one another. Rodríguez's representation of the Antilles as the breeding ground of counterrevolution was not an abstract metaphor for the corrupting effects of slavery and dictatorship; it was a shrewd commentary on the conservatives' mobilization against the revolution and the leading role of Cuban slaveowners in that process. The constant negative pole in Rodríguez's speeches was the specter of reaction that haunted Spain: the National League (Liga Nacional), an extraparliamentary association that was a grand coalition of the colonial and metropolitan right headed by the former revolutionary Francisco Serrano y Domínguez.[24]

The initial caution with which conservative metropolitan and colonial interests addressed the slavery question after the revolution soon turned to intransigent and coordinated resistance. At first, the most powerful local protests against the government's limited reform measures came from Havana. In 1871, local protests expanded and were coordinated at a broader level. Just as in 1861 when regional protectionist classes united in the Spanish Economic Circle (Círculo Económico Español) to combat the Economists' free-trade campaign, so in 1871 colonial and metropolitan groups organized to oppose the Abolitionist Society's campaign to push the government toward immediate abolition, first in Puerto Rico, then in Cuba.

This time, Cuba's Spanish party took the initiative by establishing the first Centro Hispano-Ultramarino in Madrid.[25] The president of the Madrid Center was the marquis of Manzanedo, a Spaniard who had made his fortune in Cuba as a merchant, moneylender, and slave trader. In the 1870s he was the wealthiest man in Madrid.[26] The vice-president was General José Laureano Sanz, the ultrareactionary governor of Puerto Rico when the revolution broke out and the man sent to restore "order" in 1874 once it was defeated. The secretary was the Cuban journalist Antonio G. Llorente, who had previously served the Spanish party in Havana and founded the newspaper *La Integridad Nacional* in Madrid in 1870.[27]

The Madrid Centro Hispano-Ultramarino was the backbone of the National League, formed in 1872 to check the campaign for immediate abolition in Puerto Rico. The league united metropolitan and colonial conservatives on two issues: opposition to the abolition of Puerto Rican slavery and to the monarchy of Amadeus of Savoy. Cuba's Spanish party opposed Puerto Rican abolition because they saw it as the first step toward immediate abolition in Cuba. The opposition to Amadeus's monarchy also rallied a broad coalition of antirevolutionary forces who sought a restoration of the Bourbon monarchy in the person of the young crown prince, Alfonso XII.[28]

The figurehead of the National League was Francisco Serrano y Dominguez, one of the original leaders of the revolution and the key figure in the revolution's colonial bloc. The secretary was the poet and politician Abelardo López de Ayala, a Serrano protegé and the first overseas minister after the triumph of the revolution in 1868. Serrano's and López de Ayala's leadership emphasized the degree to which the slavery question had

# AL PUEBLO ESPAÑOL

Es los momentos de peligro para las grandes causas; cuando las respetuosas súplicas que formula el patriotismo son desatendidas; cuando se olvidan promesas solemnes y de continuo reiteradas, y ante la dolorosa perspectiva de posible infortunio para la honra y la suerte de la Pátria, debe de los leales exijir el amparo poderoso, el auxilio eficaz de la Nacion.

Cumpliendo su sagrada obligacion los que suscriben, en nombre de los Comités Hispano-Ultramarino establecido actualmente en la Península; en nombre de distintas agrupaciones comerciales, de propietarios é industriales de localidades diversas; representando la opinion unánime de los buenos y esforzados españoles que en Cuba y Puerto-Rico defienden la integridad del territorio; por sí propios y como delegados que que forman parte, haciendo abstraccion cada uno y todos de diferencias de partido, y unidos en una sola aspiracion, dirijen hoy su voz sincera, enérjica, á ese pueblo, invitándole á que le preste apoyo en servicio de una causa, que es su causa, para salvar derechos que son suyos, para impedir la destruccion de su poder en el Mundo de Occidente, que peligran si á realizarse llegan proyectos que á la imprevision obedecen, á la malicia ó al error.

Y confian que este llamamiento ha de hallar éco y acojida en el país; y esperan que á él respondan cuantos aprecian la bienheredada dignidad, cuantos recuerdan la grandeza española de otros tiempos, cuantos no quieren dejar á sus hijos, con la memoria de su inercia, el cuadro desconsolador de la humi-

tuacion en daño nuestro, con olvido total de los deberes que el patriotismo impone, y prestando oido á los hipócritas lamentos de los que explotan las ideas de humanidad, finjiendo en ello á nuestra raza, condolerse de otra raza que se encuentra en situacion desventajosa, hay quienes negándoles á la voz de la razon, quieren llevar á Cuba y Puerto-Rico nueva y nuestros elementos de discordia que aumentan los sucesos, que encadenecen las pasiones y que producan la pérdida de provincias tan valiosas, y con ella la destruccion de nuestra gloria y porvenir.

No desconocen los que tal pretenden, á ménos que el fanatismo ó la ignorancia ahoguen su intelijencia en lo absoluto, que la pueril respuesta de que en nada se afecta á Cuba, y que solo á Puerto-Rico alcanzan tan erróneos planes, es un sarcasmo que ofende á los que piden aplazamiento temporal hasta el momento en que la paz y la concordia reinen en las dos Antillas, para establecer entónces las modificaciones que aconseje la prudencia y no destruyan la seguridad del territorio; no desconocen que resultan los gravísimos problemas sociales y políticos de las dos islas hermanas, prejuzgando en una lo que á la otra atañe en igual grado, se incurre en una injusticia abierta é irritante, que revela la fuerza de presion que ejerzen nuestros contrarios aleviosos, y el desprecio que se hace á los que allá por salvar los derechos de la Madre España, prodigan sus fortunas, derraman su sangre generosa y mueren en la guerra, defendiendo un suelo, que hoy vemos posible niegue acaso en venideros dias, sepultura á sus ca-

á España; que serán positivas, que serán irremediables, si, con precipitados cambios en el modo de ser político y social de aquellas islas, se atiza el fuego de la discordia en ellas y se allana el sendero que conduce á su ruina y perdicion.

No se arredran los que firman por la anunciada exigencia de Gobiernos que, se dice, pretenden inmiscuirse en nuestros asuntos interiores ó en el régimen y direccion de nuestro pueblo. ¿Desde cuándo sufre sumiso el español, la ultrajante imposicion de los extraños? ¿A dónde está la dignidad, qué se ha hecho de la independencia nacional? ¿Son ya los tiempos en que la interesada voluntad de otros poderes, constituye ley para nosotros?

Si tan oprobios pretension llegára á presentarse, suficiente fuera para rechazarla altiva, no solo la conviccion del derecho que tenemos, sino el recuerdo de que somos descendientes del pueblo de Sagunto y de Gerona, el orgullo de que es nuestra sangre la sangre de los bravos de Bailen y Zaragoza.

Nó: dignos y nobles conciudadanos nuestros, atendidos: unidos á nosotros para impedir con enérjicas protestas y firmes peticiones, que se lleven á cabo esos proyectos hoy; sus proyectos que ántes de mucho nos harían abandonar el Nuevo Mundo, el Mundo que nuestros padres descubrieron, arrancando abatidos, al emigrar de las Antillas, nuestra ganada y nuestra gloria, y mostrando en nuestros rostros la marca del oprobio y la vergüenza.

Unios á nosotros; al pié de la bandera nacional, agrupados

"Al Pueblo Español," a counterrevolutionary broadsheet issued by the Madrid Centro Hispano-ultramarino, December 1872.

radicalized and polarized the revolution. From reformers who in 1868 had sought to implement a gradual emancipation process in cooperation with Cuban slaveowners, they had turned into reactionaries.[29]

The National League and the Madrid Centro Hispano-Ultramarino defended their opposition to abolition in the name of national integrity and national honor. They argued that the government's primary duty was to suppress the rebellion in eastern Cuba and ensure Spanish sovereignty in the Antilles. Abolitionism was merely a distraction, a misguided policy that aided Spain's enemies. They affirmed their conviction in a proclamation issued in November 1872:

> The undersigned, . . . in the name of the Nation's dignity, condemn those who individually or collectively, either through error or malice, contribute to the subversion of our brothers overseas, to the ruin of those opulent islands, to the ignominy, to the shame of our glorious standard on the other side of the ocean.[30]

In December, as a vote in the Cortes on abolition approached, the Madrid Center distributed a broadsheet urging the "Spanish people" to protect Spain's honor. It recalled how the people had risen against Napoleon's forces when Charles IV compromised Spain's national integrity: "We are descendants of the people of Sagunto and Gerona, our proud blood is the blood of the valiant warriors [bravos] of Bailen and Zaragoza." Those patriotic warriors would rise again if Spain's national honor were compromised in the Antilles:

> If a careless Government failed to carry out its duties and entered into pacts that led to the loss of Cuba and Puerto Rico, may it suffer the contempt and curses of all and the disgraces that its stupidity and malice caused.[31]

That threat appeared to be carried out a few days later on December 11, when a short-lived insurrection broke out in the working-class neighborhood of Antón Martín in Madrid. Newspaper accounts reported cries of "Long live the Republic!" "Death to the enemies of the national integrity!" and "Death to the filibusters!"[32] Though no party or association claimed responsibility for the uprising, government ministers left no doubt that they believed that the National League and the Centros Hispano-Ultramarino were behind it.[33]

The Court was not the only site of conflict in Spain, however, and the Hispano-Cuban elite that made up Cuba's Spanish party and the Madrid Centro Hispano-Ultramarino were not the only groups that mobilized against abolition. Upon its formation in late 1871, the Madrid Center had sought to create a national network to defend the colonial status quo. Other centers immediately appeared throughout Spain: Barcelona, Santander, Valencia, Bilbao, and other major economic nuclei. When the Madrid Centro Hispano-Ultramarino held a national meeting in October 1872 to coordinate resistance to abolition, the most prominent provincial centers hailed from protectionist strongholds where the intitial protests against abolition had been made in 1868: Barcelona, Valencia, Palma de Mallorca, Santander, and Avilés (Asturias).[34]

The slavery and protectionist questions formed a symbiotic relationship at this particular moment of political crisis because for Spain's protectionist classes there was little difference between them. The defense of Antillean slavery was tantamount to defending the colonial market in the name of national economy. Unlike slaveowners in the U.S. South, Spanish protectionists did not offer a defense of slavery per se as a labor system morally or economically superior to free wage labor. Instead, they opposed immediate abolition because of its negative consequences for Antillean production and because of its potential political impact, that is, Cuban independence. In either case, Spain's protectionist classes foresaw abolition as disastrous for their interests.[35]

Thus, in late 1872, as Parliament prepared to vote on the abolition of Puerto Rican slavery, the Overseas Ministry again received a mass of petitions. This time, although there were again dozens favoring abolition, there were also more than one hundred antiabolitionist petitions from all over Spain, a testament to the efficacy of the Madrid Center's organizing initiative.[36] However, the antiabolitionist petitions demonstrated that not only the interests of Cuba's slaveowners were at stake, but also those of the protectionist classes active in the Liberal Union. The radicalization of colonial politics galvanized the dormant protectionist network of the Economic Circle. Hence, while the regional centers opposed abolition in the name of national integrity and honor, the protectionist associations defended their position with the familiar rhetoric of promoting the national economy.

For example, one of the antiabolitionist petitions of late 1872 was from the "Commission of Property Owners, Merchants, and Industrialists of Valladolid." Valladolid was the center of one of Spain's major cereal-producing regions, Castile. The commission claimed that Figuerola's free-trade legislation had already deprived Castile of its predominance in the national market. If Spain were to lose the Antilles through rash abolitionist policies, Castilian grain products would be left without a market.[37]

As before, the most articulate and active defense of the national economy came from Catalonia.[38] There, the nexus of antiabolitionism and protectionism was particularly clear and the discourses of national integrity and national economy were fused. For instance, Juan Güell y Ferrer was the first president of Barcelona's Centro Hispano-Ultramarino. In its 1872 petition against abolition, the Barcelona Center claimed that the "hardworking" inhabitants of Catalonia believed that slave emancipation in the Antilles "would be the death knell for those distant and rich countries as an integral part of the national territory, and thus as consumer markets for the majority of the goods produced in this Principality as well as for its shipping."[39]

Thus it was not surprising that the economic associations active in the protectionist campaigns played the most prominent role in Catalan resistance to abolition between October 1872 and January 1873. The Centros Hispano-Ultramarino of Barcelona and Villanueva y Geltrú opposed abolition.[40] The Catalan Industrial Institute (Instituto Industrial de Cataluña) and the Catalan Agricultural Institute of San Isidro (Instituto Agrícola Catalana de San Isidro, IACSI) petitioned against abolition, as did the fledgling protectionist association, El Fomento de la Producción Nacional.[41] So too did the IACSI subdelegation in Villanueva y Geltru, a town with important mercantile interests in the Antilles, especially Puerto Rico. That relationship was reflected in the range of associations in Villanueva y Geltru that petitioned against abolition: the Artisans' Circle (Casino de Artesanos); its board of directors; the Círculo Villanovés; the Centro Liberal-Monárquico; and finally the municipal government. The Artisans' Circle argued that jobs in Villanueva and throughout Spain would disappear if the colonial economy were disrupted.[42] Petitions also came from the municipal governments of Reus and Sitges (the town most represented among Catalan merchants in the Antilles)[43] and a group of "property owners, manufacturers, shipowners, merchants, and industrialists from Barcelona." Whereas in 1868 the few antiabolitionist petitions were generally signed by a dozen prominent merchants or manufacturers, in 1872 the Barcelona petition bore over a thousand signatures.[44]

The Catalans were not utterly antireformist, however.[45] They favored the same reforms for the colonies that they advocated in the protectionist campaigns. In other words, they favored the full integration of the colonial economy into the "phalanx" of the national economy. The Catalans agreed that the existing colonial economic system was contradictory and one-sided. Their solution was to harmonize the Antillean and Spanish economies by reforming the tariffs that monopolized the colonial market for peninsular goods and kept colonial products out of the metropolitan market.

In 1870, Pedro Bosch y Labrús, head of the Fomento de la Producción Nacional, had written to the Overseas Minister Víctor Balaguer, the Catalan protectionist, urging reciprocal trade *(cabotaje)* between Cuba and Spain and the protection of both markets against foreign competition. In his words, "The Island of Cuba is really a Spanish province and there should not exist customs between provinces." However, Cuban sugar and tobacco should be exceptions: sugar, because the powerful Cuban sugar complex, worked by slaves, would overwhelm Andalusia's nascent cane sugar industry, which relied on more expensive (according to Bosch) free wage labor; tobacco, because the government needed the revenue. On the other hand, Bosch y Labrús argued that the customs on foreign sugar and tobacco should be twice as high as those on Cuban sugar and tobacco, thus favoring "national" producers.[46]

Bosch y Labrús and the Fomento de la Producción Nacional advocated the same policies during the antiabolition campaign of 1872. This time, the defense of reciprocal trade was fused with the more agressive "imperial" discourse of the National League and the Madrid Centro Hispano-Ultramarino. The Fomento de la Producción Nacional stated in its protest against abolition that the government should establish a "protective fortress" around Spain and the Antilles for the greater glory of the Spanish nation:

> The tariffs for the overseas provinces should be like those of the Peninsula, a protective fortress that . . . will encourage the development of national production without privileges, fetters, or monopolies. Free trade between our shores *[cabotaje]* should be declared. By facilitating trade among all Spanish provinces, the natural laws of economy would place an inviolable stamp on the great nationality that still flies its flag in Europe, Asia, Africa, and America.[47]

Abolitionists and revolutionaries did not back down from this concerted conservative challenge. Their aim was to remake the empire on the bases of free labor, free markets, representative government, and racial unity—in other words, the imperial order they had articulated in the 1860s. Regarding "national integrity" and Spain's honor, war cries of the right, the abolitionist Joaquín María Sanromá was not troubled that National League members called themselves good Spaniards: "It does not bother me, because we are the *better* Spaniards."[48] In the Cortes, the Radical minister of state, Cristino Mártos, responded thus to conservative flag waving over Puerto Rico:

Those who are compromising the national territory are those who persist in denying the life of liberty, of law and of good administration to a peaceful, loyal province that wants to be Spanish; the life that we have offered it; the life that the Moderate governments have always denied it, and the life that the government of the September Revolution has offered and must give it.[49]

Abolitionists and revolutionaries responded with action as well as speeches. In the wake of the Madrid uprising of December 1872, the Radicals succeeded in bringing a bill for abolition in Puerto Rico to the floor of the Cortes.[50] The Abolitionist Society organized another national petition drive to demand immediate abolition in Puerto Rico *and* Cuba.[51] It also organized public parades and meetings throughout Spain to counter the publicity of the National League. During the winter of 1872–1873, *El Abolicionista Español* reported demonstrations in Madrid, Barcelona, Sevilla, Orense, Zaragoza, Lérida, and Cádiz. Demonstrators identified themselves and the revolution with the slaves of the Antilles and their fight against slavery. Abolitionism at this moment in the revolution thus denoted both liberty for the slaves and liberty for the Spanish "people" in their fight against counterrevolutionary forces.[52]

Demonstrations in late 1872 and early 1873 illustrated the interconnection of hegemonic and counterhegemonic projects. On December 21, 1872, demonstrators in Barcelona marched down the central boulevard of the city, the Rambla, to call for abolition in the Antilles in response to an antireformist demonstration held a few days earlier. The news report described the public as composed of "workers *[obreros]*, artisans, artists, merchants, bankers, etc., etc." Groups identified as the Federal Republican Circle, "workers," and the "town of Sanz," carried banners that read "Liberty for our brothers the blacks" and "The black man's sweat only makes the slaveowner richer." When the procession arrived at the governor's palace, a speaker denounced the National League and proclaimed the abolitionists to be the true defenders of Spain's national integrity:

If there is an insurrection in Cuba, it is because there is slavery. The slaveowners hide behind the farce of national integrity. . . . If they demand soldiers, it is to guard their slaves, not to save their country. Catalans, you are the most liberal people in Spain. You cannot permit a few scoundrels to get rich from the blood of the unhappy blacks, our brothers. Catalans, down with slavery! Long live reforms in the Antilles! . . . The enslaved man has the right to rebel against his master. Long live liberty![53]

"Gloria a Castelar," *La Campana de Gracia,* Barcelona, December 1872.
The image celebrates Emilio Castelar's leadership of the abolitionist
campaign in the Cortes. Press coverage of abolitionism and its
prominence in republican imagery during the September Revolution
indicates the resonance of the colonial question.

On January 12, 1873, between ten and sixteen thousand people turned
out for an abolitionist rally in Madrid. Though the abolitionists regretted
the absence of workers, they hailed the solid support of Madrid's middle
classes. Like the Catalans, the Madrid demonstrators marched through the

center of the city, from the Royal Botanical Gardens on the Paseo del Prado, to the Puerta del Sol (the symbolic center of Spain), along the calle Carretas, down Atocha and through the Plaza Antón Martín, where the uprising of December 11, 1872, had broken out, and back to the Paseo del Prado. When the parade passed the homes of the marquis of Manzanedo, head of the Madrid Centro Hispano-Ultramarino and a notorious slave trader, and of Praxedes Mateo Sagasta, leader of the Constitutional Party, the band struck up the song "Trágala" ("Swallow it"), a revolutionary anthem from the early nineteenth century.

Among the groups represented in the Madrid procession were the Abolitionist Society, the Federal Republican Party, the Tertulia Radical, and Republican and Radical newspapers like *La Discusión* and *La Tertulia*. The Abolitionist Society's standard was carried by "a young Indian from the Philippines wearing gloves and elegantly dressed." A black man carried a Masonic lodge's standard that inserted abolitionism into Spain's revolutionary tradition: "The Comuneros–The Córtes of Cádiz–The Abolitionist Society–The Puerto Rican Commission, 1866–The Cortes of 1873."[54]

Another large demonstration paraded through the center of Seville on January 26, 1873. Republican associations played an especially large role in this demonstration. The abolitionist newspaper reported that a black man carrying one of the abolitionist banners "was hailed by a black woman from a balcony. She asked for liberty for her race. The black man answered her, waving his banner. Energetic and frantic applause and cries of long live liberty for the slaves interrupted his sentences."[55]

## The First Republic and the Remaking of Empire

Thus, in the winter of 1872–1873, abolitionists and revolutionaries were well mobilized to challenge the National League in the name of metropolitan and colonial liberty. When, in the face of continued conservative resistance, Amadeus of Savoy abdicated his throne in February 1873 and the Cortes declared Spain a republic, abolitionists and revolutionaries were ready for the new political opening. One of the first acts of the First Republic (February 1873–January 1874) was to enact the abolition of slavery in Puerto Rico on March 22, 1873. Whereas the Abolitionist Society and the majority of the Puerto Rican delegation had favored immediate abolition without indemnity, they eventually compromised with conservative deputies like José Laureano Sanz and Germán Gamazo to pass the law.[56] The final law required Puerto Rico's approximately 29,000 slaves (in 1873) to sign three-year contracts with their former masters, although enforcement varied. It was also an indemnified abolition; slaveowners were to be paid 200 pesos for each slave.[57] The new government also drafted a new electoral law for Puerto Rico that broadened the franchise to include all men over twenty-one who paid a nominal tax. There were no restrictions based on color—a sharp break from earlier periods of colonial constitutionalism when Spanish liberals had excluded all nonwhites in the colonies from political society.[58]

Political expediency forced the Republic to reconsider the traditional exclusiveness of Spanish liberalism. The Cuban insurrection and slave rebellion, coupled with the counterrevolutionary activities of the Hispano-Antillean right, had forced Spanish revolutionaries to seek new allies in the colonies not only among white creoles, but also among the population of color. On the ground in the Antilles, the Spanish Republic sought to carry out a major shift in the bases of colonial hegemony. The Republic's appointee as captain general of Cuba was Cándido Pieltain, who sought to carry out conciliatory policies toward Cuban creoles. Like Dulce in 1869, he permitted freedom of the press and expanded the right of association for all classes in an effort to counter the overweening power of the Volunteers and the Spanish party. Spanish and Cuban workers formed Federal Republican clubs in Havana and openly advocated the abolition of slavery. The destruction of the Republic in 1874 brought Pieltain's initiatives to an end and returned power to the Volunteers and the Spanish party.[59]

The First Republic's most dramatic actions came in Puerto Rico, where it asserted greater control than in Cuba. The Republic's captain general was Rafael Primo de Rivera, a member of the Abolitionist Society. In his short tenure, Primo de Rivera sought to draw the new colonial pact that the abolitionists envisioned by enacting measures that would shift the balance of power in Puerto Rico dramatically away from peninsular commercial interests and toward creoles.[60]

Primo reported to Madrid that the greatest obstacle to Puerto Rico's prosperity and to republican rule was the peninsular merchants' stranglehold on commerce and credit. His condemnation of that exploitative relationship drew upon classic Radical and republican political imagery:

> Because of their profound egotism, the country's misery, decadence, and ruin matter very little to them. They only care about accumulating capital and making themselves the sole benefactors of public wealth. . . . The colonial system weakens the social body to the benefit of some of its members. These rich capitalists adore a system that rewards and protects them.[61]

Primo recommended that the government share power with the Liberal Reformist Party, the party supported by most creoles. One method of carrying out this shift in power would be to create citizens' militias to counter the conservative regular military and the Puerto Rican Volunteers. Primo saw the latter as an especially powerful threat to the Republic because they unified the island's conservative peninsular interests and were superior as a military force even to the regular army.[62]

To counter conservative mobilization, Primo argued that the government should arm liberal creoles, including free people of color (though not the recently freed slaves). Among creoles, he held, there was so little racial prejudice that to differentiate between black and white citizens would breed unnecessary resentment. Indeed, according to Primo, the Republic could find or create its staunchest supporters among the free population of color: "I believe that . . . this majority of the population is precisely where the government will find the most faithful, blind and resilient auxiliaries to its justice and law. It will combat every class of enemy."[63]

While the Republic abolished Puerto Rican slavery and sought new supporters in both Cuba and Puerto Rico, it was also under pressure from many of its supporters in the Peninsula to abolish slavery in Cuba as well. Puerto Rico was one of the bases from which abolitionists attacked Cuban slavery. Under Spanish electoral law, districts could choose representatives to the Cortes who resided elsewhere. Thus, while several members of the Puerto Rican delegation in 1873 were noted creole reformers like Manuel Corchado (from Mayagüez) and Luis Padial Vizcarrondo (from Arecibo), a number of non–Puerto Rican abolitionists were elected to represent Puerto Rico. Rafael María de Labra was the representative for Sabana Grande, Joaquín María Sanromá was elected by Humacao, and the lone Cuban member of the Abolitionist Society, José Ramón Betancourt, represented Coamo.[64]

The Puerto Rican delegation was the most aggressive proponent of decisive measures regarding reform not just in Puerto Rico but in Cuba as well. Puerto Rican deputies pushed for extending the Constitution of 1869 to both islands (Cuba still could not elect representatives to the Cortes) and for the abolition of slavery in Cuba. The Abolitionist Society also continued to petition for immediate abolition in Cuba.[65]

Abolitionists had reason to be optimistic. The Federal Republicans, who now held power, were committed to the cause of abolition; all four presidents of the First Republic, Estanislao Figueras, Francisco Pi y Margall, Nicolás Salmerón, and Emilio Castelar, were members of the Abolitionist Society. In the early days of the Republic, when a deputy asked the government when it intended to abolish Cuban slavery, the overseas minister, Francisco Suñer y Capdevila, confidently responded that the Republic would quickly abolish slavery and also move to establish constitutional rule in Cuba.[66]

Yet the Republic acted hesitantly. A month later, José Ramón Betancourt challenged the government to live up to its republican ideals: "I would celebrate if this government took the initiative. But if not, I do not lack for fellow deputies who would join me in asking that Spain liberate itself from the shame of slavery." Though the record notes that "many deputies" shouted "All of us!" in response to Betancourt's challenge, the overseas minister, Eduardo Palanca, blandly answered that the government was formulating legislation to abolish Cuban slavery and would soon submit it to the legislature.[67]

By the fall of 1873, the Republic was still vacillating in its policies toward Cuba. José María Orense, one of the early founders of Spanish republicanism, rose in September to appeal to President Emilio Castelar that the government should abolish slavery and establish the Republic in Cuba by issuing an amnesty to the insurgents. By doing so, he argued, Spain would bring itself and its colonies into harmony with Spain's major rival in the Caribbean, the United States. Castelar's response reflected the degree to which a series of political crises had compromised the initial promise of the Republic:

> We had always believed that one of the advantages of the Spanish Republic would be the tightening of the bonds of union with our Antilles. But Sr. Orense must understand . . . that regarding foreign policy . . . we can do nothing.
>
> Believe me, Sr. Orense, for four months I was in charge of our department of Foreign Affairs, and I know that unless we vigorously reestablish order in Spain, we cannot expect to establish relations with the United States or with Europe. We are alone; we are very isolated in the world.[68]

Indeed, to "reestablish order in Spain," Castelar shortly thereafter suspended the constitution and ruled unilaterally until January 1874. He had recognized by the summer of 1873 that the Republic was poorly equipped to undertake a major initiative in Cuba. Not only did it face a separatist insurgency in the east, it also had to contend with the virulently reactionary Spanish party of the west, which was armed and mobilized through the Volunteers. Moreover, civil war and regional tensions had erupted in the Peninsula. Federalist insurrections had broken out in Valencia and Murcia, as the left wing of the republican parties there sought to establish autonomous communes. More seriously, the Carlists had taken to the field again in northern Spain and a prolonged war ensued. By the time Castelar reconvened the Cortes in January, the Spanish military was ready to intervene.[69]

The various threats to the Spanish state and public order moved members of the military to precipitate the counterrevolution that civilians like Antonio Cánovas del Castillo were slowly organizing. When the Cortes was reconvened on January 3, 1874, the captain general of Madrid occupied the building and dissolved the assembly. The new head of the government was, appropriately, Francisco Serrano y Domínguez, who sought to rule in cooperation with repentant September revolutionaries, mostly from Sagasta's Constitutional Party and some Radicals. Serrano, however, failed to conclude the Carlist war, while most of the Spanish right was committed to the restoration of the Bourbon monarchy in the person of Alfonso, son of Isabel II. In December 1874, without Cánovas's approval, General Arsenio Martínez Campos declared the restoration of the Bourbons. The general enjoyed considerable support in the Spanish military and met no resistance in Madrid. Serrano and the remnants of the September Revolution were finally deposed.[70]

## Conclusion: Liberty for Whom?

In *The Overthrow of Colonial Slavery,* Robin Blackburn argues that slave emancipation in the Americas during the age of revolution (1776–1848) generally occurred in the context of metropolitan and colonial revolution:

> Slave emancipation triumphed in this period where three factors favourable to such an outcome coalesced: (i) a political crisis marginalising slaveholders and giving birth to a new type of state; (ii) the actuality or prospect of slave resistance or rebellion; (iii) social mobilisations encouraging the partisans of reform or revolution to rally popular sentiment with antislavery acts.[71]

Blackburn calls this convergence of revolution and slave rebellion *revolutionary emancipationism,* a prime example being the revolution of St. Domingue, when French Jacobins sought to ally with insurgent slaves against both the metropolitan and colonial old regime. Blackburn's model is also applicable to abolitionism and the battle against slavery in Spain and the Antilles during the revolutions of 1868.[72]

The revolutions of 1868 in Spain and Cuba and the initiatives against slavery, especially by Cuban slaves themselves, put colonial slaveowners on

"Tots som germans" ("We are all brothers!"),
*La Campana de Gracia*, Barcelona, 22 December 1872.
This shows the spirit of the Republic intervening between a glowering
Puerto Rican planter and a prostrate, grateful slave, indicating
the ambitions and tensions in "revolutionary emancipationism."

the defensive. In Cuba, while the western planters successfully mobilized
to delay emancipation, in Puerto Rico, the extent of the revolutionary state's
power forced planters to reach some sort of compromise with creole abolitionists and metropolitan revolutionaries.[73]

Moreover, the outbreak of colonial revolution, as well as counterrevolution in the form of the Volunteers, the Madrid Centro Hispano-Ultramarino, and the National League, and the actions of Cuban slaves against slavery moved the Abolitionist Society and its political allies to place immediate abolition and colonial reform at the center of the revolutionary agenda. As I have tried to demonstrate, those policies were simultaneously hegemonic and counterhegemonic in their intent and were aimed at establishing the legitimacy of the revolutionary regime and resolving tensions in colonial society that had gone unaddressed since the 1830s.

On the one hand, the abolitionists, the Radicals, and the Federal Republicans argued that the Cuban insurgency had effectively undermined colonial slavery and that the only way to reestablish Spain's legitimacy was through immediate abolition. Spanish and Puerto Rican reformers believed that immediate abolition was viable for Puerto Rico because of the possibility of indemnification, the availability of free labor, and the degree of racial mixture among the working population. Different political imperatives drove their strategy for Cuba. Abolitionism and separatism had converged in Cuba; Spanish revolutionaries hoped to split them apart through immediate abolition and thus to win the loyalty of separatists and the slave population.

Indeed, the urgency of restoring hegemony led to more inclusive visions of "Spain" in the Antilles. While Spanish and Antillean liberals had pacted in the 1860s on the basis of "whiteness," during the September Revolution slave rebellion and the abolitionism of the Cuban insurgency forced the Abolitionist Society and its revolutionary allies to reconsider the racial boundaries of the nation. One of the early acts of the September Revolution had been the abolition of the requirement of *limpieza de sangre* (purity of blood), proof of legal whiteness, for holding office and enjoying other political and civil rights.[74] The September Revolution, especially the First Republic, thus posed a series of novel answers to the questions of race, nation, and citizenship that had first been raised in the Cortes of Cádiz (1810–1814) and dramatically restated during the revolutions of the 1830s. While still defending implicit racial hierarchies, the Abolitionist Society and the First Republic acted to define and create a transatlantic Spanish nation that incorporated all members of colonial society, regardless of race.[75]

On the other hand, while the Abolitionist Society's strategies were made in response to forces in the colonies, they also responded to the polarization of politics in the Peninsula. Abolitionism figured into a broader revolutionary strategy for subverting the political and economic bases of the Hispano-Antillean right, which had organized in the National League to defend slavery. By shifting the basis of Spanish colonial hegemony away from slaveowners and peninsular merchants and instead to liberal creoles and freed slaves, abolitionists and revolutionaries hoped to solidify Spanish rule in the Antilles and the revolutionary state in the Peninsula. Primo de Rivera's short-lived administration in Puerto Rico can be seen as the boldest attempt to carry out that concurrently hegemonic and counterhegemonic project. The abolitionist defense of "liberty" was therefore made not just in reference to slaves' freedom after slavery, but also to a vision of a new imperial order that challenged the institutions of the revolutionary settlement of the 1830s.[76]

Finally, interpreting abolitionism as intersecting with colonial and metropolitan revolutions raises important questions about the unit of analysis for comprehending abolitionism. The powerful, if conflict-ridden, bonds of empire and the centrality of slavery to the imperial order unified seemingly isolated local struggles. Political initiatives for and against slavery crisscrossed the Atlantic, most obviously in hybrid organizations like the Abolitionist Society and the National League.

An observation by two anthropologists, Akhil Gupta and James Ferguson, regarding the space of colonialism is pertinent here: "The premise of discontinuity forms the starting point from which to theorize contact, conflict, and contradiction between cultures and societies."[77] As they go on to suggest, rather than thinking in terms of discontinuity, it is useful to look at the interconnections between societies and cultures, an insight I believe helpful for Spain and the Antilles. The dynamics of antislavery and slave emancipation demonstrate that the societies in Spain's Caribbean empire were acting in complex relationship to one another, and not just in terms of the hierarchical relationship between colonies and metropolis (though that dynamic was certainly important); for instance, Havana's Spanish party successfully exported counterrevolution to the Peninsula, while Puerto Rican reformers offered a crucial base from which the Abolitionist Society attacked Cuban slavery during the First Republic.

Thus, in explaining the politics of the Abolitionist Society and its allies, it is necessary to look beyond geographic boundaries and to think in terms of shifting alliances among local actors from all three countries who responded to changing political circumstances on the imperial and the Atlantic level to carry out policies that reverberated throughout the empire. The transnational perspective theorized in Blackburn's model of "revolutionary emancipationism" sheds light on how a metropolitan abolitionist like Labra could convincingly argue before revolutionary parties in Spain that the abolition of slavery would lead to freedom not only for slaves in the Antilles, but to freedom for themselves as well.[78]

# Conclusion

## THE IMPACT AND LEGACY
## OF ABOLITIONISM

On February 8, 1879, *La América,* one of the most important Spanish newspapers dedicated to Latin America and the Antilles, resumed publication
after five years of silence. The editors explained to their readers that they
had considered it their patriotic duty to remain mute on the question of
colonial reforms while the government acted to end definitively the war in
Cuba.[1]

*La América*'s silence indicated the degree to which the restored monarchy had tamed colonial politics in the Peninsula. Spanish abolitionists saw
this silencing as part of a more general reaction by Spanish conservatives.
The Economist and abolitionist Gabriel Rodríguez, for instance, called the
Restoration a period of "protectionist reaction." In his comments on protectionist demonstrations held in Barcelona in 1881, Rodríguez criticized what
he considered the false patriotism of the triumphant right:

> Instead of shouting "Long live Spain" and "Long live the cause of Span-
> ish production," the authors of the [protectionist] Manifesto should cry:
> "Sacrifice and humiliate Spain for the benefit of a few dozen favored
> industrialists. May all other Spanish production continue to live in op-
> pression or die before touching the sacred arc of our privileges."[2]

Though the protectionist reaction was particular to the Spanish Restoration, Rodríguez, in reviewing a collection of Richard Cobden's essays,
characterized it as part of a trans-European phenomenon, perceptively noting the advent of Europe's age of empire:[3] "This is an opportune moment in

which to publish this collection, as the eminent economist Mr. de Molinari states in the preface. The protectionist reaction seeks to destroy the work of Cobden throughout Europe, while militarism seeks to return us to barbarous epochs."[4]

Spanish abolitionists' pessimism reflected their own recent experience with "militarism" and reaction, as well as their marginal position in the immediate aftermath of the Bourbon Restoration. Spanish and Antillean conservatives had successfully returned legislative control of the emancipation process to traditional political leaders. The new situation reduced the Spanish Abolitionist Society to the role of parliamentary watchdog, monitoring the enforcement of laws meant to protect the interests of Cuban slaveowners. And though after the end of the Cuban war in 1878 both Cuba and Puerto Rico elected representatives to the Cortes, the metropolitan state continued to ride roughshod over creole positions, while Spanish and creole reformers frequently complained of the difficulty of harmonizing metropolitan and colonial political interests.[5]

While the Restoration had defeated the efforts of the First Republic to remake the colonial order, the revolutions of 1868 had permanently altered slavery and imperial politics. After the signing of the Pact of Zanjón in 1878, which brought the Ten Years' War to a close, the Spanish government enacted in 1880 a new emancipation law that called for an eight-year apprenticeship, known as the *patronato*, for all slaves of working age. While slavery was abolished in name, the *patronato* in fact maintained the slaveholders' traditional prerogatives.[6]

Nonetheless, a combination of forces led the government to abolish the *patronato* prematurely in 1886. Quotas set by the new legislation freed a certain number of slaves. The *patronato* regime also opened avenues for slaves and ex-slaves to purchase both their own freedom and that of family members. Moreover, the colonial state more aggressively upheld its legislation, giving slaves a third party to whom to appeal against their masters. In Spain, while the Abolitionist Society no longer enjoyed the influence it had during the September Revolution, it still issued petitions to abolish the *patronato* and sought to convince metropolitan and colonial liberal parties to support their efforts. By 1886, the population of *patrocinados* had plummeted to 25,381, from a slave population of 199,094 in 1877, and in that year the Spanish government finally acted to bring the *patronato*, and Cuban slavery, to an end.[7]

After final emancipation, many slaves in the highly developed sugar regions, such as Havana and Matanzas, became wage laborers. In less-developed or more diverse regions, some freed slaves became small proprietors or renters, while others became wage laborers. Many wage laborers, though, avoided complete proletarianization and dependence on hacienda labor by subsistence farming.[8]

Sugar planters in the 1880s sought to reorganize production and labor by dividing the agricultural and industrial components of sugar processing. Owners of mills processed sugar cane from their own fields, but they increasingly relied on cane contracted from independent farmers and renters known as *colonos*. To facilitate the division of sugar production and the growth of a *colono* class, planters favored Spanish immigration, a move they hoped would also lower wages. While in the short run Cuban planters were successful in controlling the labor of slaves until final abolition in 1886, and later in recruiting new sources of labor, the long-term effect of slave emancipation was a loosening of social control by the planter class and the colonial state, which facilitated the outbreak of the Cuban war for independence in 1895 and successful attacks on the western sugar plantations made by insurgent forces.[9]

Although the Abolitionist Society was a minor player in ending Cuban slavery after 1874, abolitionists sought to reconstruct the political alliances they had projected during the First Republic. In the late days of the September Revolution, abolitionists, republicans, and colonial liberals had theorized a new colonial order based on cross-class and cross-racial alliances that would unite popular classes both in Spain and in the colonies against the traditional Hispano-Antillean right. Tracing the efforts of Spaniards and Cubans to rebuild those alliances after the overthrow of the First Republic would lead us far afield from a study of abolitionism. Nonetheless, one effort to revive the reformist energies of the September Revolution immediately after the Pact of Zanjón directly addressed the fate of Cuban slavery.

In 1881, the distinguished Cuban reformer Nicolás Azcárate and the Spanish working-class leader Saturnino Martínez founded the Democratic Party (Partido Democrático) in Cuba as an alternative to the major colonial parties established under the post-Zanjón constitutional order: the Constitutional Union (Unión Constitucional), representing the Spanish elite, and the Liberal Party (Partido Liberal de Cuba, better known as the Autonomist Party), representing the creole elite. Azcárate and Martínez sought to build on the nascent Cuban labor movement to push for expanded political and civil rights. One of their major causes was the immediate abolition of the *patronato*. Azcárate also argued for immediate abolition as a member of the colony's Administrative Council (Consejo de Administración).[10] Ultimately, the Democratic Party convinced the Autonomists to advocate imme-

**Nicolás Azcárate (1824–1894).**
**Archivo Nacional de Cuba.**

diate abolition, which helped move the Spanish government to act.[11]

The efforts of Azcárate and the Democratic Party indicate that the Cuban and Spanish revolutions and the battles over slavery had transformed imperial politics. Before 1868, Azcárate, like Saco and Arango before him, recoiled in horror from the prospect of slave emancipation.[12] By the end of the revolutions, he was actively advocating abolition. That dramatic change in Azcárate's attitude toward slavery pointed to the persistence of the First Republic's vision of empire not just in Spain and Puerto Rico, but in Cuba as well. After Zanjón, some loyalist politicians like Azcárate sought to appeal to a broader constituency and to revive the Republic's vision of a multiracial and transatlantic Spanish nation.

Whereas abolitionism had transformed slavery and politics in Cuba, it was in Puerto Rico that the revolutionary vision of empire had its greatest (if short-lived) successes. I will briefly discuss the consequences of slave emancipation and the Bourbon Restoration so as to reassess the origins of the Abolitionist Society and its impact on Antillean slavery and the structure of the colonial empire.

### Restoration Colonialism in Post-Emancipation Puerto Rico

"The suspension of constitutional guarantees has produced a healthy effect," Captain General José Laureano Sanz reported to Madrid soon after his return to Puerto Rico in February 1874. Sanz was replacing Captain General Rafael Primo de Rivera, an abolitionist and a republican.[13] Part of that "healthy effect," apparently, was the smooth transition to free labor after abolition. In 1880, Ponce's city council voted to open a national subscription to construct a monument celebrating the abolition of slavery. The councilors projected the monument as a tribute to the justice of the Spanish nation and to the ease and success of abolition:

> Upon declaring [the abolition of slavery], the government of our nation fulfilled its duty of justice in an honorable manner. The fulfillment [of abolition] in this Province proved beyond a doubt its civic virtues. It has been perhaps the only country in the world to experience such a violent social change without the slightest alteration, with only the most insignificant unpleasantnesses, . . . even though it involved our society's most ignorant class.[14]

The Ponce proposal received enthusiastic support. Antonio Alfau y Baralt, a representative of Ponce planters resident in Madrid, negotiated with the palace to commemorate abolition.[15] The Bourbon monarch,

Monument to slave emancipation in Ponce, Puerto Rico.
Although planters built this monument to honor the end of slavery, they bitterly resisted
the transition to free labor in the aftermath of the First Republic's overthrow in 1874.
Photo: Author.

Alfonso XII, donated 1,000 pesetas to the fund. Rafael María de Labra and the Abolitionist Society also donated funds.[16] The Casino de Mayagüez (Mayagüez had the second largest slave population in Puerto Rico in 1872 after Ponce) sent a large donation raised at a charity ball and the proceedings from the comic play *El Gíbaro,* composed for the occasion by Ramón Mendez y Quiñones. Moreover, Mendez y Quiñones donated four hundred copies of his play to the Ponce commission to help raise money for the monument.[17]

The self-congratulatory air of Ponce's and Mayagüez's sugar planters, however, glossed over their earlier determined resistence to abolition and the transition to free labor after the overthrow of the First Republic. The abolition of slavery and the *libreta* (also ended in 1873) led Puerto Rico's sugar planters to scramble to reorganize labor and production. Their immediate response was to turn to the colonial state for help in coercing free labor, help that in the immediate aftermath of the counterrevolution was forthcoming. Planters' resistance to the effects of abolition, coupled with the renewed intransigence of the colonial administration toward creole reformism after 1874, demonstrates through juxtaposition the profound challenge posed by abolitionism and revolutionary colonial policy to the colonial order consolidated in the 1830s.

### *Politics*

Sanz was an appropriate representative of counterrevolution. During the September Revolution, after a tenure as captain general of Puerto Rico marked by persecution of liberal creoles, he served as a conservative deputy for Puerto Rico in the Cortes and as vice-president of the Madrid Centro Hispano-Ultramarino. His politics strongly favored Spaniards over creoles. Eventually, in reward for his service in Puerto Rico, the restored monarchy bestowed upon him the title of marquis of San Juan Bautista de Puerto Rico.[18]

Sanz inaugurated his second tenure as captain general by purging all prorevolutionary elements from the colonial administration, rewarding conservative Spaniards, and creating new pro-Spanish paramilitary forces. For instance, he recommended for various honors and decorations pro-Spanish members of the Church, the Volunteers, and the colonial administration, such as the leader of Puerto Rico's Spanish Party, the marquis of Esperanza, and Pedro Diz Romero, a vociferously reactionary Spanish bureaucrat.[19] He organized a new Public Order Corps (Cuerpo de Ordén Público) and reinforced the Civil Guard. He also fired teachers in Puerto Rico's primary schools and replaced them with teachers from the Peninsula to ensure a "Spanish" education.[20]

In his summary of his second tenure, Sanz reported that he had restored peace and order in Puerto Rico and brought to an end the disruptive politics of the revolutionary period. He recommended that Madrid suspend elections indefinitely so as not to disturb the peace, in effect hoping to return Puerto Rico to the pre-1868 days of extraordinary rule. "Unfortunately," he wrote to the overseas minister, "the announcement of the elections of deputies to the Cortes has arrived; . . . every party has considered abstaining to demonstrate to the nation that this island renounces the exercise of political rights and that it wants nothing more than to conserve the peace and union that it enjoys."[21]

Captain generals after Sanz continued his effort to deaden politics and creole initiatives in Puerto Rico. The most infamous of such efforts was the brutal repression of the Autonomist Party, successor to the Liberal Reform Party (Partido Liberal Reformista), in 1887. The southern city of Juana Diaz, located near Ponce, was the seat of the new party headed by Román Baldorioty de Castro.[22]

The founding of the Autonomist Party took place in the midst of an islandwide boycott of peninsular stores and goods. As tensions mounted, Spanish conservatives prevailed upon Captain General Romualdo Palacios to take action. The result was a raid on a party meeting in Juana Diaz by the Civil Guard and the imprisonment and torture of numerous Autonomists. Though Madrid quickly reprimanded Palacios and replaced him, the incident reflected the limited political space open to creole reformers under the Restoration.[23]

Repression was not always so intentional or obvious; other obstacles existed. In a letter to Rafael María de Labra, who represented Puerto Rico and Cuba in the Cortes until 1898, the Puerto Rican liberal Antonio Corton complained of the difficulties in aligning colonial and metropolitan political parties.[24] In Spain, the republicans had splintered into various factions after the disaster of the First Republic, some parties favoring cooperation with the restored Bourbon monarchy, others seeking to continue, unsuccessfully, the tradition of civilian-military *pronunciamientos*.[25] Corton apologized to Labra for his inability to muster support for Labra and Nicolás Salmerón's Centralist Republican Party (Partido Republicano Centralista). He explained that Manuel Ruiz Zorrilla and Emilio Castelar, leaders of other republican parties, enjoyed more support in Puerto Rico—the former because he was president when the September Revolution abolished slavery in Puerto Rico, the latter because of his prominence in the abolitionist campaign.[26]

Corton's and Labra's frustration also reflected the limits of colonial politics under the Restoration. Political changes had occurred that made the Restoration's colonial order different from that of the 1833–1868 period. Most important, Puerto Rico enjoyed some semblance of constitutional rule and political representation in the Spanish Cortes. Nonetheless, the colonial state continued to lean heavily toward Spanish interests, while creole liberals had difficulties in negotiating with the fragmented and generally marginal forces of Spanish republicanism. In short, the First Republic's strategy of shifting colonial hegemony to Puerto Rico's creoles was a thing of the past.

### Labor

More important changes occurred in the Puerto Rican economy that distinguished it from the prerevolutionary order. Most obviously, all labor was now theoretically free, though as we shall see, sugar planters sought to reinstate forms of coercion. Perhaps of greater significance for Puerto Rico's position in the Spanish Empire and the broader Atlantic economy was the continued stagnation and indeed decline of the Puerto Rican sugar sector and the dramatic ascendance of coffee, a sector that used free wage labor, as Puerto Rico's major export crop. In 1876, coffee represented 17.6 percent of the total value of Puerto Rico's exports and sugar 62.5 percent. By 1896, that balance had been dramatically reversed: coffee now made up 76.9 percent of the value of exports and sugar 20.7 percent.[27] Moreover, Puerto Rican coffee found its major markets within the imperial economy: between 1890 and 1895, Puerto Rico exported 35 percent of its coffee to Cuba and 23 percent to Spain. Puerto Rico's relationship to the imperial economy was in marked contrast to that of Cuba, whose main sugar markets were in the United States.[28] (See table 5.) Historians leave little doubt that the decline of Puerto Rican sugar resulted from the abolition of slavery and the problems in contracting free labor after emancipation.

Sanz was horrified by the laxity with which Primo de Rivera had enforced the three-year contracts with former owners, other employers, or the government, to which all freed slaves (libertos) were subject. According to Sanz, in the postemancipation regulation published by Primo de Rivera, ex-slaves had the right "to rescind their contracts at their will." Moreover, Primo had appointed prominent creole liberals and abolitionists like Pedro Gerónimo Goico and Salvador Carbonell as freedmens' protectors (protectores de libertos) to monitor the emancipation process.[29] Sanz published a new regulation in which the three-year contracts became binding.[30]

He also deployed new ways of controlling now free laborers. Sanz reported to Madrid that vagrancy had increased dramatically since the abolition of slavery. Landowners and local governments complained of the difficulty of recruiting labor and maintaining public order. To counter what he perceived as a growing political and economic crisis, Sanz promulgated a stiff vagrancy law and a new workers' regulation, *(reglamento de trabajadores)* similar to the *libreta* system. The latter measure in particular he formulated in response to the pleas of growers from sugar regions like Mayagüez and Arecibo for a return to the *libreta* system.[31] The targets of Sanz's new measures were all landless wage laborers. If workers or freedmen could not prove that they were gainfully employed, local governments could punish them with fines and force them to labor on public works.[32]

Madrid responded with ambivalence to Sanz's measures, confirming his vagrancy law but striking down the proposal to reinstate the *libreta*. In its opinion on Sanz's proposals, the Council of State (Consejo de Estado), an administrative body that deliberated on the legality of all government measures, agreed that tighter vagrancy laws were a wise measure during a period of political and economic reorganization. The council added, however, that its approval was provisional and that it would reconsider the vagrancy laws when the Spanish penal code was promulgated in Puerto Rico and Cuba.[33]

Regarding the return to the *libreta,* the council based its rejection on the reports gathered by Captain Generals Messina and Marchesi in the mid-1860s. That islandwide survey had revealed general discontent with the *libreta* system among landowners because it did not permit them flexibility in hiring and firing workers.[34] The Council of State held that the earlier surveys had demonstrated that any interference with the formation of a free labor market only hindered Puerto Rican production to the detriment of all classes:

> Anything that limits personal activity . . . alters the economic laws of supply and demand, the interest of capital and the worker . . . ; this is an alteration whose undeniable consequences are the depreciation of wealth, the languishing of production, and the decadence of all the arts and industries in general.[35]

Most Puerto Rican sugar planters disagreed with Madrid's views on the labor market. Many planters through the 1850s and 1860s had insisted on the importance of coercing labor through slavery, the *libreta,* or indenture to keep down production costs. Because of the difficulty in obtaining credit to invest in new processing technology and the ever increasing competitiveness of the world sugar market, many continued to see cheap and coerced labor as the key to profitability even after abolition. While abolitionists like

Acosta and Baldorioty de Castro continued to advocate investment in new technology and the division of sugar production into separate cultivating and processing units, many planters appealed to the captain general and to Madrid to help them organize labor through extraeconomic measures like workbooks or extended contracts for freed slaves.[36]

Thus, when the three-year mandatory contracts were due to expire in 1876, planters prevailed upon Captain General Segundo de la Portilla to extend the freedmen's obligations. Portilla responded favorably. In January 1876, he formed a commission to deliberate on methods for regulating their labor. He named the marquis de la Esperanza, an arch-conservative, to head the committee.[37] Not suprisingly, the commission advocated extending the freedmens' contracts, a recommendation that Portilla forwarded to Madrid. While Madrid pondered its decision, Portilla permitted employers to sign new contracts with ex-slaves.[38]

The contracts clearly showed resistance to converting to market relations between former masters and slaves. For example, in Mayagüez, on February 24, 1876, one Lucas Rivera, a cook by trade who had belonged *(pertenece)* to Don Isidro Caballer, signed a contract to continue working as a cook. His salary was six pesos per month, and he received maintenance and clean clothes from his employer. Rivera had to live in his employer's house, and in case of illness he was to bear his own expenses. Also in Mayagüez in February 1876, another ex-slave named Félix signed a contract with Doña Ursula Affigne that reads as follows:

> Señora Affigne is obliged to give land to the freedman to work in halves. She will supply him with the necessary seeds, as well as oxen. She will support him until the fields produce. In case of illness, the employer *[contrante]* will tend to the freedman. . . . The freed slave has to live in his employer's house. Both are subject to penal sanction.[39]

The contracts, however, were short-lived. The Council of State struck them down almost immediately, objecting to the interference in the labor market and to the violation of the former slaves' civil rights. The council recommended that Portilla and the slaveowners rely upon Sanz's 1874 vagrancy law to maintain public order and to encourage work.[40]

Sugar planters were not content with the decision. In 1877, Antonio Alfau, a representative of the Ponce Agricultural Society (Sociedad de Agricultura de Ponce), who a few years later would help raise funds in Spain for the monument to slave emancipation, submitted a plan to the government for regulating labor that again resembled the *libreta* system. Among other proposals, workers had to prove gainful employment, they must have fixed residences, and they had to carry records of their employment and conduct.[41]

In 1879, Captain General Eulogio Despujol supported Alfau and the Agricultural Society. He argued that unless the government regulated the relationship between capital and labor, the island's prosperity would decline and the freed slaves would sink into sloth and misery.[42] Moreover, Despujol queried Madrid about the fate of Sanz's 1874 vagrancy law, since the Spanish constitution of 1876 and the penal code would be promulgated in the colonies when the Cuban insurrection came to an end. He was concerned about the decriminalization of vagrancy, as well as the shift of jurisdiction from the executive to the judicial branch. Both measures, he argued, would seriously disrupt Puerto Rico's public order.[43]

Despite Despujol's concerns, the Council of State acted again to impede restrictions on free labor. It turned down Alfau's request for labor regulation and informed Despujol that the Spanish penal code was unequivocal concerning the noncriminal status of vagrancy. Regarding Alfau's request, the council observed that Puerto Rico's "public wealth" had increased since abolition (though studies now show that Puerto Rican sugar was indeed in crisis) and that the freedmen, despite Alfau and Despujol's characterizations of them as lazy and uncivilized, had proven themselves worthy of civil rights, as Puerto Rico enjoyed the "most complete order."[44]

Thus with little choice but to reconcile themselves to Madrid's position, sugar planters turned to informal methods of binding and attracting labor to the sugar plantations, such as granting usufruct rights and debt peonage. Luis Figueroa observes in his study of postemancipation Guayama that most freed slaves returned to plantation labor. Given Puerto Rico's population density, flight from plantation zones and squatting were difficult alternatives. Nonetheless, ex-slaves were still free to choose where they worked. Their new mobility forced planters to devise strategies for recruiting labor. Andrés Ramos Mattei documents how the hacienda "Mercedita" in Ponce maintained its work force. The means included ceding land and dwellings to freedmen and allowing them to cultivate their own farm plots, advancing salaries in food grown on a farm cultivated by the hacienda for that purpose, and issuing pay tokens redeemable only in the hacienda store.[45]

Those efforts had only limited results for planters. Figueroa, for instance, contends that Puerto Rican sugar exports after emancipation dropped significantly not only in 1874, the year after abolition, but also in 1877, the year after Sanz's strict enforcement of the three-year contracts expired.[46] Although sugar exports enjoyed a brief, though substantial, resurgence in 1879, the long-term trend was one of decline.[47] All evidence indicates that unfree labor was central to Puerto Rican sugar production and that slave emancipation led to crisis.[48]

## The Politics of Slavery and Antislavery

The evidence also shows that the abolition of Puerto Rican slavery was a tortuous political process. A glance at recent explanations for the rise of antislavery in the British Empire illustrates this point. Seymour Drescher and David Eltis calculate that slavery in the British Empire was still profitable and on the verge of expanding when both the slave trade and slavery were abolished. They conclude that the rise of British antislavery must be explained through political and ideological changes, as opposed to changes in the profitability or effiency of slavery itself.[49]

While slavery in Puerto Rico was not as vigorous as it had been in the British Empire on the eve of abolition, it was still an important pillar of Puerto Rican prosperity. The end of the slave trade at midcentury and the Moret Law of 1870 no doubt set the stage for Puerto Rican slavery's demise. But the efforts of planters and Spanish governors to coerce free labor after the September Revolution indicate that the ultimate timing of slavery's destruction resulted from the actions of the Abolitionist Society and the revolutionary regime, especially the First Republic, against Antillean planters. And while abolitionists and revolutionaries failed in their goal of immediately abolishing slavery in western Cuba, they failed because of the success of the Cuban and Spanish right in mobilizing to defend slavery. Slavery persisted in Cuba not only because of its economic viability, but also because of the political will of the Hispano-Antillean right to protect it. Studies that emphasize transformations in markets, technology, immigration, and the slave trade are fundamental for understanding Antillean slavery's demise; but in the last instance, the actions of people throughout the Spanish colonial empire for and against slavery determined that institution's fate.[50]

This point about the politics of slavery and antislavery leads me to several other conclusions. First, it is crucial to understand the rise of Antillean slavery and its destruction within the context of a renewed imperial order. Spanish rule in Cuba and Puerto Rico was not that of a decayed, moribund power but a complex restructuring of both metropolitan and colonial societies that responded to interests and initiatives in both the Peninsula and the Antilles.[51] Though the "second empire" consolidated Antillean slavery, it also paradoxically created new opportunites for attacking slavery because of the powerful interconnections between the colonies and metropolis.

Cuban planters had to worry not only about their own slaves but also about abolitionists in Madrid and Puerto Rico, who mobilized against Cuban slavery because of its centrality to the imperial order. Thus, initiatives against protectionism in Spain and slavery in Puerto Rico dovetailed with revolutionary challenges to the Spanish centralized state and bonded labor in Cuba because those diverse struggles were unified by the particular structures of capital accumulation and political power in the Spanish colonial empire. The transatlantic nature of revolutionary politics during the September Revolution, especially during the First Republic, demonstrates the counterhegemonic possibilities within the second empire.[52]

Second, we should see Atlantic antislavery movements as arising from the interaction of metropolitan and colonial actors and interests. The dominant explanations for the rise of these abolitionist movements in the Atlantic world generally focus on ideological and social changes occurring in the imperial metropolis.[53] In the case of the Abolitionist Society, transformations in Madrid liberalism and associational life and the public sphere in Spain were crucial in laying the foundations for abolitionism. But this focus ignores the clearly hybrid nature of the Abolitionist Society and its deeper origins in creole resistance to the consolidation of the imperial order of the 1830s. The interaction of Cuban and Puerto Rican reformers with Madrid liberals, each group seeking to further its specific interests by exploiting transatlantic alliances during the broader crisis of Antillean and American slavery in the 1860s, produced abolitionism. The intersection of abolitionism with revolutionary challenges to the imperial order in Cuba and Spain after 1868 led to the Abolitionist Society's determined attacks on Antillean slavery.

## Race, Nation, and Empire

That interaction in the 1860s also produced alternative visions of empire. Reformers who addressed inequities in political and economic institutions united in criticizing the political economy of Spanish imperialism. However, they also found themselves divided over the question of race and its significance for slave emancipation.

While Puerto Rican, Cuban, and Spanish reformers addressed the question of racial difference from distinct positions and with conflicting interests, they at times were able to subsume those differences in a common vision of reformed Spanish rule in the Antilles. They did so in the 1860s between the outbreak of civil war in the United States and the eruption of revolutions in Spain and the Antilles. In that period, they revived the liberal conception of the transatlantic Spanish nation that equated Spanishness with "whiteness."[54]

Because the Spanish Abolitionist Society was a hybrid association of metropolitan and colonial actors, it fused disparate strategies for representing and reinforcing the boundary between whites and nonwhites. Cuban creoles like José Antonio Saco saw extreme racial difference as a menace to white hegemony in Cuba. He and others proposed "whitening," through European immigration and miscegenation, as a method of lessening the racial difference between elites and workers while still maintaining distance between the "white" elite and "whitened" workers. Though Puerto Rican reformers like José Julián Acosta held similar views about "whitening," they argued by midcentury that Puerto Rico's laboring population was sufficently "whitened" and that the threat of race war had been overcome. And while the discourse of "whitening" constructed race as a variable and shifting condition, it drew a hard line between whites and nonwhites, making explicit a racial hierarchy in which "whiteness" was desirable and "blackness" was undesirable.[55]

Spanish liberals' attitudes toward slavery, race, and the place of people of color in the Spanish state and nation had changed significantly since the Cortes of Cádiz, when those questions first appeared on the political agenda. The novel context of mid-nineteenth-century Madrid liberalism and its middle-class associational life provided new ways of formulating those questions. Abolitionists like Rafael María de Labra and Segismundo Moret y Prendergast saw the question of racial difference through the lens of metropolitan class politics. In their visions of postemancipation society in the Antilles, they mapped their ideal of class relations onto colonial race relations. In other words, they believed that racial difference in the colonies would translate into class difference: black proletarians and peasants would work peacefully for white landowners and capitalists. Even at the height of the First Republic's counterhegemonic colonial policies, when Spanish abolitionists and revolutionaries envisioned a "Spain" on both sides of the Atlantic that was more inclusive than earlier liberal constructions of the Spanish nation, that vision of Spain in the Antilles was still saturated with notions of racial difference. They thus saw racial difference not as an obstacle to social peace but as a "natural" hierarchical division in colonial society.[56]

Nancy Stepan observes that even as abolitionism was winning the battle against slavery in the Atlantic world, it was losing the war against racism. That observation pertains to the abolitionist struggles both in Spain and in the Antilles. If abolitionism threatened repressive institutions in the Span-

ish colonial empire, it simultaneously reinforced conceptions of racial division and hierarchy that undermined claims of universal liberty and equality.[57]

Yet to dismiss Spanish and Antillean abolitionists as unwitting defenders of racial dominance would imply too static a conception of ideology and
political action. Abolitionists responded to new conditions and unexpected
initiatives with flexibility. During the constitutional periods of the first third
of the nineteenth century (1810–1814, 1820–1823, 1833–1840), Spanish liberals had specifically excluded any person of African heritage, even if free,
from active citizenship. Moreover, Cuban and Puerto Rican deputies forecast bloody race wars at the very mention of abolition. Thus, the Abolitionist Society's plan to include slaves as active citizens in a transatlantic Spanish nation, even if that role were limited, was unprecedented in Spain's
nineteenth-century colonial project. Undoubtedly, the majority of the
Hispano-Antillean elite in the late nineteenth century continued to fear the
possibility of race war.[58] But the emergence within the metropolitan and
colonial elite of political activists who fought against slavery and for
broader conceptions of the Cuban, Puerto Rican, and Spanish nations represented a major shift in the politics of empire. Thus, to capture the dyna-
mism of racial ideologies and antislavery politics, it is more appropriate to
conclude that while Hispano-Antillean abolitionists never escaped racist
assumptions, the struggle for freedom and for rights after slavery on a
transatlantic scale constantly altered their conceptions of race, nation, and
empire.

# NOTES

Unless otherwise indicated, all translations are by the author.

### Abbreviations and Terms Used in Notes

| | |
|---|---|
| AGPR | Archivo General de Puerto Rico (San Juan) |
| AHMP | Archivo Histórico Municipal de Ponce |
| AHN/U | Archivo Histórico Nacional, Sección de Ultramar (Madrid) |
| ANC | Archivo Nacional de Cuba (Havana) |
| BNJM | Biblioteca Nacional José Marti (Havana) |
| leg. | *legajo* (bundle of documents) |
| exp. | *expediente* (file) |

### Introduction

1. Sanromá, *La esclavitud en Cuba,* 21, emphasis in the original.

2. Murray, *Odious Commerce;* Scott, *Slave Emancipation in Cuba;* Bergad, "The Economic Viability of Sugar Production Based on Slave Labor in Cuba" and *Cuban Rural Society;* Tomich, "World Slavery and Caribbean Capitalism"; and Bergad Iglesias, and Carmen Barcía, *The Cuban Slave Market, 1790–1880.*

3. On Spanish involvement in the Antillean economy, see Maluquer de Motes, "El mercado colonial antillano en el siglo XIX" and *Nación e inmigración;* Moreno Fraginals, *El Ingenio,* 1:259–309; Bergad, *Coffee* and *Cuban Rural Society,* 89–259; Fradera, *Indústria i mercat;* Scarano, ed., *Inmigración y clases sociales;* and Bahamonde and Cayuela, *Hacer las Américas.*

4. The chief archives for these sources are the Archivo Histórico Nacional (Madrid), the Archivo Nacional de Cuba (Havana), and the Archivo General de Puerto Rico (San Juan).

5. See Sewell, "Toward a Post-materialist Rhetoric for Labor History"; see also Althusser, "Ideology and Ideological State Apparatuses (Notes towards an Investigation)," in *Lenin and Philosophy and Other Essays,* 127–86; Laclau and Mouffe, *Hegemony and Socialist Strategy;* Reddy, *Money and Liberty in Modern Europe,* esp. 60; and Sewell, *A Rhetoric of Bourgeois Revolution,* 1–40.

6. See Scott, *Slave Emancipation in Cuba,* 5–6.

7. Tomich, "The 'Second Slavery.'"

8. Many scholars have contributed to this general reevaluation of Spanish colonialism in the nineteenth century. See especially Fradera, "Quiebra imperial y reorganización política."

9. This focuses on Spain's Antillean empire. The Philippines were the other major Spanish colony after the Spanish American revolutions, but the politics of colonialism in the Caribbean and the Pacific did not converge significantly until the 1870s and most particularly during the revolutionary 1890s. For an overview, see Fradera, "La importáncia de tenir colonias"; and Schmidt-Nowara, "Imperio y crisis colonial."

10. On Cuban slave imports, see Eltis, *Economic Growth*, 249. On the slave trade to Spanish America up to the late eighteenth century, see Curtin, *The Atlantic Slave Trade*, 25.

11. See Maluquer de Motes, "La burgesia catalana i l'esclavitud colonial"; Serrano, *Final del imperio;* and Espadas Burgos, *Alfonso XII y los orígenes de la Restauración.*

12. Paquette, *Sugar Is Made with Blood*, 89, 114–15; and Martínez-Fernández, *Torn between Empires*, 5. See also Bergad, *Cuban Rural Society*, 335.

13. Scott, *Slave Emancipation in Cuba*, xii–xiii, 5–6, 281–82, and *passim.*

14. For other studies on the politics of slavery and colonialism that follow the works of Moreno Fraginals, Maluquer de Motes, Scott, Scarano, Bergad, Fradera and others, see Figueroa, "Facing Freedom"; Náter Vázquez, "Los autonomismos"; Casanovas Codina, "Labor and Colonialism in Cuba"; Ferrer, "To Make a Free Nation"; Findlay, "Domination, Decency, and Desire"; Garcia, "Tradició liberal i política colonial a Catalunya"; and García Mora, "El Ateneo de Madrid y el problema colonial."

15. Jürgen Habermas, quoted in Eley, "Nations, Publics, and Political Cultures," 290.

16. On Madrid, see Gil Novales, "Abolicionismo y librecambio"; on free trade and protectionism, see Costas Comesaña, *Apogeo del liberalismo.*

17. See Díaz Soler, *Historia de la esclavitud negra en Puerto Rico,* esp. 373–75.

18. On Puerto Rican slavery and politics, see Figueroa, "Facing Freedom"; Findlay, "Domination, Decency, and Desire"; Morales Carrión, *Auge y decadencia;* Picó, *Libertad y servidumbre;* Curet, "From Slave to 'Liberto'"; Ramos Mattei, *La hacienda azucarera;* Bergad, *Coffee;* Scarano, *Sugar and Slavery in Puerto Rico;* and Cubano Iguina, *El hilo en el laberinto.*

19. In formulating these concerns, I found these works to be crucial: Wolf, *Europe and the People without History;* Mintz, *Sweetness and Power;* Gupta and Ferguson, "Beyond 'Culture'"; Trouillot, *Silencing the Past;* Hall, "When Was the 'Post-colonial'?"; and Cooper and Stoler, "Between Metropole and Colony."

20. See Ferrer, "To Make a Free Nation"; González, *El país de cuatro pisos;* Pérez, "Between Baseball and Bullfighting"; Helg, *Our Rightful Share;* de la Fuente, "Race and Inequality in Cuba"; Kinsbruner, *Not of Pure Blood;* and Scarano, "The *Jíbaro* Masquerade."

21. See Mintz, introduction to *Caribbean Transformations,* esp. 5–8, 20; and Scott, *Gender and the Politics of History,* 2.

22. On constructions of racial difference in the Americas, see Martínez-Alier, *Marriage, Class and Colour;* Roediger, *The Wages of Whiteness;* Wade, *Blackness and Race Mixture;* and Cope, *The Limits of Racial Domination.* On colonialism and the articulation of racial difference, see Hall, "When Was the 'Post-colonial'?," 249–51; Arjun Appadurai, *Modernity at Large,* 11–16; and Stoler, "Sexual Affronts and Racial Frontiers: European Identities and the Cultural Politics of Exclusion in Southeast Asia."

23. On the politics of slavery and antislavery in the late eighteenth and nineteenth-century Atlantic world, see James, *The Black Jacobins;* Davis, *The Problem of Slavery in the Age of Revolution;* and Blackburn, *The Overthrow of Colonial Slavery.*

24. See Pérez, *Cuba: Between Reform and Revolution,* 86; and Bergad, *Coffee,* 69.

25. On racial ideology in the Spanish Empire, see Cope, *The Limits of Racial Domination,* 3–26, 161–65.

26. See Cepero Bonilla, *Azúcar y abolición;* Paquette, *Sugar Is Made with Blood,* esp. chap. 3; Ferrer, "To Make a Free Nation."

27. On Spanish and Latin American liberal attitudes toward race, nation, empire, and citizenship at Cádiz and after, see King, "The Colored Castes"; Rodríguez, *The Cádiz Experiment,* 53–74; Gudmundson, "Society and Politics in Central America"; and Fradera, "Why Were Spain's Special Overseas Laws Never Enacted?" For more general discussions of racial attitudes in Spain and Latin America, see Martínez-Alier, *Marriage, Class and Colour,* 130–39; Wade, *Blackness and Race Mixture;* and Cope, *The Limits of Racial Domination,* 3–26, 161–65.

28. See Drescher, "Epilogue: Reflections"; see also Blackburn, *The Overthrow of Colonial Slavery,* esp. 519–50. See also Tomich's critique of both Williams and Drescher in "Spaces of Slavery."

29. See Williams, *Capitalism and Slavery;* see also Drescher, "Eric Williams," on the context in which Williams wrote his study.

30. See Drescher, *Econocide;* and Eltis, *Economic Growth.*

31. Davis, *The Problem of Slavery in the Age of Revolution,* 213–54, 262–73, 523–56; Davis, *The Problem of Slavery in Western Culture,* 291–390; Davis, *Slavery and Human Progress,* 107–68; Davis, "Slavery and 'Progress.'"

32. Davis, "Reflections on Abolitionism," 799; Davis, *The Problem of Slavery in the Age of Revolution,* 373–522. See also *The Antislavery Debate,* ed. Bender; and Eltis, *Economic Growth,* 20. Also on the limits of British free labor ideology, see Holt, "'An Empire over the Mind'" and *The Problem of Freedom.*

33. Davis writes in "Reflections on Abolitionism," "I was trying to suggest a far more complex model in which the colonial plantation system served as a projective screen or experimental theater for testing the ideas of liberation, paternalism, and controlled social change that were prompted in part by domestic anxieties" (805). See also Davis, *The Problem of Slavery in the Age of Revolution,* 455–68.

34. Drescher, "Cart Whip and Billy Roller," 18; see also Drescher, *Capitalism and Antislavery,* chaps. 5–7, and "Whose Abolition?"

35. Drescher, "Two Variants of Anti-slavery," 57–59; see also Drescher, "Brazilian Abolition in Comparative Perspective," 35–38.

36. Drescher, "The Long Goodbye," 68. See also the essays in *Fifty Years Later,* ed. Oostinde.

37. This argument is indebted to Tomich, "The 'Second Slavery'" and "World Slavery and Caribbean Capitalism"; as well as to Blackburn, *The Overthrow of Colonial Slavery.*

38. See esp. Drescher, "The Long Goodbye"; and Davis, *The Problem of Slavery in the Age of Revolution.*

39. See James, *The Black Jacobins;* Blackburn, *The Overthrow of Colonial Slavery,* 24–28; and Tomich, "Spaces of Slavery," 77–79.

40. On the Quakers and antislavery, see Davis, *The Problem of Slavery in Western Culture,* 291–332. On the "displacement" of metropolitan struggles, see Drescher, *Capitalism and Antislavery,* 3; and Davis, "Reflections on Abolitionism," 805.

41. On "hybridity" see Hall, "When Was the 'post-colonial'?," 249–51.

42. On the intersection of local interests with larger scale political and economic processes, see Gupta and Ferguson, "Beyond 'Culture'"; Cooper and Stoler, "Between Metropole and Colony"; and Cooper, "Race, Ideology, and the Perils of Comparative History."

## Chapter 1. The Limits of Revolution

1. "Carta de José Luis Alfonso a José Antonio Saco, fecha Habana, 27 de Enero de 1836," BNJM, CM/Alfonso, no. 17, emphasis in the original.

2. On the Haitian revolution, see James, *The Black Jacobins;* on the transatlantic dynamic of the destruction of slavery, see Blackburn, *The Overthrow of Colonial Slavery;* on the growth of Antillean slavery in response to the decline of slavery in other areas, see Tomich, "The 'Second Slavery.'"

3. Corwin, *Spain and the Abolition of Slavery in Cuba,* 63–64.

4. The commission's final report is in Saco, *Examen analítico del informe de la Comisión Especial.*

5. On the liberal revolution, centralization, and capitalist development, see Herr, "Spain"; Marichal, *Spain (1834–1844);* López Garrido, *La Guardia Civil;* Artola, *La burguesía revolucionaria;* Fontana, *La crisis del antiguo régimen;* Fradera, *Cultura nacional en una societat dividida* and *Jaume Balmes;* and Cruz, *Gentlemen, Bourgeois, and Revolutionaries.* On Carlism, see Carr, *Spain,* 155–209, 337–42, 674–75; Barahona, *Vizcaya on the Eve of Carlism;* and Fradera, Millan, and Garrabou, eds., *Carlisme i moviments absolutistes.*

6. See Fradera, "Why Were Spain's Special Overseas Laws Never Enacted?" 335–37.

7. Ibid., 338–47. See also Lynch, *The Spanish American Revolutions;* Anna, "Institutional and Political Impediments to Spain's Settlement of the American Rebellions"; Andrews, "Spanish American Independence"; Costeloe, *Response to Revolution;* and Kinsbruner, *Independence in Spanish America.*

8. On the relative position of the Cuban elite in the late eighteenth and early nineteenth centuries, see Knight, *Slave Society in Cuba,* 3–46; Moreno Fraginals, *El ingenio;* Domínguez, *Insurrection or Loyalty;* and Kuethe, *Cuba, 1753–1815.*

9. On slaveowner ideology in Cuba, see Cepero Bonilla, *Azúcar y abolición;* Lewis, *Main Currents in Caribbean Thought,* 140–70; Paquette, *Sugar Is Made with Blood;* Moreno Fraginals, *Cuba/España,* 145–231.

10. See Fradera, "Why Were Spain's Special Overseas Laws Never Enacted?" and "Quiebra imperial y reorganización política."

11. This was only a temporary peace. The Carlists mobilized again in 1849, more significantly between 1872 and 1876, and finally, during the Spanish Civil War (1936–1939) in support of the so-called nationalist forces. See Carr, *Spain,* 155–209, 337–42, 674–75.

12. See Vázquez Sotillo, "La represión política en Puerto Rico."

13. The epithet *ayacucho* referred to Spain's final military defeat in South America at Ayacucho by Sucre. See Christiensen, *The Origins of Military Power in Spain.*

14. "Reales órdenes, consultas y correspondencia del General Don Miguel Tacón. Tacón al Secretario de Estado, La Habana, 4 de Abríl de 1837," ANC, Asuntos Políticos, leg. 132, no. 17. Tacón's cryptic reference to Methodists suggests that he equated Methodists with Anglo-American abolitionists.

15. On the new 1835 ban and the development of the trade in this period, see Murray, *Odious Commerce,* 92–113.

16. See Pérez, *Lords of the Mountain.*

17. See Saco's autobiography in the *Revista Cubana* 20 (1894); Pérez de la Riva, *Correspondencia reservada del Capitan General D. Miguel Tacón,* 331–35; and Torres-Cuevas, *José Antonio Saco.*

18. See Saco, "Justa defensa de la Academia Cubana de Literatura," in *Colección de pápeles,* 3:25–65.

19. See Torres-Cuevas, *José Antonio Saco;* Moreno Fraginals, *Cuba/España,* 170–205; Jensen, *Children of Colonial Despotism;* and Luis, *Literary Bondage.*

20. On racial thought and politics in Cuba, see Paquette, *Sugar Is Made with Blood,* chap. 3; Martínez-Alier, *Marriage, Class and Colour;* and Helg. On the idea of "whitening" in Latin America, see Wade, *Blackness and Race Mixture.*

21. Arango y Parreño, "Representación al Rey." See also Kuethe, *Cuba,* 155–70.

22. Arango y Parreño, "Representación al Rey," 532–33.

23. Saco, "Noticias del Brasil," 213–30, discusses Cuba in particular and the dangers of a general African revolution in the Caribbean.

24. See Saco, *La vagancia en Cuba* and *Memoria sobre caminos en la isla de Cuba.*

25. See "Población blanca," *Memorias de la Real Sociedad Patriótica de la Habana,* no. 6 (April 1836); and "Ingenios sin esclavos," ibid., no. 22 (August 1837).

26. Domingo del Monte, "Al público," first published in *La Aurora,* Matanzas, 29 April 1834. BNJM, CM/Morales, no. 6. On del Monte, one of Cuba's leading political and intellectual figures until his premature death in 1853, see Paquette, *Sugar Is Made with Blood;* and Luis, *Literary Bondage.*

27. Del Monte, *La isla de Cuba tal cual está,* AHN/U, leg. 4462, exp. 17.

28. Fradera, "Why Were Spain's Special Overseas Laws Never Enacted?," 347–49; see also Jensen, *Children of Colonial Despotism.*

29. See the following pamphlets by Saco published while in Spain: *Carta de un patriota, Mi primera pregunta,* and "Paralelo entre la Isla de Cuba."

30. Comunicación reservada de Tacón, Habana, 31 July 1837, in "El Regente de la Audiencia de Puerto Príncipe remite un paquete con el sello de las armas reales con ejemplares de impresos subversivos venido por el último correo marítimo," 30 July 1837. ANC, Asuntos Políticos, leg. 39, No. 29.

The metropolitan government was also alarmed by Saco's work. See the order banning Saco's pamphlets: "Real Orden fecha Madrid 30 Julio 1837, 'Enterado de la carta 372 y manda impedir que circula impresos alarmantes.'" ANC, Asuntos Políticos, leg. 39, no. 28.

31. On the Santiago regime, see Navarro García, *Entre esclavos y constituciónes.* Pérez de la Riva considered the Santiago regime a precursor of the independence movement launched in Oriente Province in 1868. See *Correspondencia reservada,* 57.

32. Navarro García, *Entre esclavos y constituciónes,* 73–106.

33. Manuel Lorenzo, "Cubanos," *Suplemento al Cubano Oriental* (Santiago de Cuba), 19 November 1836, emphasis in the original.

34. Pérez de la Riva, *Correspondencia reservada,* 37–57. The Santiago liberals were not abolitionists. Saco certainly defended slavery as a necessary evil, even in a less developed zone like Oriente. See also the advertisments for slaves in the Santiago regime's official newspaper, "Aviso que da D. José de Oñate a los señores habitantes españoles y estrangeros que gusten aprovecharlo," *Diario Constitucional de Santiago de Cuba,* 8 October 1836.

35. "El Diputado [Ramón Arango] de la Real Junta de Fomento en Cuba, informa sobre las causas de la decadencia de la Provincia, y acerca de los medios de aumentar los ingresos de las Arcas Reales," Santiago de Cuba, 20 August 1849, in "Expediente para que las diversas autoridades de la provincia de Santiago de Cuba se rinda un informe acerca de la decadencia de aquella y sus causas, proponiendo medidas para mejorar la riqueza pública. En los informes rendidos se atribuye principalmente a las ocurrencias políticas de 1836 y a las ideas abolicionistas de los siguientes años, 18 Abríl 1849," ANC, Asuntos Políticos, leg. 43, no. 30.

36. "Acta capitular del Ayuntamiento de Cuba atestando el buen estado de tranquilidad de la Prov.a" in "Testimonio de espediente instruído para calificar de un modo positivo la tranquilidad pública, bienestar, cáracter manso y buena índole que constantamente han disfrutado de la Ciudad y Provincia de Cuba, 26 de Octubre de 1836," ANC, Asuntos Políticos, leg. 37, no. 10.

37. "Certificación de la acta del Ayuntamiento de Baracoa acerca del buen estado de paz y tranquilidad de la Prov.a," in "Testimonio de espediente instruído," ANC, Asuntos Políticos, leg. 37, no. 10.

38. Navarro García, *Entre esclavos y constituciones*, 107–29.

39. The report is reproduced in Saco, *Examen analítico*, 4.

40. See ibid., 5. On Spanish imperialism and racial categories, see Fradera, "Why Were Spain's Special Overseas Laws Never Enacted?," 339–41; and Cope, *The Limits of Racial Domination*, 3–26, 161–65.

41. See Spain, Cortes, *Diario de las Sesiones de Cortes*, no. 62, 7 March 1837; see also Fradera, "Why Were Spain's Special Overseas Laws Never Enacted?"

42. See Fradera, "Why Were Spain's Special Overseas Laws Never Enacted?," 339–41; King, "The Colored Castes"; Rodríguez, *The Cádiz Experiment*, 53–74; and Martínez-Alier, *Marriage, Class and Colour*.

43. The protest is noted in the *Diario de las Sesiones de las Cortes*, no. 62, 7 March 1837, 3:51. The special commission first presented its report on 10 February 1837. The final vote took place on 7 March, 128 votes in favor, 12 votes against. For the published protest see "Protesta de los diputados electos por la Isla de Cuba a las Cortes Generales de la Nación," *El Mundo*, Madrid, 22 February 1837, suplemento al no. 266.

44. Saco, *Examen analítico*, 17.

45. Ibid., 21.

46. See Fradera, "Why Were Spain's Special Overseas Laws Never Enacted?," 347–49; and García Balaña, "Tradició liberal i política colonial a Catalunya."

47. See Solé Tura, *Constituciones y periodos constituyentes en España*.

48. See Saco, "Paralelo entre la Isla de Cuba," 69–70.

49. "Carta de José Luis Alfonso a José Antonio Saco, fecha: Habana, Nov.e 3 de 1849," BNJM, CM/Alfonso, no. 28.

50. See Guerra y Sánchez, *La guerra de los diez años;* and Scott, *Slave Emancipation in Cuba,* 45–197.

51. On slaveowners' reactions to abolition, see Scott, *Slave Emancipation in Cuba*, 172–226; and Bergad, *Cuban Rural Society*, 263–88.

52. "Carta de José Luis Alfonso a José Antonio Saco, fecha: Habana, Octubre 14 de 1878," BNJM, CM/Alfonso, no. 33, emphasis in the original. The plan apparently was not apocryphal. In 1851, Domingo del Monte, Alfonso's brother-in-law, reported to Saco of Alfonso's meeting with Palmerston in London about it. See "Carta de Domingo del Monte a José Antonio Saco, fecha: Londrés, 13 Agosto 1851," in ANC, Donativos y Remisiónes, fuera de caja 47-10.

53. See Villaverde, *General Narciso López.* (Villaverde was one of Cuba's greatest novelists and López's personal secretary.) See also Chaffin, *Fatal Glory.*

54. On annexationism during this period, see Paquette, *Sugar Is Made with Blood;* Guerra y Sánchez, *Manual de historia de Cuba,* 407–552; Murray, *Odious Commerce,* 208–40; Martínez-Fernández, *Torn between Empires,* 114–41; May, *The Southern Dream of a Caribbean Empire,* 22–76; and Chaffin, *Fatal Glory.*

55. See Murray, *Odious Commerce;* Bethell, *The Abolition of the Brazilian Slave Trade;* Temperley, *British Antislavery.*

56. On the Chinese in Cuba, see Scott, *Slave Emancipation in Cuba,* 28–35.

57. Claudio Antón Luzuriaga, *Diario de Sesiones de la Cortes Constituyentes,* 8 March 1855, 2760.

58. See Eltis, *Economic Growth,* 249. On British diplomatic and naval pressure, see Murray, *Odious Commerce,* 72–158.

59. See for instance, "Real Orden, fecha Madrid 8 febrero 1841, acusando el recibo de una exposición de la Junta de Fomento acerca de las inconvenientes que puede causar la presencia y opiniones del nuevo Cónsul inglés Mr. David Turnbull, y sobre las medidas que deberán ponerse en práctica," ANC, Asuntos Políticos, leg. 40, no. 60; and "Junta de Comercio de Cataluña," Barcelona, 16 June 1841, AHN/U, leg. 3547, exp. 9, no. 6.

60. "Minuta del informe fecha Habana 25 Octubre 1841, del Censor de la Real Sociedad Patriótica, Sr. Manuel Martínez Serrano, sobre el convenio propuesto por el Gobierno de S.M.B. para la abolición del tráfico de esclavos," ANC, Asuntos Políticos, leg. 41, no. 18.

61. On European immigration to nineteenth-century Cuba, see Maluquer de Motes, *Nación e inmigración;* Yáñez Gallardo, *La emigración española;* and Naranjo Orovio and García González, *Racismo y inmigración.*

62. The regent of Spain from 1840 to 1843 was Espartero, the leader of the *ayacucho* faction of the Spanish military; see Carr, *Spain,* 215–27.

63. "Copia de la comunicación reservada dirigida por el Capitan General de la Ysla al Ministro de Ultramar, fecha Habana 30 Abríl 1841 sobre ciertos proyectos de la Junta de Fomento que disgustaron al Gobierno," ANC, Asuntos Políticos, leg. 41, no. 3.

64. The Palacio Aldama was a frequent target of Spanish resentment and vengeance. After the outbreak of the Ten Years' War in 1868, Spaniards burned and sacked a section of the palace. See "Carta de Miguel de Aldama a Domingo Dulce, fecha: Ingenio Santa Rosa, Enero 27, 1869," BNJM, CM/Ponce, no. 445.

65. On the Aldamas' involvement in railroad construction, especially in Matanzas, see Bergad, *Cuban Rural Society,* 113.

66. "Carta de José Luis Alfonso a José Antonio Saco, fecha, Habana, Mayo 13 de 1843," BNJM, CM/Alfonso, no. 27. See also letters from Alfonso to Saco dated Guanabacoa, 4 July 1844, and Havana, 13 May 1844, both BNJM, CM/Alfonso, no. 27. Bergad, however, observes that the Alfonsos were "notorious" slave traders, (*Cuban Rural Society,* 113). Scott also notes the disjuncture between discourse and actual practice regarding the slave trade in the case of the *hacendado* Tomás Terry (*Slave Emancipation in Cuba,* 39, n. 94).

67. "Carta de José Luis Alfonso a José Antonio Saco, fecha Habana, Mayo 13 de 1843," BNJM, CM/Alfonso, no. 27. On Turnbull and his attempts to end the slave trade and abolish slavery, see Paquette, *Sugar Is Made with Blood,* 131–57; and Murray, *Odious Commerce,* 133–58.

68. See Paquette, *Sugar Is Made with Blood;* Murray, *Odious Commerce,* 159–80. On the persecution of Cuba's large free black population, see Deschamps Chapeaux, "Flebotomianos y dentistas," 83–96; and Paquette, *Sugar Is Made with Blood,* 104–28. La Escalera took its name from the ladders *(escaleras)* to which prisoners were bound and flogged during interrogation.

69. Murray, *Odious Commerce,* 166–68. On del Monte and Everett, see Paquette, *Sugar Is Made with Blood,* 189–94.

70. On the repression carried out by O'Donnell, see Paquette, *Sugar Is Made with Blood,* 209–32.

71. See Martínez-Fernández, *Torn between Empires,* 114–41; and Murray, *Odious Commerce,* 178–80.

72. See for example, Opatrny, *Antecedentes históricos,* 109–21.

73. Letter from Narizotas [Gaspar Betancourt Cisneros] to José Antonio Saco, New York, 30 August 1848, in Fernández de Castro, *Medio siglo de historia colonial de Cuba,* emphasis in the original.

74. "Thoughts upon the Incorporation of Cuba into the American Confederation in contra-position to those published by José Antonio Saco," *A Series of Articles,* 20.

75. On the Drake family, see Ely, *Cuando reinaba su majestad el azúcar,* 342–84; and Bahamonde and Cayuela Fernández, *Hacer las Américas,* 183–200.

76. Conde de Vega-Mar, *Informe del excmo. Señor Conde de Vega-Mar,* 7–8.

77. See Bahamonde Magro and Cayuela Fernández, "La creación de nobleza en Cuba" and *Hacer las Américas.*

78. Many of Saco's antiannexationist writings were collected in 1853 in *Obras de Don José Antonio Saco.*

79. See Martínez-Fernández, *Torn between Empires,* 136.

80. Saco, "Réplica de D. José Antonio Saco a los Anexionistas," in *Obras,* 2:145.

81. "Carta de Domingo del Monte a José Antonio Saco, fecha: Madrid, 12 Junio 1851," ANC, Donativos y Remisiónes, fuera de caja 47-10.

82. On del Monte, Plácido, and Manzano, see Paquette, *Sugar Is Made with Blood,* chaps. 3–4 and *passim;* Jensen, *Children of Colonial Despotism;* and Luis, *Literary Bondage.* See also del Monte's defense of the Academia Cubana de Literatura in *La Aurora* (Matanzas), 29 April 1834, in BNJM, CM/Morales/ tomo 12, no. 6; and Manzano, *Autobiography of a Slave.*

83. Letter from Domingo del Monte to José Antonio Saco, Madrid, 27 March 1850, in Fernández de Castro, *Medio siglo de historia colonial en Cuba,* 149–50, emphasis in the original.

84. The debate was touched off by a review of the Cuban Junta de Fomento's proposal for increased European immigration that argued against immigration. See Vázquez Queipo, *Informe fiscal.* Saco responded in "Carta de un cubano a un amigo suyo en que se hacen algunas observaciónes al informe fiscal sobre fomento de la población blanca de la isla de Cuba, etc.," *Obras,* vol. 1.

85. Saco, "Carta de un cubano," 254.

86. Vázquez Queipo, *Contestación a la carta de un cubano;* see also his response in the Madrid daily *El Clamór Público,* 7 and 22 July 1847; and Saco's final word, "Réplica a la contestación del Señor fiscal de la Real Hacienda de la Habana, D. Vicente Vázquez Queipo," in *Obras,* vol. 1.

87. "Carta de Domingo del Monte a José Antonio Saco, fecha: Madrid, 19 Octubre 1851," ANC, Donativos y Remisiónes, fuera de caja 47-10, emphasis in the original.

88. See, for instance, the article by José Luis Retornillo, *El Constitucional* (Madrid), 21 December 1851, and Saco's response, 2 January 1852. See also Saco's pamphlets, "La situacion política de Cuba y su remedio" [Paris, 1851] and "Cuestion de Cuba. O sea contestacion al *Constitucional* de Madrid y a Don José Luis Retornillo, impugnadores del folleto intitulado 'La situacion política de Cuba y su remedio'" [Paris, 1852], in *Obras,* vol. 2.

89. On Spanish interest in colonialism in the 1850s, see López-Ocón, *Biografia de "La América."*

90. See Kiernan, *The Revolution of 1854;* on the Spanish colonial administration at midcentury, see Cayuela, *Bahía de Ultramar.*

91. El Marqués de Albaida, *Diario de Sesiones,* 18 de Diciembre de 1854, 706.

92. Salustiano Olózaga, ibid., 709.

93. Ramón de la Sagra, ibid., 708. See his pamphlet in support of Tacón and in favor of excluding colonial deputies from the Cortes: Sagra, *Apuntes destinados.*

## Chapter 2. "Cuestión de brazos"

1. On race and colonial identities in Puerto Rico, see Gónzalez, *El pais de cuatro pisos;* Díaz-Quiñones, "Salvador Brau"; Scarano, "The *Jíbaro* Masquerade"; and Kinsbruner, *Not of Pure Blood.*

2. See Scarano, *Sugar and Slavery.*

3. See Drescher, review of Blackburn, *The Overthrow of Colonial Slavery.*

4. Scarano, *Sugar and Slavery,* xxii, emphasis in the original.

5. See Díaz Soler, *Historia de la esclavitud negra,* 373–75.

6. See Scarano, *Sugar and Slavery;* Curet, "From Slave to 'Liberto'"; Ramos Mattei, *La hacienda azucarera;* Figueroa, "Facing Freedom"; and Martínez-Vergne, *Capitalism in Puerto Rico.*

7. See Curet, "From Slave to 'Liberto,'" 254–60.

8. The following works have shaped my perspective: Gupta and Ferguson, "Beyond 'Culture'"; Cooper, "Race, Ideology, and the Perils of Comparative History"; Cooper and Stoler, "Between Colony and Metropole"; and Tomich, "Spaces of Slavery."

9. On the *libreta,* see Picó, *Historia general de Puerto Rico,* 173–74; Mintz, "Slavery and Forced Labor"; Bergad, *Coffee,* 53–67; and Dietz, *An Economic History of Puerto Rico,* 42–50.

10. See the description of the ceremony in "Sobre el sorteo celebrado entre los jornaleros de esta villa y adjudicación del premio a Rafael Barbosa fue premiado por la suerte. Año 1850" (AHMP, Ayuntamiento, Secretaría, Seguridad Pública, Premios, Jornaleros, 1850–1917, Caja S-125, exp. 1).

11. "Sobre el sorteo celebrado entre los jornaleros de esta villa y adjudicación del premio a Manuel Ramos fue premiado por la suerte. Año 1854" (ibid., exp. 3).

12. On the slave trade to Puerto Rico and its demise, see Morales Carrión, *Auge y decadencia;* and Scarano, *Sugar and Slavery,* 120–43.

13. On Ponce slaveowners, see Scarano, *Sugar and Slavery;* Ramos Mattei, *La hacienda azucarera;* and Curet, "From Slave to 'Liberto'" and *Los amos hablan.*

14. "Antecedentes de la conspiración que se fraguaba para proclamar la independencia," San Juan, 16 August 1838, AHN/U, leg. 5062, exp. 16. See also Cruz Monclova, *Historia de Puerto Rico,* 1:302–12.

15. On slave rebellions and slave resistance in Puerto Rico, see Baralt, *Esclavos rebeldes.*

16. Yrizarry, "Informe dado por el alcalde Don Pedro de Yrissari al Ayuntamiento de la Capital," in Ramírez Avellano, *Instrucciónes al diputado Don Ramón Power y Giralt,* 15–16.

17. "Sobre introducción de papeles subversivos," 1841, AHN/U, leg. 5063, exp. 35.

18. See "Política," *Boletín Instructivo y Mercantil de Puerto Rico* (San Juan), 4, no. 104 (28 December 1842): 825–26.

19. On slave conspiracies in Ponce and Vega Baja in 1848, see Baralt, *Esclavos rebeldes,* 127–44.

20. "[El Conde de Reus] participa los sucesos acaecidos en la Martinica por mero

consecuencia de la emancipación de los eslcavos, y las medidas energícas que ha tomado para preservar esta Isla de tal contagio," San Juan, 10 June 1848, AHN/U, leg. 5069, exp. 3.

21. "[El Conde de Reus] participa la insurreción de los esclavos de la Isla Danesa de Sta. Cruz, y ausilios que facilitó para reprimirla a petición de su Gobernador General con la demas que espresa," San Juan, 10 July 1848, AHN/U, leg. 5069, exp. 4.

22. Bergad, *Coffee*, 69.

23. Díaz Soler, *Historia de la esclavitud negra*, 122–23, 256. See also Morales Carrión, *Auge y decadencia*, 187–211.

24. For data on slaves and registered laborers in Ponce, see "Estados trimestrales del alta y baja de jornaleros, de esclavos, frutos mayores y menores y del ganado vacuno del partido," AHMP, Ayuntamiento, Secretaría, Seguridad Pública, Listas, Jornaleros, 1864–1871; caja S-109, exp. 5.

25. Bergad, *Coffee*, 68–71.

26. See *Proyecto de inmigración africana*. On foreign contract laborers in Puerto Rico, see Ramos Mattei, "La importación de trabajadores."

27. "Resumen se los acuerdos celebrados por la Sociedad Económica de Amigos del País, desde 27 de Enero de 1859 a 1862," *Acta de la Junta Pública efectuada por la Sociedad Económica*, 14.

28. See Pedro Yrizarry, "Informe dado por el alcalde Don Pedro Yrisarri al Ayuntamiento de la Capital," in Ramírez de Arellano, *Instrucciónes al diputado Don Ramón Power y Giralt*.

29. *Junta General de la Sociedad Económica*, 23–24.

30. *Acta de la Junta Pública tenida por la Sociedad Económica de Amigos de País de Puerto Rico*, 14–15.

31. See Acosta y Quintero, *José J. Acosta y su tiempo*.

32. Cruz Monclova, *Historia de Puerto Rico*, 1:361. Micault Pignateli and Aurelio Núñez died in Spain.

33. Documents pertaining to the selection of Acosta and Baldorioty can be found in AHN/U, leg. 308, exp. 5–10. Acosta, however, was from a notable family recognized by the king of Spain in the early nineteenth century. See Soliván de Acosta, "Genealogía de Don José Julián de Acosta y Calbo." Thanks to David Stark for providing me with this article.

34. See Acosta's journal from his stay in Madrid in Acosta y Quintero, *José J. Acosta y su tiempo*, 63. Del Monte was a frequent visitor to the Real Academia de Historia in Madrid. He and Saco voraciously collected documents pertaining to the history of slavery in Cuba and the Americas. See del Monte's description of Cubans in Madrid and his activities at the Real Academia in "Carta de Domingo del Monte a José Antonio Saco, fecha: Madrid, 1851," ANC, Donativos y Remisiónes, fuera de caja 47-10.

35. José J. Acosta to Félix M. Tanco, Paris, 31 October 1852, in Acosta y Quintero, *José J. Acosta y su tiempo*, 86–87.

36. J. J. Acosta y Calbo, "Prólogo," in Abbad y Lasierra, *Historia geográfica*, iv.

37. Ibid., v–vii.

38. See Alonso, *El gíbaro*.

39. Julio L. de Vizcarrondo, "Al lector," in Ledrú, *Viaje a la Isla de Puerto-Rico*, 6.

40. "Informe dado por el alcalde Don Pedro Yrizzary", 12–14.

41. On the *jíbaro*, see Pedreira, "La actualidad del jíbaro"; Bergad, *Coffee*, 60–67; and Scarano, "The *Jíbaro* Masquerade."

42. See Acosta, "Viaje por la Isla de Puerto Rico," in Acosta y Quintero, *José Julián Acosta y su tiempo*, 114.

43. See, for instance, *El Ponceño* 2, nos. 41 and 61, 9 April and 27 August 1853. On Chinese indentured laborers in Cuba, see Pérez de la Riva, *El barracón*, 55–140; Scott, *Slave Emancipation in Cuba*, 28–35; and Helly, intro. to *The Cuba Commission Report*, 3–30.

44. J. J. Acosta y Calbo, "Cuestión de brazos para el cultivo actual de las tierras de Puerto Rico," in *Colección de artículos publicados*, 4–6. Originally published in *El Boletín Mercantil* (San Juan). On the transfer of slaves from Puerto Rico to Cuba in the 1850s, see Morales Carrión, *Auge y decadencia*, 187–211.

45. Acosta, "Cuestión de brazos," 7.

46. See for instance, Julio Vizcarrondo, "Sociedad Libre de Economía Política de Madrid. Año octavo—1864 a 1865. Novena reunión, celebrada el 20 de febrero 1865," *El Abolicionista Español* (Madrid), 1, no. 3 (15 September 1864): 50; and the Junta Informativa de Reformas para Puerto Rico, quoted in Baldorioty de Castro, *Interpelación del diputado Don Luis Padial*, 16–17.

47. Acosta, "Cuestión de brazos," in *Colección de artículos publicados*, 8–9.

48. Ibid., 10–11.

49. Ibid., 15.

50. See, for instance, a response from Guayama, "Sobre la necesidad de brazos en este país," *El Ponceño* 2, no. 72 (12 November 1853).

51. Puerto Rico specialized in muscovado sugar extracted from sugar cane which through the nineteenth century was gradually replaced by beet sugar as the chief source of unrefined sugar in the world market. See Ramos Mattei, "Technical Innovations and Social Change," 161. On the world sugar market in the nineteenth century, see Moreno Fraginals, "Plantations in the Caribbean," 8–14; and Tomich, "World Slavery and Caribbean Capitalism." See also Mintz, *Sweetness and Power*.

52. Acosta, "Artículo segundo," in *Colección de artículos publicados*, 32.

53. Ibid., 34–37.

54. On criticisms of the *libreta* and abuses of the system, see Dietz, *An Economic History of Puerto Rico*, 47–50.

55. See Messina's circulars in AHN/U, leg. 5114, exp. 42, nos. 4, 6, 7.

56. AHN/U, leg. 5114, exp. 47.

57. "Corregimiento y Municipalidad de San Germán, respuesta al decreto de Gobernador sobre libreta," 15 May 1866, AHN/U, leg. 5114, exp. 49, no. 1. One of the members of the San Germán commission was Francisco M. Quiñones, who joined Acosta as an early advocate of abolition as members of the Junta de Información, which met in Madrid from 1866 to 1867.

58. Carlos Cabrera, Ponce, 22 May 1866, AHN/U, leg. 5114, exp. 47. As noted, the number of laborers subjected to the *libreta* was rising in Ponce in the 1860s.

59. Carlos de Rojas to Marchesi, San Juan, 1 June 1866, AHN/U, leg. 5114, exp. 48, no. 3.

60. Acosta, "Notas. 1. Agricultura," in Abbad y Lasierra, *Historia geográfica*, 329–30.

61. Abbad y Lasierra, "Cáracter y diferentes castas de los habitantes de la isla de San Juan de Puerto Rico," ibid., 400.

62. Acosta, "Notas. Cáracter, costumbres y cultura intelectual de los habitantes de Puerto Rico," ibid., 409–10.

63. Acosta, "Notas. 1. Comercio," ibid., 337–54. A colonial bureaucrat had advocated free trade between Spain and Puerto Rico as a means of improving the Puerto Rican economy. He noted that Puerto Rico had flourished under the period of free trade between 1812 and 1835, while it languished under the current protectionist system. See "Relaciónes mercantiles

entre España y Puerto Rico; estado actual de la agricultura y comercio de la Antilla; producciónes, su valoración y proyecto de reforma en los aranceles de la Peninsula respecto a la importación de los artículos coloniales, por el secretario cesante de la Junta de Comercio y Fomento, Don Andrés Viña" [Madrid, 1850], *Boletín Histórico de Puerto Rico* 7 (1920). On the Spanish protectionist system, see Maluquer de Motes, "El mercado colonial antillano."

64. Acosta, "Notas. 1. Agricultura," in Abbad y Lasierra, *Historia geográfica*, 330–31.

65. Ibid., 332–33. Acosta especially favored the cultivation of coffee as an export crop. He wrote to a friend, "Regarding my essay *El Café* I can only say that I wrote it out of my love for that wonderful plant" (Acosta y Quintero, *José J. Acosta y su tiempo*, 89). "El Café" is in *Colección de artículos publicados*, 105–11. On the growth of the coffee sector in Puerto Rico from the mid to the late nineteenth century when coffee became Puerto Rico's chief export crop, see Picó, *Amargo Café*; Bergad, *Coffee*, esp. 68–223; and Cubano Iguina, *El hilo en el laberinto*, 120–44.

66. On the crisis of the 1860s, see Cepero Bonilla, *Azúcar y abolición;* Murray, *Odious Commerce*, 298–326; and Martínez-Fernández, *Torn between Empires*, 153–226.

67. See Acosta, "Cuestión de brazos," 7; Vizcarrondo, "Sociedad Libre de Economía Política," 50; Baldorioty de Castro, *Interpelación del diputado*, 16–17; See also the arguments about race and labor made by the Spaniard who represented Puerto Rico in the Cortes after 1868: Labra y Cadrana, *La abolición de la esclavitud en el órden económico*, 231–33.

68. See "Manifestación de los señores comisionados de Puerto-Rico pidiendo la inmediata abolición de la esclavitud," Madrid, 8 November 1866, in *Información sobre reformas en Cuba y Puerto Rico* 1:47–48; and "Sección segunda. Negros libres," ibid., 121–28.

69. See Curet, "From Slave to 'Liberto,'" 254–60.

70. On Cuban planters, see Scott, *Slave Emancipation in Cuba;* and Bergad, *Cuban Rural Society*.

71. See Gil Novales, "Abolicionismo y librecambio."

## Chapter 3. Free Trade and Protectionism

1. Larra, "¿Quién es el público y donde se encuentra?"; and El Curioso Parlante [Ramón de Mesonero Romanos], *Panorama Matritense*, v.

2. Hartzenbusch, *Periódicos de Madrid*.

3. On Madrid from the early to mid-nineteenth century, see Bahamonde and Toro, *Burguesía;* Ringrose, *Madrid and the Spanish Economy;* Shubert, "'Charity Properly Understood'"; Baker, *Materiales para escribir Madrid;* Fernández, *Apology to Apostrophe;* Juliá et al., *Madrid; Madrid: Atlas histórico;* and Cruz, *Gentlemen*.

4. Mesonero Romanos, *Nuevo Manual*, v.

5. Mesonero Romanos, *Manual de Madrid*, 56–61.

6. Mesonero Romanos, *Nuevo Manual*, 491–502. On the Ateneo, see also Labra, *El Ateneo de Madrid*.

7. Mesonero Romanos, *Nuevo Manual*, 569–79. See also Madoz, *Diccionario Geográfico-estadístico-histórico*, vol. x, 776–863.

8. *Diccionario de la lengua castellana* (1832), 613.

9. *Diccionario de la lengua castellana* (1869), 640, emphasis in the original.

10. Rodríguez, "La idea y el movimiento antiesclavista."

11. Gil Novales, "Abolicionismo y librecambio," 162.

12. Ibid.

13. See Hobsbawm, *The Age of Capital;* Habermas, *The Structural Transformation of the Public Sphere;* and Eley, "Nations, Publics, and Political Cultures."

14. "Mr. Cobden's Speech at Cadiz," in Schwabe, *Reminiscences of Richard Cobden,* 32–33, emphasis in the original.

15. See Tortella Casares, *Banking, Railroads, and Industry,* 506–50; and Lluch, "La 'gira trionfal,'" 78–80.

16. Cruz, *Gentlemen.*

17. See Eley, "The British Model," esp. 76–90. See also Mayer, *The Persistence of the Old Regime;* Reddy, *Money and Liberty in Modern Europe,* 1–33; Sewell, *A Rhetoric of Bourgeois Revolution,* 1–40; and Cruz, *Gentlemen,* 272.

18. My thanks to Seymour Drescher for urging me to clarify this issue.

19. See Marichal, *Spain;* and Cánovas Sánchez, "Los partidos políticos."

20. See Cánovas Sánchez, "Los partidos políticos," 373–410; López Garrido, *La Guardia Civil;* and Artola, *La burguesía revolucionaria,* 211–22.

21. See Cánovas Sánchez, "Los partidos políticos," 411–85; Artola, *La burguesía revolucionaria,* 222–38; Kiernan, *The Revolution of 1854 in Spanish History;* Tortella Casares, *Los orígenes del capitalismo en España;* Harrison, *An Economic History of Modern Spain,* 42–67; and Carr, *Spain,* 257–304.

22. See Hobsbawm, *The Age of Capital.*

23. For an overview of European free trade and protectionist organizations and initiatives in this period, see Bairoch, "European Trade Policy," 8:1–51. On protectionist ideology in nineteenth-century Europe, see Szporluk, *Communism and Nationalism.*

24. Tortella Casares, *Banking, Railroads, and Industry,* 506–50. For a discussion of trade policies throughout the nineteenth century, see Carrera Pujal, *La economía de Cataluña en el siglo XIX.*

25. See Lluch, "La 'gira trionfal,'" 78–80; on Valencia see Piqueras and Sebastià, *Agiotistas, negreros y partisanos,* 9–60, passim.; on the short-lived free-trade enthusiasm of the Castilian wheat growers, Varela Ortega, "El proteccionismo," 18–20. For a brief overview, see Tortella Casares, *El desarrollo,* 167–75.

26. See Tortella Casares, *El desarrollo,* 167–75; and Artola, ed., *Los Ferrocarriles.*

27. On the Spanish school of political economy, see Costas Comesaña, *Apogeo del liberalismo;* and Gil Novales, "Abolicionismo y librecambio," 161–63. See also the Economists' celebration of their cohesiveness in "Introducción," *Gaceta Economista* (Madrid), 1, no. 12 (May 1861): 1–3.

28. "Introducción," *El Economista* 1, no. 1 (5 February 1856).

29. "Exposición de la Comisión Catalana a los Cortes Constituyentes sobre la reforma de aranceles," ibid., 1, no. 2 (20 February 1856): 34, emphasis in the original.

30. Ibid., 34.

31. On Figuerola, see Costas Comesaña, *Apogeo del liberalismo,* 40–48.

32. See the letter from Figuerola to Agustí Aymar y Gelabert, 16 January 1869, in "Papers personals i correspondència política de Agustí Aymar y Gelabert," Biblioteca de Catalunya, Ms. 1260.

33. See Costas Comesaña, *Apogeo del liberalismo,* 34–48, 128–69.

34. Hobsbawm, *Nations and Nationalism,* 29.

35. Nadal, *El fracaso de la revolución industrial,* 188–225; Maluquer de Motes, "The Industrial Revolution in Catalonia"; and Thomson, *A Distinctive Industrialization.*

36. On the response of less-developed industrializing nations to British economic power

in the nineteenth century, see Hobsbawm, *Nations and Nationalism*, 23–31; Tomich, "The 'Second Slavery,'" 104–07; and esp. Szporluk, *Communism and Nationalism*, esp. 96–166, for a discussion of the leading mid-nineteenth-century theorist of economic protectionism and national economy.

37. I have castilianized many Catalan names in this chapter to conform to the original sources (for instance, Juan Güell y Ferrer rather than Joan Güell i Ferrer, or Villanueva y Geltrú instead of Vilanova i la Geltrú).

38. On Güell, see McDonogh, *Good Families of Barcelona*, 84–107; on Bosch y Labrús, Puig Llagostera, and the Fomento del Trabajo Nacional, see Izard, *Manufactureros, industriales y revolucionarios*, 223–62.

39. McDonogh, *Good Families of Barcelona*, 108–40, discusses the Barcelona bourgeoisie's complex relationship with Spanish and Catalan nationalism. See also Hobsbawm, *Nations and Nationalism*, 14–45, on theories of regional nationalisms in the nineteenth century.

40. On Aribau, see Lluch, "'La economía política'"; on Balaguer, Feu, and the Renaixença, see Fradera, *Cultura nacional en una societat dividida*, 23–233, passim.

41. Riquer, "El conservadurisme polític català," notes a similar compromise between conservative Catalan legal scholars like Duran i Bas, Permanyer, Reynals, and the industrial bourgeoisie.

42. Blanch y Cortada, "Necesidad y defensa del sistema proteccionista—II. Influencia de la Inglaterra" *Revista Industrial* 1, no. 6 (7 February 1856); and Juan Güell y Ferrer, "Adam Smith, proteccionista," *Escritos económicos* (Barcelona: Imprenta Barcelonesa, 1880). See also Szporluk, *Communism and Nationalism*, 134–39, for List's similar analysis of the German economy and the role of the state in economic growth.

43. "Exposición de la comisión catalana de Aranceles a la Asamblea Constituyente," *Revista Industrial* 1, no. 14 (3 April 1856): 106–07.

44. "Asociaciónes industriales—II." ibid., 1, no. 20 (15 May 1856): 153–54.

45. "*La Revista Industrial* de Barcelona," *El Economista* 1, no. 14 (20 October 1856): 239–40, emphasis in the original.

46. "La prosperidad nacional depende de la protección a la industria," *Revista Industrial* 1, no. 4 (24 January 1856): 27.

47. "Continúan las esposiciónes de la comisión catalana de Aranceles a la Asamblea Constituyente," ibid., 1, no. 10 (6 March 1856): 75.

48. "Instrucción de la clase obrera—artículo primero," ibid., 1, no. 14 (3 April 1856).

49. "Instrucción de la clase obrera—artículo cuarto," ibid., 1, no. 24 (12 June 1856).

50. "Una palabra a la *Revista Industrial* de Barcelona," *El Economista* 1, no. 18, (20 October 1856): 300–01, emphasis in the original.

51. On the disentailments and the consolidation of capitalist agriculture in the first half of the nineteenth century, see García Sanz, "Crisis de la agricultura tradicional"; and articles in *Historia agraria de la España contemporánea*, ed. Garrabou et al., vol. 1; and Herr, "Spain."

52. Bernal and Drain, "Progreso y crisis."

53. On cereal production and protectionist policies in Andalusia, see ibid.; for Castile, Varela Ortega, "El proteccionismo," 7–60.

54. Laureano Figuerola, "La cuestión de cereales— Conferencias librecambistas" *Gaceta Economista* (Madrid), 2, no. 14 (14 June 1862): 428–29.

55. Héran, "Tierra y parentesco."

56. On the Seville economy in the nineteenth century, see Bernal y Drain, "Progreso y

crisis"; Héran, "Tierra y parentesco"; and Tedde de Lorca, "On the Historical Origins of Andalusian Underdevelopment."

57. Genaro Morquecho y Palma, "Economistas y labradores," *La Agricultura Española* (Sevilla), 2, no. 55 (21 July 1859): 25–27.

58. Genaro Morquecho y Palma, "Nuestro plan y nuestras tendencias," ibid., 2, no. 53 (7 July 1859): 2.

59. "Defensa industrial. II," ibid., 1,, no. 42 (21 April 1859): 558–59.

60. Genaro Morquecho y Palma, "Nuestro plan y nuestras tendencias," ibid., 2, no. 53 (7 July 1859): 2.

61. Genaro Morquecho y Palma, "El Círculo de Labradores de Sevilla y el Instituto Agrícola Catalan de San Isidro," ibid., 2,, no. 65 (29 September 1859).

62. On the IACSI, see Planas, "Els propietaris i l'associacionisme agrari a Catalunya."

63. Morquecho y Palma, "El Círculo de Labradores de Sevilla".

64. Gil Novales, "Abolicionismo y librecambio"; and Rodríguez, "La idea y el movimiento antiesclavista en España durante el siglo XIX."

65. The extensive membership lists are scattered through various numbers of *La Verdad Económica* (Madrid), vols. 1–3 (1861).

66. For example, *Impugnación de las doctrinas librecambistas* (Madrid: Imprenta de Manuel Tello, 1862).

67. Buenaventura Carlos Aribau, "Consideraciónes generales sobre el objeto y motivo de esta publicación" *La Verdad Económica* (Madrid), 1 (1861): 9.

68. *La Verdad Económica* (Madrid), 1 (1861): 4 (no title or author), emphasis in the original.

69. "Esposicion que el Círculo económico ha elevado a la Córtes," ibid., 1 (1861): 149–53.

70. Juan Güell y Ferrer, "Bolsa de Madrid. Cuestion sobre los principios proteccionistas," ibid., 3 (1861): 110–11.

71. *La Verdad Económica* (Madrid), 1 (1861): 4–5 (no title or author).

72. See Keane, ed., *Civil Society and the State*, and Krieger, *The German Idea of Freedom* on German conceptions of the state and civil society.

73. José Román Leal, "Qué es el proteccionismo," *La Verdad Económica* (Madrid), 1 (1861): 23–25. Again, see Szporluk, *Nationalism and Communism,* for a comparison with German economic thought.

74. See Eley, "The British Model"; Reddy, *Money and Liberty;* Szporluk, *Communism and Nationalism;* and Cruz, *Gentlemen, Bourgeois, and Revolutionaries.*

75. See Carrera Pujal, *La economía de Cataluña,* 1, 295–385; and Tortella Casares, *El desarrollo,* 167–75.

76. Vilar, "Spain and Catalonia," 560.

77. Maluquer de Motes, "El mercado colonial antillano."

78. Cubano Iguina, *El hilo en el laberinto,* 120–44.

79. Maluquer de Motes, "El mercado colonial antillano," 337–49.

80. See Murray, *Odious Commerce;* Fradera, "La participació catalana"; Bahamonde and Cayuela, *Hacer las Américas.* For examples of Spanish entrepeneurs, especially the Zuluetas, see ibid., 223–77; and Bergad, *Cuban Rural Society,* 21–182, *passim.*

81. Maluquer de Motes, "Inmigración y comercio catalan." Percentages for Havana and Matanzas calculated from statistics on p. 173.

82. Ibid., 166.

83. Ibid., 173–74. Percentage of Catalan merchants calculated from statistics on p. 174.

For a regional and occupational breakdown of Spanish immigration to Cuba, see Maluquer de Motes, *Nación e inmigración.*

84. Cubano Iguina, *El hilo en el laberinto;* and Bergad, *Coffee.*

85. Maluquer de Motes, "Inmigración y comercio catalan," 174.

86. Fradera, *Indústria i mercat.*

87. On Güell and López, see McDonogh, *Good Families of Barcelona,* 84–107.

88. Maluquer de Motes, *Nación e inmigración, passim;* and Yáñez Gallardo, *Saltar con red.*

89. Maluquer de Motes, "Inmigración y comercio catalan," 175–79.

90. Eley, "The British Model."

## Chapter 4. Family, Association, and Free Wage Labor

1. See the speech of Segismundo Moret y Prendergast on June 20, 1870, in *Diario de Sesiones de las Cortes Constituyentes* 14 (1870): 8998–99.

2. On the centrality of religion in British and North American antislavery, see Davis, *The Problem of Slavery in Western Culture,* 291–390; and Davis, *The Problem of Slavery in the Age of Revolution,* 213–54; Drescher, "Two Variants of Anti-slavery"; and *Capitalism and Antislavery,* 111–34. Liberal political economy was also of course crucial in Anglo-American abolitionism. See Foner, *Free Soil;* and Holt, *The Problem of Freedom,* 13–112.

3. See Eley, "The British Model"; see also Hobsbawm, *The Age of Capital.*

4. See Gil Novales, "Abolicionismo y librecambio," 161–63; and Scanlon, *La polémica feminista,* 30–41; and Palacio Morena, *La institucionalización de la reforma social.*

5. On the Economists, see Costas Comesaña, *Apogeo del liberalismo.*

6. López-Morillas, *The Krausist Movement,* 1–10.

7. See ibid.; Trend, *The Origins of Modern Spain;* and Pike, "Making the Hispanic World Safe from Democracy"; see also Krause, *Ideal de la humanidad para la vida.*

8. On the origins of the Partido Demócrata, see Castro Alfín, "Orígenes y primeras etapas del republicanismo en España," and "El Partido Demócrata." On divisions within the Democrats and the later Republican parties, see Trías and Elorza, *Federalismo y reforma social en España;* and Duarte, *El Republicanisme català.*

9. Pérez Ledesma, "'Ricos y pobres"; and Navarro, "De la esperanza a la frustración, 1868–1873," in *El republicanismo en España,* 102–09.

10. On Pi y Margall and the "socialists," see Martí, *Orígenes del anarquismo en Barcelona;* Hennessey, *The Federal Republic in Spain;* and Termes, *Anarquismo y sindicalismo en España.*

11. See Harrison, *An Economic History of Modern Spain,* 42–67.

12. See Benet and Martí, *Barcelona a mitjan del segle XIX;* on the right of association, see Alarcón Caracuel, *El derecho de asociación obrera en España,* 49–115.

13. "Un obrero económico—Crónica económica," *Gaceta Economista* (Madrid) 2, no. 11 (March 1862): 230–31.

14. Segismundo Moret y Prendergast, "Las necesidades y los recursos de la clase obrera," *Fomento de las Artes* (Madrid) 4, no. 73 (5 February 1863): 562.

15. See, for instance, Joaquin María Sanromá, "Cuestion de principios," *La Verdad Económica* (Madrid), 2 (1861): 324–29; Moret y Prendergast, "Perjuicios que causa el proteccionismo a las clases obreras"; or Joaquin María Sanromá, *Política del taller* (Madrid: Imprenta de Víctor Saiz, 1876).

16. Villacorta Baños, "Teoría y práctica del obrerismo democrático."

17. "Un obrero economista—Crónica económica" *Gaceta Economista* (Madrid), 2, no. 11

(March 1862): 231.

18. See Lorenzo's comments on Castro and the Fomento in his memoirs, *El proletariado militante*, 31–37; see also *Fomento de las Artes* (Madrid), 4, no. 86 (20 August 1863): 646.

19. See Labra's reflections on his involvement with the Fomento and social reform in general, "La cuestión obrera y el Fomento de las Artes," *Fomento de las Artes* (Madrid), 28 October 1888.

20. On Republican associations and their relationship to working class politics see Duarte, *El Republicanisme català*, 21–98; and Duarte, *Pere Coromines;* Kaplan, "Positivism and Liberalism"; and Guereña, "Hacia una historia socio-cultural."

21. On Barcelona Republican politics, see Duarte, *El Republicanisme català;* and Alvarez Junco, *El Emperador del Paralelo*.

22. Clemente Selvas to Rafael María de Labra, Barcelona, 28 Octuber 1894. Labra family private archive, Madrid.

23. Castelar, "Utilidad de la propaganda libre-cambista en España," 334.

24. Ibid., 340–48. Protectionist intellectuals also pointed to the apparent contradiction between the Economists' economic radicalism and their political conservatism. See Genaro Morquecho y Palma, "Economistas y conservadores," *La Verdad Económica* 2 (1861): 353–60.

25. Castelar, *La formúla del progreso*, 91–97.

26. Castelar, "Del cáracter general de las escuelas socialistas," *Historia del movimiento republicano en Europa*, 1:182–84.

27. Ibid., 186–87.

28. On Barcelona Republicanism, see Duarte, *El republicanisme català;* and Gabriel, "Insurreción y política. El republicanismo ochocentista en Cataluña," in *El republicanismo en España*, ed. Townson, 341–71; and for the 1854–1874 period, see Martí, *Orígenes del anarquismo en Barcelona;* and Termes, *Anarquismo y sindicalismo en España*.

29. See especially Ceferino Tressera, "Al Sr. D. José Anselmo Clavé," and José Leopoldo Feu, "Algunas palabras sobre la educacion del obrero," *El libro del obrero* (Barcelona: Narciso Ramírez, 1862).

30. 22,000 signatures were from Catalonia, the rest from other cities such as Sevilla, Alcoy, or Valladolid. Only 600 were from Madrid. See Alarcon Caracuel, *El derecho de asociación obrera*, 108.

31. "Influencia de las asociaciónes—V," *Eco de la Clase Obrera* (Madrid), 1, no. 11 (14 October 1855): 162–65.

32. "Impugnación al Proyecto de Ley por el Ministro de Fomento a las Cortes sobre Ejercicio, Policía, Sociedades, Jurisdicción e Inspección de la Industria Manufacturera," ibid., 1, no. 19 (Madrid, 16 December 1855): 6.

33. "Señores Diputados de las Cortes Constituyentes," Madrid, 29 December 1855, Archivo del Congreso, Serie General, leg. 106, no. 3.

34. Lorenzo, *El proletariado militante*, 43.

35. Lorenzo won a first prize in Spanish grammar in 1863 (*Fomento de las Artes* 4, no. 86 [20 August 1863]: 646). Printers were the quintessential Madrid labor radicals in the nineteenth century. The original nucleus of the Spanish Workers' Socialist Party (PSOE), founded in 1879, was a printers' trade union (Asociación del Arte de Imprimir) headed by Pablo Iglesias. Iglesias was also a member of the First International but of the Marxist faction gathered around the newspaper *La Emancipación* and Marx's son-in-law, Paul Lafargue who fled to Spain after the suppression of the Paris Commune. Lorenzo and his comrades adhered to the Bakuninist faction of the International. See Pérez Ledesma, *El obrero consciente*

on anarchists, socialists, and the First and Second Internationals in Spain; and Morato, *Lideres del movimiento obrero español,* for biographies of anarchist and socialist leaders.

36. Lorenzo, *El proletariado militante,* 31–32.

37. Ibid., 65–69.

38. Ibid., 70–74.

39. See Alvarez Junco, *La Comuna en España.*

40. Gabriel Rodríguez, "Extracto de la discusión sobre la Internacional en el Congreso de los Diputados de España. Sesion del 7 de Octubre de 1871," *La Defensa de la Sociedad* 1, no. 6 (20 May 1872): 247.

41. See *Defensa de la Sociedad* 1, no. 5 (10 May 1872), for its governing board and collaborators. Another important abolitionist, Concepción Arenal, a conservative Catholic social reformer who was a severe critic of liberal market society, founded the journal *La Voz de la Caridad* in response to the International. Arenal and her collaborators urged the reestablishment of paternalistic social bonds between "rich" and "poor" that had been severed by the middle-class revolution. On Arenal and her place within conservative Spanish social theory, see Pérez Ledesma, "'Ricos y pobres."

42. Nicolás Salmerón y Alonso, "Extracto de la discusión sobre la Internacional en el Congreso de los Diputados de España. Sesión del 7 de Octubre de 1871," *La Defensa de la Sociedad* 1, no. 6 (20 May 1872): 249–54.

43. See ibid., 253–54; and Montero Ríos, "Extracto de la discusión sobre la Internacional," ibid., 1, no. 8 (10 June 1872): 329.

44. Francisco Pi y Margall, "Extracto de la discusión sobre la Internacional," ibid., 1, no. 7 (1 June 1872): 291.

45. Fernando Garrido, "Extracto de la discusión sobre la Internacional," ibid., 1, no. 5 (10 May 1872): 207.

46. Ibid., 1, no. 5 (10 May 1872): 209–10. Garrido was interrupted by the Carlist Cándido Nocedal who claimed, "The pope is not a foreigner." Garrido responded: "Now I hear that the pope is not a foreigner. Next they'll tell me that he was born in Carabanchel [a small village south of Madrid]." See the speech of Fernando Garrido, 17 October 1871, *Diario de las Sesiones de Cortes,* 1872, 4:30.

47. Garrido, for instance, in 1871 had proposed in the Cortes the creation of a commission to investigate working and living conditions throughout Spain in preparation for profound social reforms. Questionnaires were printed, but the commission never carried out its investigations, probably because of the political instability of the revolutionary period. See the questionnaire in *Las clases obreras.*

48. Lorenzo, *El proletariado militante,* 88–92.

49. Ibid.; Alvarez Junco, *La ideología política,* 408–09, 377–448.

50. Alvarez Junco, *La ideología política,* 311–35.

51. "La manifestación abolicionista de Madrid," *El Abolicionista* (Madrid), 5, no. 10 (20 January 1873), in *El proceso abolicionista en Puerto Rico,* 1:423.

52. *La Revista Social* (Manresa), quoted in Izard, *Manufactureros, industriales y revolucionarios,* 173.

53. "La esclavitud de los negros en Cuba," *La Federación* 4, no. 176 (Barcelona, 28 December 1872).

54. For a comparison with the class divisions in British antislavery, see Drescher, "Cart Whip and Billy Roller," esp. 18.

55. Hunt, *The Family Romance,* 202.

56. On liberal gender ideology in nineteenth-century Spain, see Scanlon, *La pólemica femenista*, 30–77; Aldaraca, "'El angel del hogar'"; and Kirkpatrick, *Las Románticas*.

57. Moret y Prendergast, "Perjuicios que causa el proteccionismo a las clases obreras," 153.

58. These particular debates were occasioned by the publication of Jules Simon's *L'Ouvrière* (1861). See Scott, "'L'ouvrière!'"

59. Laureano Figuerola, "'¿Es justa y legítima la influencia que ejerce la industria moderna para arrancar a la mujer del hogar doméstico?" *Gaceta Economista* (Madrid), 1, no. 2 (June 1861): 127.

60. Moret's statement was was an exact echo of Jules Simon's verdict: "The woman who becomes a worker is no longer a woman." Quoted in Scott, "'L'Ouvrière,'" 155.

61. Segismundo Moret y Prendergast, "Del porvenir de las clases obreras de mujeres," *Gaceta Economista* (Madrid), 1, no. 3 (July 1861): 184–88. See also José Giraldez, "¿Es justa y legítima la influencia que ejerce la industria modern para arrancar a la mujer del hogar doméstico?" ibid., 1, no. 4 (August 1861): 292–93. Giraldez also argued that women workers' ignorance of housekeeping had negative consequences for the working population in general.

62. Luis María Pastor, "'¿Es justa y legítima la influencia que ejerce la industria moderna para arrancar a la mujer del hogar doméstico?," ibid., 1, no. 2 (June 1861): 128.

63. On the maleness of the individual in classical liberalism, see Pateman, *The Sexual Contract*.

64. See Smith, *Ladies of the Leisure Class*, for a discussion of French male liberals' anxieties over women's antiliberalism, particularly during the Third Republic.

65. Castro y Pajares, *Discurso que en la inauguración*, 3–4.

66. Ibid., 6. ("Society" is capitalized in the original.)

67. Ibid., 3.

68. Ibid., 8–10.

69. Ibid., 11–12.

70. See Moret y Prendergast, *Influencía de la madre;* and Pi y Margall, *La misión de la mujer en la sociedad.*

71. Sanromá, *Educación social de la mujer*, 10–11.

72. Ibid., 14–15.

73. Ibid., 20–21.

74. Labra y Cadrana, *La mujer y la legislación*, 21–24.

75. Ibid., 24.

76. Ibid., 29–30.

77. Ibid., 33.

78. See the discussion in Kirkpatrick, *Las Románticas*, of the ambiguities within midcentury liberal discourse concerning the relationship between the public and the private.

79. Saez de Melgar, *Memoria del Ateneo de Señoras*, 5–16.

80. Fernando de Castro, *Discurso que en la inauguración*, 8–9. Emphasis in the original.

81. Arenal, "A las mujeres," 418.

82. Ibid.

83. Cepero Bonilla, *Azúcar y abolicion;* Corwin, *Spain and the Abolition of Slavery in Cuba*, 107–71; Murray, *Odious Commerce*, 298–326; López-Ocón, *Biografía de "La América";* and Martínez-Fernández, *Torn between Empires*, 153–226.

84. See Labra y Cadrana, *La emancipación de los esclavos en los Estados-Unidos.*

85. For similar interpretations, see Rodríguez, "La idea y el movimiento antiesclavista en España"; and Gil Novales, "Abolicionismo y librecambio."

## Chapter 5. The Colonial Public Sphere

1. Drescher, "The Long Goodbye," 68. See also the conclusion to Blackburn, *The Overthrow of Colonial Slavery,* 517–50, on the politics of abolition during the "age of revolution."

2. See Davis, *The Problem of Slavery in the Age of Revolution* and "Reflections on Abolitionism and Ideological Hegemony"; Williams, *Capitalism and Slavery;* and Holt, "Explaining Abolition."

3. On the crisis of the 1860s see Scott, *Slave Emancipation in Cuba,* 45–62; Cepero Bonilla, *Azúcar y abolicion;* and Murray, *Odious Commerce,* 298–326.

4. See Habermas's discussion of the "bourgeois public sphere" and "public opinion" in *The Structural Transformation of the Public Sphere,* esp. parts 1–4.

5. Casanovas Codina, "Labor and Colonialism," chap. 4.

6. See Jiménez de Wagenheim, *El Grito de Lares;* Poyo, "Evolution of Cuban Separatist Thought" and *"With All and for the Good of All";* and Estrade, *Les ecrits de Betances.*

7. See Bergad, *Coffee,* 69; and Pérez, *Cuba: Between Reform and Revolution,* 86.

8. On slavery and the attitudes of sugar planters in Ponce, see Curet, "From Slave to 'Liberto.'"

9. See Murray, *Odious Commerce,* 298–99; Scott, *Slave Emancipation in Cuba,* 3–41; and Bergad, "The Economic Viability of Sugar Production."

10. See Murray, *Odious Commerce,* 298–326.

11. "Carta de José Luis Alfonso a José Antonio Saco, facha: Madrid 13 de Mayo de 1864," BNJM, CM/Alfonso, no. 32, emphasis in the original.

12. On Vega-Mar and O'Gavan's properties in Spain, see Angel Bahamonde Magro y José Gregorio Cayuela Fernández, "La creación de nobleza en Cuba durante el Siglo XIX," *Historia Social* 11 (fall 1991): 57–82, esp. 80.

13. See José Luis Alfonso a José Antonio Saco, Madrid, 28 May 1864, in *Medio siglo de historia colonial en Cuba,* ed. Fernández de Castro, 316–18.

14. "Carta de José Luis Alfonso a José Antonio Saco, fecha: Madrid, Abril 22 de 1864," BNJM, CM/Alfonso, no. 32. See Bahamonde and Cayuela, "La creación de nobleza en Cuba durante el Siglo XIX," on the politics of titles in nineteenth-century Cuba.

15. Conde de Vega-Mar, *Informe del excmo. Conde de Vega-Mar* (Madrid: T. Fortanet, 1868), 16–20. In AHN/U, leg. 3553, exp. 2.

16. See letters from Vega-Mar to the overseas minister, 16 October and 5 December 1868, in AHN/U, leg. 3553, exp. 5, nos. 8, 17.

17. As illustration, Alfonso told Saco that even the most decided slave traders *(negreros)* were turning to Chinese contract laborers. See "Carta de José Luis Alfonso a José Antonio Saco, fecha: Habana, Mayo 6 de 1865," BNJM, CM/Alfonso/ no. 32. Alfonso himself, while in Paris, inquired about recruiting laborers from French colonies in Cochin China. French experts informed him that the Cochin Chinese were too weak for plantation labor. In the same letter, he pondered the possiblity of importing contract laborers from the Philippines, another Spanish colony. See "Carta de José Luis Alfonso a José Antonio Saco, fecha: Paris, Diciembre 22 de 1866," BNJM, CM/Alfonso, no. 32.

18. "Carta de José Luis Alfonso a José Antonio Saco, fecha: Paris, Noviembre 26 de 1866," BNJM, CM/Alfonso, no. 32, emphasis in the original. On the trade in Yucatecan

Indians in the 1860s, see Estrade, "Los colonos yucatecos." Between 1847 and 1874, 125,000 Chinese contract laborers were brought to Cuba. See Scott, *Slave Emancipation in Cuba*, 29.

19. See Piqueras and Sebastià, *Agiotistas, negreros y partisanos*, 252, 286. On Serrano and Dulce's administrations in Cuba, see Murray, *Odious Commerce*, 309–14.

20. On politics and public life in Havana during the Serrano and Dulce administrations, see Casanovas Codina, "Labor and Colonialism," chap. 4.

21. On the reformist clique of *El Siglo*, see Cepero Bonilla, *Azúcar y abolición*, 85–116.

22. "Al Ministro de la Guerra y de Ultramar. Reservado." Havana, 20 de Junio de 1862. AHN/U, leg. 3551, exp. 2, no. 4.

23. "Se llama la atención sobre la discusión en los periódicos de la Peninsula de los asuntos referentes a esta Isla especialmente la esclavitud," Havana, 30 October 1863. AHN/U, leg. 3551, exp. 5, no. 2.

24. "Al Exmo. Sr. Presidente del Consejo de Ministros y Ministro de Ultramar." Havana, 14 May 1863. AHN/U, leg. 3552, exp. 8, no. 9.

25. Dulce, "Informe del Excmo. Sr. D. Domingo Dulce," *Información sobre reformas en Cuba y Puerto Rico*, 219.

26. Ibid., 223–24.

27. Francisco Serrano y Domínguez, "Contestación del Sr. General D. Francisco Serrano y Domínguez," *Información sobre reformas en Cuba y Puerto Rico*, 200–04.

28. On the Junta, see Corwin, *Spain and the Abolition of Slavery in Cuba*, 189–214.

29. For a list of the delegates, see ibid., 186.

30. The Cuban representatives were upset that the "social question," rather than economic or political reforms, was first on the agenda. See the letter from the head of Cuban delegation, José Morales Lemus, to Miguel de Aldama complaining of the government's duplicity: Madrid, 13 November 1866, in *El proceso abolicionista en Puerto Rico*, 2:27.

31. "Informe sobre la abolición inmediata de la esclavitud en la isla de Puerto Rico presentado en la Junta de Información sobre reformas ultramarinas el 10 de Abril de 1867 por los comisionados de la expresada isla Don Segundo Ruiz Belvis, Don José Julián Acosta y Don Francisco Mariano Quiñones," in *Boletín Histórico de Puerto Rico*, ed. Coll y Toste, 3:323–67. See the correspondence among Acosta, Quiñones, and Ruiz Belvis as they set their strategies before leaving Puerto Rico in Acosta y Quintero, *José J. Acosta y su tiempo*, 169–77.

32. José Morales Lemus to Miguel de Aldama, Madrid, 13 November 1866, *El proceso abolicionista en Puerto Rico*, 2:29.

33. On the Cuban proposal, see Corwin, *Spain and the Abolition of Slavery in Cuba*, 203–05.

34. Acosta y Quintero, *José J. Acosta y su tiempo*, 212–30.

35. See Sánchez-Albornoz, "El trasfondo económico de la Revolución"; and Fontana, *Cambio económico*, 99–145.

36. See Saco, "Réplica de D. José Antonio Saco a los Anexionistas que han impugnado sus Ideas sobre la Incorporación de Cuba en los Estados-Unidos," in *Obras*, 2:145.

37. See also Schmidt-Nowara, "'Spanish' Cuba."

38. On Spain and the Americas after independence, see Van Aken, *Pan-Hispanism*; Costeloe, *Response to Revolution*; López-Ocón, *Biografía de "La América"*; and Brading, *The First America*, 535–82.

39. See Fradera, "La importància de tenir colònies."

40. On Spain and Santo Domingo, see Martínez-Fernández, *Torn between Empires*, 208–22.

41. Saco had reached similar conclusions in the 1830s as he sought to counter Spain's

consolidation of the "second empire," though he characteristically remained silent on English antislavery (see "Paralelo entre la Isla de Cuba y algunas colonias inglesas"); see also Saco's comment on English colonialism made in the 1860s in "La política absolutista."

42. Bona, *Cuba, Santo Domingo y Puerto Rico,* 11.

43. Ibid., 41–45.

44. Ibid., 44.

45. Laureano Figuerola, "El tema relativo a las reformas coloniales," *Gaceta Economista* (Madrid), 2, no. 11 (March 1862): 212, emphasis in the original.

46. See Maluquer de Motes, "El problema de la esclavitud"; Whitney, "The Political Economy of Abolition"; and Cubano Iguina, *El hilo en el laberinto.*

47. On the strategic use of national identity, see Sahlins, *Boundaries,* 291; Klor de Alva, "The Postcolonization of the (Latin) American Experience"; and Appadurai, *Modernity at Large,* 12–16, 139–57.

48. Agüero, *Biografías de cubanos distinguidos,* 1:83, emphasis in the original.

49. Antonio Angulo y Heredia, "A los Cubanos. Nuestros propósitos y nuestros principios sobre la cuestión de Cuba," *Revista Ibérica* 6, no. 2 (30 January 1863): 92.

50. See Fradera, "Why Were Spain's Special Overseas Laws Never Enacted?," esp. 339–41.

51. Eduardo Asquerino, "Nuestro pensamiento," *La América* (Madrid), 1, no. 2 (24 March 1857).

52. Ibid.

53. Castelar, "La unión de España y América," *La América.* Castelar's depiction of Anglo-Saxon, particularly North American, particularism and materialism was similar to the famous critique made by the Uruguayan writer José E. Rodó in *Ariel* (1900). In fact, Charles Hale suggests that Rodó wrote *Ariel* partly in response to the finale of the Spanish-Cuban-American War ("Political and Social Ideas," in *Latin America,* ed. Bethell, 272–74).

54. Bona, *Cuba, Santo Domingo y Puerto Rico,* 46.

55. Luis María Pastor, "Sobre reformas coloniales," *Gaceta Economista* (Madrid), 2, no. 12 (April 1862): 281.

56. See Fradera, "Why Were Spain's Special Overseas Laws Never Enacted?"

57. "Exposición presentada al Senado por varios dueños de ingenios con esclavos en la Isla de Cuba," *Revista Hispano-Americana* (Madrid), 3, no. 33 (12 April 1866). See Julio Vizcarrondo on the slave trade, cited in Murray, *Odious Commerce,* 320.

58. Armas y Céspedes, *De la esclavitud en Cuba.*

59. Francisco de Armas y Céspedes, "La inmigración en Cuba." *Revista Hispano-Americana* 3 (27 July 1866), supplement. 4.

60. Calixto Bernal, "La quinta y la inmigración blanca en las Antillas españolas," *Revista Hispano-Americana* (Madrid), 2 (27 December 1865): 130.

61. Ibid.

62. Antonio Angulo y Heredia, "Movimiento reformista en Cuba.—El primer paso de la reforma," *Revista Hispano-Americana* 2 (12 October 1865): 407, emphasis in the original.

63. On "hybridity," see Hall, "When Was the 'Post-colonial'?," 249–51.

64. See the society's announcement of intentions in "Prospecto," *El Abolicionista Español* (Madrid), 1 (15 August 1865).

65. See Corwin, *Spain and the Abolition of Slavery in Cuba,* 159.

66. For a discussion of women and antislavery in the British case, see Midgley, *Women against Slavery.*

67. "Expresivo y respetuoso mensaje dirigido a las señoras de Madrid por las que

constituyen la Sociedad de Amigos de los Negros en Birmingham," *El Abolicionista Español* (Madrid), 1, no. 5 (15 November 1865): 73.

68., Ibid., 74.

69. Sociedad Abolicionista Española, "Al Congreso," Madrid, 17 May 1866, AHN/U, leg. 3552, exp. 9, no. 20.

70. Luis María Pastor, "Al Senado. Proyecto de ley sobre la abolición de la esclavitud," Madrid, 27 May 1867, AHN/U, leg. 3552, exp. 9.

71. Julio Vizcarrondo, "Sociedad Libre de Economía Política de Madrid. Año octavo— 1864 a 1865. Novena reunión, celebrada el 20 de febrero de 1865," *El Abolicionista Español* (Madrid), 1, no. 3 (15 September 1865): 50.

72. Ibid.

73. The belief in the universality of the market and its effects was central to British and North American antislavery and to the policies of the post-emancipation administrations. See Holt, "'An Empire over the Mind.'"

74. See, for instance, "Prospecto," *El Abolicionista Español* (Madrid), 1 (15 August 1865).

75. Ferrer de Couto was a Spanish military official who published the newspaper *La Crónica* in New York as a counter to Antillean separatist activity in the United States. During the U.S. war he published several proslavery tracts, including *Los negros en sus diversos estados.*

76. Laureano Figuerola, "Sociedad Libre de Economía Política de Madrid. Décima cuarta reunión celebrada el 20 de Mayo de 1865," *El Abolicionista Español* (Madrid), 2, no. 9 (15 March 1866): 162–63.

77. Sánchez Ruano, "Sociedad Libre de Economía Política de Madrid. Décima reunión celebrada el 8 de Marzo de 1865," ibid., 1, no. 3 (15 September 1865): 52.

78. "El motín en la isla de Jamaica," ibid., 1 (15 November 1865); and "Los negros de la insurreción cubana," ibid. (1 November 1872). See also Labra y Cadrana, *La emancipación de los esclavos en los Estados Unidos* and "El negro Santos de Santo Domingo." On British responses to Morant Bay, see Hall, "The Economy of Intellectual Prestige"; and Holt, *The Problem of Freedom,* chaps. 8–9.

79. See Fradera, "Why Were Spain's Special Overseas Laws Never Enacted?," 339–41.

80. See Holt, "'An Empire over the Mind,'" on the relationship between the class and racial ideologies of British and North American "emancipators."

81. Garrido, *Historia de las clases trabajadoras. I. El esclavo,* 191.

82. Labra y Cadrana, *La abolición de la esclavitud en las Antillas españolas,* 72.

83. Ibid., 54–61. See also Ladra y Cadrana, *La brutalidad de los negros.*

84. Labra y Cadrana, "El negro Santos de Santo Domingo," 87.

85. See Scott, *Slave Emancipation in Cuba,* 45–62; Fradera, "Why Were Spain's Special Overseas Laws Never Enacted?"; Schmidt-Nowara, "'Spanish' Cuba"; Ibarra, *Ideología mambisa;* and Ferrer, "To Make a Free Nation."

86. Drescher, "Brazilian Abolition in Comparative Perspective," 34–36. Drescher states, "Spain was the most extreme example of the 'continental' variant of abolitionism" (36).

87. Ibid., 36–37.

88. Here I am following works that stress the persistence of slave labor in Puerto Rico against earlier interpretations that held that slavery never took firm root in the island's economy. For the latter view, see Díaz Soler, *Historia de la esclavitud negra en Puerto Rico,* esp. 373–75; for the former, see Curet, "From Slave to 'Liberto'"; and Scarano, *Sugar and Slavery in Puerto Rico.*

89. On the influence of regional demographic and economic changes on Brazilian abolitionism, see Drescher, "Brazilian Abolition," 25–33. See also Conrad, *The Destruction of Brazilian Slavery;* and Scott, "Defining the Boundaries of Freedom."

90. See Drescher, *Capitalism and Antislavery,* 2–3.

91. See Williams, *Capitalism and Slavery;* Davis, *The Problem of Slavery in the Age of Revolution;* and Holt, *The Problem of Freedom.*

92. Tomich's work on the Atlantic world's uneven transition to free labor helped me to formulate this argument. See "The 'Second Slavery'" and "World Slavery and Caribbean Capitalism."

93. Saco was the greatest admirer of the Canadian model. See "Paralelo entre la isla de Cuba y algunas colonias inglesas"; see also Bona, *Cuba, Santo Domingo y Puerto Rico.*

94. On British and North American emancipators' gloomy responses to the transition to free labor, see Holt, "'An Empire over the Mind'" and *The Problem of Freedom,* 263–309.

95. Blackburn, *The Overthrow of Colonial Slavery,* 522.

96. On the parties involved in the revolutionary movement, see Carr, *Spain,* 290–304. See also Hennessey, *The Federal Republic in Spain;* Sánchez-Albornoz, "El trasfondo económico de la Revolución"; and Artola, *La burguesía revolucionaria,* 363–97.

97. Antonio Angulo y Heredia to José Antonio Saco, Madrid, 24 March 1866, in *Medio siglo de historia colonial en Cuba,* ed. Fernández de Castro, 343.

## Chapter 6. Revolution and Slavery, 1868–1870

1. See Maluquer de Motes, "El problema de la esclavitud"; Jiménez de Wagenheim, *El Grito de Lares;* and Guerra y Sánchez, *La Guerra de los Diez Años.*

2. On the balance of the revolutionary forces, see Hennessey, *The Federal Republic in Spain;* Carr, *Spain;* Artola, *La burguesía revolucionaria,* 363–97; and Navarro, "De la esperanza a la frustración." On Serrano and the revolution, see Espadas Burgos, *Alfonso XII.* On the colonial dimension of the revolution, see Piqueras Arenas, *La revolución democrática.* On the broader Euopean context of the September Revolution, see Hobsbawm, *The Age of Capital;* and Eley, "Liberalism, Europe, and the bourgeoisie."

3. See Guerra y Sánchez, *La Guerra de los Diez Años.*

4. On slave participation in the war, see Scott, *Slave Emancipation in Cuba,* 45–62; Robert, "Slavery and Freedom in the Ten Years' War"; and Ferrer, "To Make a Free Nation," 15–127. On resistance in the west to the revolutions, see Guerra y Sánchez, *La Guerra de los Diez Años,* 1:169–212; Cepero Bonilla, *Azúcar y abolición,* 203–20; and Quiroz, "Loyalist Overkill."

5. See Jiménez de Wagenheim, *El Grito de Lares;* and Bergad, *Coffee,* 134–44.

6. On the attitudes of Ponce slaveowners in 1868, see    Curet, "From Slave to 'Liberto,'" 254–60; see also Acosta y Quintero, *José J. Acosta y su tiempo,* 277–80.

7. My thinking on revolution and antislavery has been shaped by James, *The Black Jacobins;* and Blackburn, *The Overthrow of Colonial Slavery.*

8. Corwin, *Spain and the Abolition of Slavery in Cuba,* 217–18.

9. See "Al Gobierno Provisional," Madrid, 3 October 1868, AHN/U, leg. 3553, exp. 5, no. 1. The petitoners included Labra; the Economists Joaquín María Sanromá, Félix de Bona, José Echegaray, Luis María Pastor, and Gabriel Rodríguez; and the Puerto Ricans Alejandro Tapía y Rivera, José and Julio de Vizcarrondo, and Eugenio de Hostos.

10. "Puerto Riqueños residentes en esta capital," Madrid, 15 October 1868, AHN/U, leg. 3553, exp. 5, no. 5.

11. See the list of petitions favoring caution from Santander, Asturias, Vigo, Palma de Mallorca, Villanueva y Geltrú *[sic]*, Valencia, and Barcelona. "Qué antes de someter a la deliberación de las Cortes la cuestión de esclavitud se [illegible word] a los propietarios grandes y pequeños sobre la manera de extinguirla," AHN/U, leg. 3553, exp. 2, no. 1.

12. See Vega-Mar's letter to the overseas minister, Madrid, 16 October 1868, AHN/U, leg. 3553, exp. 5, no. 8.

13. See Corwin, *Spain and the Abolition of Slavery in Cuba*, 218.

14. See the petitions, dated between December 1868 and February 1869, in AHN/U, leg. 3553, exps. 2–4.

15. Janué i Miret, *La Junta Revolucionaria de Barcelona*, 135.

16. Ibid., 109.

17. Saco, *L'Esclavage à Cuba*, 11–12.

See also Valiente, *Réformes dan les isles de Cuba et Porto-Rico*, for a similar position. Valiente, like Saco, had been a representative of the short-lived Santiago regime of 1836 and later served on the Junta de Información.

18. "Carta firmada de N. Azcárate a José Morales Lemus, fecha: Madrid, Mayo 13 de 1868," ANC, Donativos y Remisiónes, leg. 150, no. 10-83.

19. Azcárate, *Votos de un cubano*, 9. *La Voz del Siglo* was a newspaper founded by Azcárate and Segismundo Moret y Predergast in 1868.

20. Azcárate, *Votos de un cubano*, 14.

21. See Bernal, *Vindicación*. See also Betancourt y Betancourt, *Las dos banderas* for a similar interpretation of the Cuban conflict. For Betancourt, the Spaniards of the west were the true obstacle to peace.

22. "Carta de Calixto Bernal a José Antonio Echeverría, fecha: Madrid, 27 de Septiembre de 1874," BNJM, CM/Ponce, no. 249.

23. See Tomich, "The 'Second Slavery,'" 103–17; Hobsbawm, *The Age of Capital;* and Bairoch, "European Trade Policy," 1–51.

24. See Maluquer de Motes, "La burgesia catalana"; Whitney, "The Political Economy of Abolition"; and Scott, *Slave Emancipation in Cuba*, 284.

25. See Tortella Casares, *Banking, Railroads, and Industry in Spain*, 506–50; and Costas Comesaña, *Apogeo del liberalismo*, 83–127.

26. "Qué antes de someter a la deliberación de las Cortes la cuestión de esclavitud se [illegible word] a los propietarios grandes y pequeños sobre la manera de extinguirla," AHN/U, leg. 3553, exp. 2, no. 1.

27. "Al Gobierno Provisional de la Nacion," Barcelona, October 1868, AHN/U, leg. 3553, exp. 5, no. 3.

28. On the Fomento, see Izard, *Manufactureros, industriales y revolucionarios*, 223–53.

29. Gräell, *Historia del Fomento del Trabajo Nacional*, 296. Izard argues that Gräell and other protectionists greatly exaggerated the cross-class nature of Catalan resistance to free trade during the September Revolution (*Manufactureros, industriales y revolucionarios*, 221–22).

30. Güell y Ferrer, "Dos palabras al Señor Moret" [1869], in *Escritos económicos*, 894, emphasis in the original.

31. Güell y Ferrer, "Rebelión cubana" [1871], in ibid., 986.

32. Ibid., 1002.

33. See Scott, *Slave Emancipation in Cuba*, 46–48; and Guerra y Sánchez, *La Guerra de los Diez Años*, 1:305–32.

34. See Bergad, *Cuban Rural Society,* 183–89.

35. On the west and the Volunteers, see Guerra y Sánchez, *La Guerra de los Diez Años,* 1:169–212; and Quiroz, "Loyalist Overkill." On Concha, the Volunteers, and conservative Spanish slave traders in the 1850s, see Cayuela Fernández, *Bahía de Ultramar,* 219–41.

36. On Aldama and western reformers, see Cepero Bonilla, *Azúcar y abolición,* 229–42; and esp. Dionisio Poey Baró, *La entrada de los Aldamistas.*

37. "Carta de Miguel Aldama a Domingo Dulce, fecha: Ingenio Santa Rosa, Enero 27, 1869," BNJM, CM/Ponce, no.445.

38. "Carta de Miguel de Aldama a José Morales Lemus, fecha: Ingenio Santa Rosa, Unión, Febrero 18 de 1869," BNJM, CM/Aldama, no.1.

39. Aldama, Morales Lemus, and other creoles who had supported the reformism of the 1860s left for the United States. Though they nominally supported the revolution in the east, they also remained open to annexation or reconciliation with Spain. See Cepero Bonilla, *Azúcar y abolición,* 221–76; and Poey Baró, *La entrada de los Aldamistas.*

40. On the social origins of the Grito de Lares, see Bergad, *Coffee,* 134–44; on the planning and implementation of the rebellion, see Jiménez de Wagenheim, *El Grito de Lares.* Also on the coffee regions of Lares and Utuado, see Picó, *Amargo café.*

41. See Acosta y Quintero, *José J. Acosta y su tiempo,* 231–87.

42. On the centrality of slave labor in the Puerto Rican sugar sector, see Ramos Mattei, *La hacienda azucarera,* 96–106.

43. Letter from Gustavo Cabrera to J. J. Acosta, 21 November 1868, in Acosta y Quintero, *Jose J. Acosta y su tiempo,* 377–78, emphasis in the original.

44. Letter from J. J. Acosta to Gustavo Cabrera, 27 November 1868, in ibid., 380.

45. See for instance Acosta's arguments in "Cuestión de brazos para el cultivo actual de las tierras de Puerto Rico" [1853], in *Colección de artículos publicados.*

46. See Padial's speech in Baldorioty de Castro, *Interpelación del diputado Don Luis Padial y sus consecuencias.*

47. See Corwin, *Spain and the Abolition of Slavery in Cuba,* 241–43.

48. "Junta de Reformas de Puerto Rico," 31 October 1869, AHN/U, leg. 5095, exp. 5, no. 20.

49. Quoted in Baldorioty de Castro, *Interpelación del diputado Don Luis Padial y sus consecuencias,* 16–17.

50. See Scott, *Slave Emancipation in Cuba,* 64; and Corwin, *Spain and the Abolition of Slavery in Cuba,* 245–47.

51. See Scott, *Slave Emancipation in Cuba,* 77–78, 91; Corwin, *Spain and the Abolition of Slavery in Cuba,* 255–72; and Figueroa, "Facing Freedom," 175–80.

52. See the speech of Emilio Castelar in *Diario de Sesiónes de las Cortes Constituyentes,* 1870, 14:8984.

## Chapter 7. Abolitionism and a New Imperial Order

1. Labra y Cadrana and Rodríguez, *Una sesión de la Tertulia Radical de Madrid,* 32, emphasis in the original.

2. On the maneuverings of the Abolitionist Society and the Puerto Rican delegation in the Cortes, see "La cuestión de la esclavitud en el año 1872," *El Abolicionista Española* 2, no. 9, Madrid (10 January 1872); and Rafael María de Labra's eulogy of Joaquín María Sanromá in *Velada celebrada en honor de D. Joaquín Ma. Sanromá.* On the polarization of the revolu-

tion, see Espadas Burgos, *Alfonso XII;* and Riquer, "El conservadurisme polític català."

3. On Ruiz Zorilla, see Alvarez Junco, *El Emperador del Paralelo,* 91–131. On Radical and Federal Republican ideology, see Hennessey, *The Federal Republic in Spain;* Pérez Ledesma, "'Ricos y pobres'"; and Navarro, "De la esperanza a la frustración."

4. Blackburn's discussion of the link between antislavery and revolutionary political legitimacy has influenced my interpretation of the September Revolution; see *The Overthrow of Colonial Slavery,* esp. 522.

5. On politics in Puerto Rico during the September Revolution, see Díaz Soler, *Historia de la esclavitud negra,* 289–371; Cubano Iguina, *El hilo en el laberinto;* and Scarano, *Puerto Rico,* 443–53.

6. Captain General Gabriel Baldrich al Ministro de Ultramar, AHN/U, San Juan de Puerto Rico, 10 March 1871, leg. 5113, exp. 48, no. 4.

7. See the overseas minister and Baldrich's criticism of Spanish conservatives in "Instrucciónes para el Gobernador superior civil de Puerto-Rico, Mariscal de campo Don Gabriel Baldrich," Madrid, 13 May 1870, AHN/U, leg. 5113, exp. 46, no. 1; and Baldrich to the Ministro de Ultramar, San Juan de Puerto Rico, 25 July 1871, AHN/U, leg. 5113, exp. 3, no. 1. See also Baldrich's outrage when conseratives undermined the parliamentary elections that he had rigged to give equal representation to all Puerto Rican parties. See AHN/U, leg. 5113, exp. 5, no. 15.

8. See "La central de Ponce," *El Progreso,* Puerto Rico, 3 no. 11 (26 January 1872); and "La central en la costa del Norte," ibid., 3, no. 14, 2 February 1872. See also Acosta's arguments made before the revolution in his annotated edition of Abbad y Lasierra, *Historia geográfica,* esp. 330–33. On *centrales* in Puerto Rico, see Curet, "From Slave to 'Liberto,'" 275; Ramos Mattei, "Technical Innovations and Social Change"; and Martínez-Vergne, *Capitalism in Colonial Puerto Rico.*

9. "La central de Ponce," *El Progreso.*

10. Ibid.

11. See "Bibliotecas populares," *El Progreso* 3, no. 57 (15 May 1872); "Centros de obreros," ibid., 3, no. 16 (7 February 1872); or "La cuestión del trabajo en Puerto-Rico," ibid., 2, no. 134 (12 November 1871). The *Almanaque Aguinaldo,* an annual publication in the 1850s and 1860s, also offers an interesting collection of writings on work and morality by abolitionists like Baldorioty de Castro and Acosta.

12. "Centro de obreros," *El Progreso.*

13. Carta de Manuel Fernández Juncos a José Pablo Morales, Vega-Baja, 10 April 1873, in AGPR, Colecciónes Partiuclares, Colección José Pablo Morales Otero, CP-33, exp. 98, caja 2. See also "Nuestros diputados en Madrid," *El Progreso* 3, no. 151 (22 December 1872).

14. Labra y Cadrana, *La abolición de la esclavitud en el órden económico,* 231.

15. Ibid., 233, emphasis in the original.

16. See for instance, Labra y Cadrana, *La abolición de la esclavitud en las Antillas españolas,* 102–05; and *La abolición y la Sociedad Abolicionista Española,* 36–37.

17. Garrido, *Historia de las clases trabajadores,* 1:183, emphasis in the original.

18. See the speech of Emilio Castelar, in Spain, Cortes, *Diario de las Sesiones de las Cortes Constituyentes (1870),* 14:8990.

19. Labra y Cadrana, *La abolición de la esclavitud en las Antillas españolas,* 33.

20. Labra y Cadrana, *Carta que a varios electores,* 15–16. See also "Los negros de la insurreción cubana," *El Abolicionista Española* 1, no. 3, Madrid (1 November 1872).

21. See the speech of Emilio Castelar in Spain, Cortes, *Diario de las Sesiones de la Cortes*

*Constituyentes (1870)*, 14:898l.

22. For a representative denunciation of the colonial status quo during the September Revolution, see Sanromá, *La esclavitud en Cuba.*

23. Ladra y Cadrana and Rodríguez, *Una sesión de la Tertulia Radical de Madrid,* 11–12.

24. On the Liga Nacional, see Maluquer de Motes, "El problema de la esclavitud y la revolución de 1868"; Espadas Burgos, *Alfonso XII;* and Riquer, "El conservadurisme polític català."

25. Maluquer de Motes, "El problema de la esclavitud y la Revolución de 1868."

26. On Manzanedo, see Bahamonde and Cayuela, *Hacer las Américas,* 201–22.

27. On Llorente, see Piqueras Arenas, *La revolución democrática,* 391–92.

28. On the pro-Alfonsist coalition, see Espadas Burgos, *Alfonso XII,* 265–398; and Varela Ortega, *Los amigos políticos,* 20–85.

29. See the criticism of López de Ayala made by Labra y Cadrana, *La cuestión colonial;* and the Abolitionist Society's criticism of Serrano, López de Ayala, and the Liga, "El primer tropiezo," *El Abolicionista* (Madrid), 1, no. 7 (20 December 1872): 50.

30. "Exposición que al gobierno de S. M. dirige el Centro Hispano-Ultramarino de Madrid," Madrid, 25 November 1872, AHN/U, leg. 3554, exp. 1, no. 10, 3.

31. "Al pueblo español," Madrid, 8 December 1872, AHN/U, leg. 3554, exp. 1, no. 33.

32. See *Anti-Slavery Reporter* 18 (January 1873), 97.

33. See the speech of Cristino Mártos in *Diario de Sesiones de las Cortes,* 12 December 1872, 329.

34. "Resoluciónes adoptadas por los señores delegados de los Centros Hispano-ultramarinos en la junta celebrada en Madrid a 14 de Octubre de 1872," AHN/U, leg. 3554, exp. 1, no. 11. Also represented were Cádiz, Zaragoza, Málaga, Bilbao, and Cáceres.

35. See for instance Güell y Ferrer, "Rebelión cubana" [1871], in *Escritos económicos.* On the defense of slavery in the U.S. South, see Genovese, *The Slaveholders' Dilemma.*

36. See "Esposiciónes contra las reformas en las Antillas," AHN/U, leg. 3554, exp. 1, no. 7.

37. "La Comision de Propietarios, Comerciantes e Industriales de Valladolid," Valladolid, 8 December 1872, AHN/U, leg. 3554, exp. 1, no. 31.

38. See García Balaña, "Tradició liberal i política colonial a Catalunya," 94–102.

39. Círculo Hispano Ultramarino de Barcelona, Barcelona, 2 December 1872, AHN/U, leg. 3554, exp. 1, no. 18.

40. "Centro Hispano-ultramarino de Barcelona," AHN/U, leg. 3554, exp. 1, no. 18; and "Centro Hispano-Ultramarino de Villanueva y Geltru," leg. 3554, exp. 3, no. 14.

41. IACSI and Instituto Industrial de Cataluña, AHN/U, leg. 3554, exp. 3, nos. 8–9. Fomento de la Producción Nacional, AHN/U, leg. 3554, exp. 1, no. 44.

42. "Casino Artesano de Villanueva y Geltrú," Villanueva y Geltrú, 3 December 1872, AHN/U, leg. 3554, exp. 3, no. 12.

43. Maluquer de Motes, "Inmigración y comercio catalan," 167–68.

44. "Propietanos, fabricantes, navieros, comerciantes, industriales vecinos de Barcelona," Barcelona, 5 December 1872, AHN/U, leg. 3554, exp. 3, no. 7.

45. García Balaña, "Tradició liberal i política colonial a Catalunya," 94–102, and *passim.*

46. Letter from Pedro Bosch y Labrús, Secretario del Fomento de la Producción Nacional, to Víctor Balaguer, Barcelona, 19 April 1870. Biblioteca-Museu Balaguer, Vilanova i la Geltrú, Epistolari de Víctor Balaguer, 1870/396.

47. "La Junta Directiva del Fomento de la Producción Nacional," Barcelona, 12 Decem-

ber 1872, AHN/U, leg. 3554, exp. 1, no. 44.

48. Sanromá, *La esclavitud en Cuba*, 7, emphasis in the original.

49. See the speech of Cristino Mártos, *Diario de Sesiónes de las Cortes*, 11 December 1872, 306.

50. See Corwin, *Spain and the Abolition of Slavery in Cuba*, 285–87.

51. See the abolitionist petitions in AHN/U, leg. 3553, exp. 7.

52. See Drescher, "Cart Whip and Billy Roller," on the complex uses of antislavery language and symbolism in Great Britain. Drescher has argued that workers supported antislavery so as to protest their own "wage slavery." In Spain, antislavery arose not as a protest to proletarianization but to political subordination.

53. "Manifestaciónes antireformistas y reformistas en Barcelona," *El Abolicionista Español* 1, no. 8 (30 December 1872): 67–68.

54. "La manifestación abolicionista de Madrid," ibid., 2, no. 10 (20 January 1873): 83–84.

55. "Manifestaciónes abolicionistas. Sevilla," ibid., 2, no. 12 (10 February 1873): 105–06.

56. See Cruz Monclova, *Historia de Puerto Rico (Siglo XIX)*, 2:268–77.

57. The Spanish state did not complete the indemnification until 1890, thus mitigating the impact of the capital that slaveowners had counted on. On abolition and indemnification, see Diaz Soler, *Historia de la esclavitud negra*, 349–71.

58. Cruz Monclova, *Historia de Puerto Rico (Siglo XIX)*, 2:282; and Fradera, "Why Were Spain's Special Overseas Laws Never Enacted?"

59. See Casanovas Codina, "Labor and Colonialism in Cuba," 212–23; see also "La Sociedad Abolicionista de Cuba," *El Abolicionista* (Madrid) 2, no. 32 (10 November 1873), 215.

60. On the period of the republic in Puerto Rico, see Cruz Monclova, *Historia de Puerto Rico (Siglo XIX)*, 2:257–373; Díaz Soler, *Historia de la esclavitud negra*, 315–48; and Figueroa, "Facing Freedom," chap. 4.

61. Primo to Ministro de Ultramar, 26 July 1873, AHN/U, leg. 5113, exp. 23, no. 2.

62. See "Reservado. Da cuenta de organización militar e indica la conveniencia de organizar la milicia ciudadana," 2 Septembrer 1873, AHN/U, leg. 5103, exp. 64, no. 11.

63. See "Hace referencia a su contestación al telegrama sobre entrega de armas a los naturales del país," 3 January 1874, AHN/U, leg. 5103, exp. 64, no. 14. Moreover, in 1870, the Spanish government had abolished the requirement of "limpieza de sangre" for holding public office. See Díaz Soler, *Historia de la esclavitud negra*, 300–01.

64. The list of deputies during the First Republic can be found in the index to *Diario de Sesiones de las Cortes Constituyentes*, 4:169. See also "La abolición en Cuba," *El Progreso* (San Juan) 4, no. 95 (10 August 1873).

65. See for instance Manuel Corchado's urging of the Minister of Ultramar to submit legislation concerning immediate slave emancipation in Cuba, 22 August 1873, no. 74, *Diario de Sesiones de las Cortes Constituyentes*, 3:1783–84; and the petitions sent by the Abolitionist Society, 16 June 1873, no. 15, ibid., 1:166; and 19 July 1873, appendix to no. 44, ibid., 2:2. See also "A las Cortes Constituyentes," *El Abolicionista* (Madrid) 2, no. 19 (11 June 1873): 157–58.

66. See the session of 28 June 1873, no. 26, ibid., 1:398–99.

67. See the session of 26 July 1873, no. 50, ibid., 2:952–53.

68. See the session of 17 de Setiembre de 1873, no. 95, ibid., 4:2331–32.

69. On the collapse of the Republic, see Carr, *Spain*, 336–42.

70. See Espadas Burgos, *Alfonso XII*, 301–98; and Varela Ortega, *Los amigos políticos*, 22–85.

71. Blackburn, *The Overthrow of Colonial Slavery*, 522.

72. Ibid., 161–264.

73. On Cuban and Puerto Rican slaveowners, see Scott, *Slave Emancipation in Cuba*, 63–124; Bergad, *Cuban Rural Society*, 183–89; and Curet, "From Slave to 'Liberto,'" 226–60. On slave participation in the Cuban insurgency, see Scott, *Slave Emancipation in Cuba*, 45–62; Robert, "Slavery and Freedom in the Ten Years' War"; and Ferrer, "To Make a Free Nation," 15–172.

74. See Díaz Soler, *Historia de la esclavitud negra*, 300–01. See also the discussion of *limpieza de sangre* in Martínez-Alier, *Marriage, Class and Colour in Nineteenth-Century Cuba*, 71–81.

75. See also Ferrer, "To Make a Free Nation," 15–268, on the struggles over the racial boundaries of the Cuban nation set off by the Ten Years' War.

76. In addition to Blackburn's *The Overthrow of Colonial Slavery*, the following works have helped me formulate the relationship between colonial slavery and metropolitan conceptions of liberty: Drescher, "Cart Whip and Billy Roller," passim; James, *The Black Jacobins*; and Davis, *The Problem of Slavery in the Age of Revolution*.

77. See Gupta and Ferguson, "Beyond 'Culture,'" 6.

78. Hall, "When Was 'the Post-Colonial'?," 242–60; Cooper, "Race, Ideology, and the Perils of Comparative History"; and Cooper and Stoler, "Between Metropole and Colony."

## Conclusion

1. "A nuestros colaboradores, corresponsales y suscritores," *La América* 20, no. 1, Madrid (8 February 1879).

2. Gabriel Rodríguez, "Prólogo," in *Cataluña y la cuestión arancelaria*, iii.

3. On politics and economic change in the Restoration, see Kern, *Liberals, Reformers, and Caciques;* Varela Ortega, *Los amigos políticos;* Carr, *Spain*, 347–563; Serrano Sanz, "El proteccionismo"; Palomas and Bravo, "Víctor Balaguer"; and Pan-Montojo, *Más se perdió en Cuba*. On late nineteenth-century Europe, see Hobsbawm, *The Age of Empire*, esp. chap. 2, for a discussion of protectionism; Schumpeter, *Imperialism and Social Classes;* Mayer, *The Persistence of the Old Regime;* Schorske, *Fin-de-siècle Vienna*, esp. 116–80; and Eley, *Reshaping the German Right*.

4. Gabriel Rodríguez, "Cobden en España," *La América* 21, no. 2, Madrid (28 January 1880).

5. For example, see Labra y Cadrana, "A mis electores de Cuba y Puerto-Rico."

6. See Scott, *Slave Emancipation in Cuba*, 127–40.

7. See ibid., 194, 127–97. On the legislative aspect of the *patronato* and the role of abolitionist deputies in the Cortes, see Corwin, *Spain and the Abolition of Slavery in Cuba*, chap. 16; and García Mora, "Tras la revolución."

8. See Scott, "Defining the Boundaries of Freedom," 83, 85–86.

9. On the restructuring of the Cuban sugar industry, see Scott, *Slave Emancipation in Cuba*, 127–278; and Bergad, *Cuban Rural Society*, 263–302. On the new political and military possibilities wrought by emancipation, see Scott, *Slave Emancipation in Cuba*, 287–93; Ibarra, *Ideología mambisa;* Casanovas Codina, "Labor and Colonialism in Cuba," chs. 6 and 7; Helg, *Our Rightful Share;* and Ferrer, "To Make a Free Nation," chaps. 5–7.

10. See "Voto particular de Nicolás Azcárate," Consejo de Administración, La Habana, 8 August 1884, AHN/U, leg. 4926, exp. 141.

11. On the Partido Democrático and Cuban antislavery after Zanjón, see Casanovas Codina, "Labor and Colonialism," 240–68. See also the biography by Azcárate's grandson, Rafael Azcárate Rosell, *Nicolás Azcárate, el reformista*.

12. See Azcárate, *Votos de un cubano*. See also his letter to José Morales Lemus, Madrid, 13 May 1868, in ANC, Donativos y Remisiónes, leg. 150, no. 10-83.

13. "Da cuenta de haber disuelto la Diputación y ayuntamientos, nombrando las personas que deben constituir estas corporaciónes," 11 February 1874, AHN/U, leg. 5113, exp. 20.

14. "Trata sobre la creación de un monumento conmemoratorio de la abolición de la esclavitud en Puerto Rico," 14 May 1880, AHMP, Ayuntamiento, Secretaría, Obras públicas, Proyecto, monumentos, 1880–1919; caja S-320-1; exp. 1.

15. See letters from Antonio Alfau y Baralt to the mayor of Ponce, Madrid, 18 and 28 May 1882, in AHMP, caja S-320-1, exp. 1.

16. See letters from Rafael María de Labra, Madrid, 12 May and 18 June 1881, AHMP, caja S-320-1, segunda pieza, nos. 202 and 261.

17. See letter from R. B. López, Presidente, Casino de Mayagüez, 4 October 1881, in AHMP, caja S-320-1, segunda pieza, no. 279. On Ramón Méndez y Quiñones and the nineteenth-century literature on the *gíbaro,* see Pedreira, "La actualidad del jíbaro."

18. On Sanz's administration, Cruz Monclova, *Historia de Puerto Rico (siglo XIX),* 2:413–40; and Gómez Acevedo, *Sanz, promotor de la conciencia separatista.* Sanz received his title in 1883. See the personal dossier of José Laureano Sanz y Posse, Archivo Militar, Segovia.

19. See the list of those to receive honors in AHN/U, leg. 5106, exps. 36–48.

20. See "Memoria de su mando," 2 December 1875, AHN/U, leg. 5113, exp. 28, no. 8.

21. Ibid.

22. On the Autonomist Party and its origins, see Náter Vázquez, "Los autonomismos"; and Scarano, *Puerto Rico,* chaps. 18–19.

23. On the events of 1887, see Cruz Monclova, *Historia de Puerto Rico (siglo XIX),* 3:78–176; and Brau, *Historia de Puerto Rico,* 253–55. On the social and economic background of creole and Spanish conflicts in the 1880s and 1890s, see Cubano Iguina, *El hilo en el laberinto,* 136–44.

24. On the disagreements between creole and Spanish liberals over colonial reforms during the Restoration, see Náter Vázquez, "Los autonomismos," 148–51; and García Mora, "El Ateneo de Madrid." See also García Mora, "Tras la revolución."

25. On the Republican parties during the Restoration, see Duarte, *El republicanisme català;* and Alavarez Junco, *El Emperador del Paralelo.*

26. Letter from A. Corton to Rafael María de Labra, San Juan, 10 April 1891, Labra family archive, Madrid.

27. See Dietz, *Economic History of Puerto Rico,* 27. On coffee in Puerto Rico, see Picó, *Amargo café;* and Bergad, *Coffee.*

28. See Cubano Iguina, *El hilo en le laberinto,* 123.

29. See *Gaceta de Puerto Rico,* 24 April 1873, in AHN/U, leg. 5111, exp. 20.

30. See "Decreto sobre contratación de libertos," 10 April 1874, AHN/U, leg. 5111, exp. 20, no. 32. The most thorough study of the enforcement of contracts under Primo de Rivera and Sanz is Figueroa, "Facing Freedom," chap. 4.

31. See the petitions from the municipal governments of Mayagüez and Arecibo made in February 1874 in AHN/U, leg. 5114, exp. 51, nos. 2–3. Mayagüez had the second highest

concentration of slaves in Puerto Rico on the eve of abolition. In 1872, the government reported a slave population of 6,323 in Mayagüez out of a total island population of 31,041. Ponce had the largest slave population at 7,238; Arecibo had 2,801. See "Provincia de Puerto Rico. Resumén general de los esclavos de la misma existentes en el Registro del corriente año, clasificados por oficios, sexos, estados, edades, y Departamentos a que corresponden," AHN/U, leg. 5111, exp. 23, no. 22.

32. See "Acompaña el Bando sobre vagancia," 18 April 1874, AHN/U, leg. 5114, exp. 42, no. 17; and "Bando," 15 April 1874, AHN/U, leg. 5114, exp. 41, no. 2.

33. Consejo de Estado, Madrid, 10 October 1874, AHN/U, leg. 5114, exp. 42, no. 1. Spain waited until the end of the Cuban war to publish the peninsular penal code in the colonies. Under the penal code of 1870, vagrancy was not a crime.

34. The reports are summarized in a letter from Carlos de Rojas, secretary of the government, to Captain General Marchesi, 1 June 1866, AHN/U, leg. 5114, exp. 48, no. 3.

35. Consejo de Estado, Madrid, 10 October 1874, AHN/U, Leg. 5114, exp. 42, no. 1.

36. On the obstacles to modernization of production and the strategies of *hacendados,* see Figueroa, "Facing Freedom," chaps. 4–7; Curet, "From Slave to 'Liberto,'" 275; Ramos Mattei, *La hacienda azucarera,* 100–06, and "La importación de trabajadores"; and Martínez-Vergne, *Capitalism in Colonial Puerto Rico.*

37. See the *Gaceta de Puerto Rico,* 25 January 1876, in AHN/U, leg. 5111, exp. 21, no. 26.

38. See "Remitiendo proyecto de reglamentación del trabajo en esta Isla," AHN/U, leg. 5111, exp. 21, nos. 25 and 27.

39. Both contracts can be found in "Alcaldía Municipal de la Villa de Mayagüez," AGPR, Fondo de Gobernadores, Political and Civil Affairs, Esclavos, 1870–76, entry 23, box 78, no. 730. See Figueroa, "Facing Freedom," chap. 4.

40. Consejo de Estado, Madrid, 12 April 1876, AHN/U, leg. 5111, exp. 20, no. 1.

41. "Antonio Alfau, Sociedad de Agricultura de Ponce," Madrid, 12 August 1877, AHN/U, leg. 5115, exp. 52, no. 2.

42. "Informando sobre las bases propuestas por Don Antonio Alfau y Baralt," Puerto Rico, 7 February 1879, AHN/U, leg. 5115, exp. 52, no. 4.

43. "Consultando si una vez publicado en la Isla el Código Penal la vagancia puede continúar como hasta aquí, sometida para su persecución y castigo a la acción gubernativa, o si debe confiarse su repressión a los tribunales de justicia," Puerto Rico, 6 October 1879, AHN/U, leg. 5115, exp. 5, no. 2.

44. Consejo de Estado, Madrid, 9 June 1880, AHN/U, leg. 5115, exp. 52, no. 1.

45. See Figueroa, "Facing Freedom," chaps. 6–7; Ramos Mattei, *La hacienda azucarera,* 100–06; and Mintz, "The Culture History of a Puerto Rican Sugar Cane Plantation."

46. Figueroa, "Facing Freedom," 495.

47. See Bergad, *Coffee,* 68–73.

48. On sugar and labor after slavery, see Curet, "From Slave to 'Liberto'"; Ramos Mattei, *La hacienda azucarera;* Figueroa, "Facing Freedom." See also Scarano, *Puerto Rico,* 462–66; and Bergad, "Agrarian History of Puerto Rico," 64–67.

49. Drescher, *Econocide* and *Capitalism and Antislavery;* and Eltis, *Economic Growth.* See also Tomich's critique of Drescher's interpretation in "Spaces of Slavery, Times of Freedom."

50. Here, I am following Rebecca Scott's emphasis on the diverse mobilizations, in relationship to social and economic tranformations, against slavery (see *Slave Emancipation in Cuba,* 5–6). The dominant social and economic explanations are those of Moreno Fraginals,

*El Ingenio;* and Bergad, *Cuban Rural Society,* esp. 334–42. For a more general discussion of the politics of Atlantic slavery, see Blackburn, *The Overthrow of Colonial Slavery,* 26–30, 520.

51. See Fradera, "Quiebra imperial y reorganización política."

52. My view on the relationship between capitalist development, state formation, and slavery has been influenced by the following works: Blackburn, *The Overthrow of Colonial Slavery,* 519–50; Tomich, "The 'Second Slavery'" and "World Slavery and Colonial Capitalism."

53. See esp. Drescher, *Capitalism and Antislavery,* 2–3. See also Blackburn's observation in *The Overthrow of Colonial Slavery,* 26–29.

54. See the discussion in Fradera, "Why Were Spain's Special Overseas Laws Never Enacted?," 339–41.

55. On constructions of race and the discourse of whitening in Cuba and Puerto Rico, see Lewis, *Main Currents in Caribbean Thought,* 140–70; Paquette, *Sugar Is Made with Blood,* chap. 3; Martínez-Alier, *Marriage, Class and Colour;* Gónzalez, *El país de cuatro pisos;* Díaz Quiñones, "Salvador Brau"; Helg, *Our Rightful Share;* and Kinsbruner, *Not of Pure Blood.* For a comparison with the discourse of whitening and whiteness in Latin America and the United States, see Roediger, *The Wages of Whitness;* Wade, *Blackness and Race Mixture;* and Cope, *The Limits of Racial Domination.*

56. On the intersection of class and racial ideologies in other colonial contexts, see Holt, *The Problem of Freedom,* and "'An Empire over the Mind'"; see Hall, "The Economy of Intellectual Prestige"; Stoler, *Race and the Education of Desire;* Hall, "When Was the 'Post-colonial'?"; and Thorne, "The Conversion of Englishmen."

57. See Stepan, *The Idea of Race in Science,* 1; see also Holt, *The Problem of Freedom,* xii–xxv.

58. See Helg, *Our Rightful Share,* 23–90; and Ferrer, "To Make a Free Nation," 128–330.

# BIBLIOGRAPHY

## Archival Sources

### SPAIN

Archivo del Congreso, Madrid
Archivo Histórico Nacional, Madrid
  Sección de Ultramar
Archivo Militar, Segovia
Biblioteca de Catalunya, Barcelona
  Agustí Aymar and Gelabert Collection

Biblioteca-Museu Balaguer, Vilanova i la
  Geltrú
  Epistolari de Víctor Balaguer
Fundación Antonio Maura, Madrid
Labra family private archive, Madrid

### CUBA

Archivo Nacional de Cuba, Havana
  Asuntos Políticos
  Consejo de Administración
  Donativos y Remisiónes
  Liceo Artístico y Literario de la Habana

Biblioteca Nacional José Martí, Havana
  Colección Cubana
  Colección de Manuscritos/Aldama
  Colección de Manuscritos/Alfonso
  Colección de Manuscritos/Bachiller
  Colección de Manuscritos/Morales
  Colección de Manuscritos/
    Ponce de Leon

### PUERTO RICO

Archivo General de Puerto Rico, San Juan
  Fondo de Gobernadores
  Colecciónes Particulares
    Colección José Pablo Morales Otero
Archivo Histórico Municipal de Ponce, Ponce
  Ayuntamiento

Centro de Investigaciónes Históricas,
  Universidad de Puerto Rico,
  Río Piedras
  Colección María del Pilar Acosta

## Periodicals

*El Abolicionista Español*, Madrid
*La Agricultura Española*, Seville
*Almanaque Aguinaldo*, San Juan
*La América*, Madrid
*Anales de Ciencias, Agriculutra, Comercio y Arte*, Havana
*Anti-Slavery Reporter*
*La Azucena*, San Juan
*Boletín Histórico de Puerto Rico*, San Juan
*Boletín Instructivo y Mercantil de Puerto Rico*, San Juan
*Boletín Mercantil*, San Juan
*La Campana de Gracia*, Barcelona
*El Clamór del Público*, Madrid
*El Condenado*, Madrid
*El Cubano Oriental*, Santiago de Cuba
*La Defensa de la Sociedad*, Madrid
*La Democracia*, Madrid
*El Diario Constitucional de Santiago de Cuba*, Santiago de Cuba
*El Diario de Barcelona*, Barcelona
*El Diario de la Marina*, Havana
*El Diario de Manila*, Manila
*La Discusión*, Madrid
*El Eco de la Clase Obrera*, Madrid
*El Economista*, Madrid

*La Emancipación*, Madrid
*La Federación*, Barcelona
*El Fomento de las Artes*, Madrid
*El Fomento de la Producción Nacional*, Barcelona
*Gaceta de los Caminos de Hierro*, Madrid
*Gaceta Economista*, Madrid
*La Ilustración Español y Americana*, Madrid
*El Imparcial*, Madrid
*Memorias de la Real Sociedad económica de los amigos del país de la Habana*, Havana
*El Mundo*, Madrid
*El Noticiero*, Ponce
*El Ponceño*, Ponce
*El Progreso*, San Juan
*El Protector del Pueblo*, Barcelona
*Revista Bimestre Cubana*, Havana
*Revista de Ambos Mundos*, Madrid
*Revista Hispano-Americana*, Madrid
*Revista Ibérica*, Madrid
*La Revista Industrial*, Barcelona
*La Tribuna*, Madrid
*La Verdad Económica*, Madrid
*La Voz de la Caridad*, Madrid
*La Voz del Siglo*, Madrid

## Primary Works

### NOTE ON SOURCES

Most of these source materials may be found in the Biblioteca Nacional (Madrid), the Ateneo de Madrid, the Hemeroteca Municipal (Madrid), the Biblioteca Nacional José Martí (Havana), the Colección Puertorriqueña at the Universidad de Puerto Rico (Río Piedras), the Biblioteca de Catalunya (Barcelona), and the Biblioteca Arús (Barcelona). The Puerto Rican sources, especially newspapers, are found almost exclusively in the Colección Puertorriqueña in Puerto Rico. Many Cuban sources, by contrast, are in Spain's Biblioteca Nacional.

Abbad y Lasierra, Inigo. *Historía geográfica, civil y natural de la isla de San Juan Bautista de Puerto Rico, por Fray Iñigo Abbad y Lasierra*. Ed. José Julián Acosta y Calbo. Puerto Rico: Imprenta y Librería de Acosta, 1866.
Acosta y Calbo, José Julián. *Colección de artículos publicados*. Puerto Rico: Imprenta de Acosta, 1869.

Acosta y Quintero, Angel. *José J. Acosta y su tiempo.* Puerto Rico: Sucesión de J. J. Acosta, 1899.

*Acta de la Junta Pública efectuada por la Sociedad Económica el 22 de enero de 1863.* Puerto Rico: Imprenta del Boletín Mercantil, 1863.

*Acta de la Junta Pública tenida por la Sociedad Económica de Amigos del País de Puerto Rico.* Puerto Rico: Establecimiento tipográfico de D. Ignacio Guasp, 1859.

Agüero, Pedro de. *Biografías de cubanos distinguidos.* Vol. 1: *Don José Antonio Saco.* London: Imprenta de W & A Webster, 1858.

Alonso, Manuel. *El gíbaro. Cuadro de costumbres de la Isla de Puerto Rico.* 2nd ed. Puerto Rico: José González Font, 1882.

*Anti-Slavery Reporter.* London: Kraus Reprint, 1969.

*Apuntes sobre la cuestión de la reforma política y de la introducción de africanos en las islas de Cuba y Puerto Rico.* Madrid: T. Fortanet, 1866.

Arango y Parreño, Francisco. *Obras de D. Francisco Arango y Parreño.* 2 vols. Havana: Ministerio de Educación, 1952.

———. "Representación al Rey sobre la extinción del tráfico de negros y medios de mejorar la suerte de los esclavos coloniales," in *Obras,* vol. 1.

Arenal, Concepción. "A las mujeres." In Centro de Investigaciones Históricas, *El proceso abolicionista en Puerto Rico: Documentos para su estudio,* vol. 1. San Juan, 1974.

Armas y Céspedes, Francisco de. *De la esclavitud en Cuba.* Madrid: T. Fortanet, 1866.

Azcárate, Nicolás. *Noches literarias en casa de Nicolás Azcárate.* 2 vols. Habana: Imprenta la Antilla, 1866.

———. *Votos de un cubano.* Madrid: Imprenta de C. Moliner y Compañía, 1869.

Baldorioty de Castro, Román. *Interpelación del diputado Don Luis Padial y sus consecuencias.* Madrid: Imprenta de la Gaceta de los Caminos de Hierro, 1869.

Bernal, Calixto. *La democracía o el individualismo.* Madrid, 1859.

———. *Vindicación: cuestión de Cuba, por un español cubano.* Madrid: Imprenta de Nicanor Pérez Zuloaga, 1871.

Betancourt y Betancourt, José Ramón de. *Las dos banderas: apuntes históricas sobre la insurreción de Cuba.* Sevilla: Establecimiento tipográfico del Círculo Liberal, 1870.

Bona, Félix de. *Cuba, Santo Domingo y Puerto Rico.* Madrid: Imprenta de Manuel Galiano, 1861.

Cabrera, Raimundo. *Cuba and the Cubans.* Trans. Laura Guiteras. Philadelphia: The Levytype Company, 1896.

*El cancionero del esclavo.* Madrid: Publicaciónes Populares de la Sociedad Abolicionista Española, 1866.

Castelar, Emilio. *La formúla del progreso.* 2nd ed. Madrid: Julián Peña, 1870.

———. *Historia del movimiento republicano en Europa.* 2 vols. Madrid: Casa Editorial de M. Rodríguez, 1873–1874.

———. "La unión de España y América," *La América.*

———. "Utilidad de la propaganda libre-cambista en España," *Conferencias libre-cambistas.*

Castro y Pajares, Fernando de. *Discurso que en la inauguración de las Conferencias dominicales para la Educación de la Mujer leyó en la Universidad de Madrid el Dr. Fernando de Castro.* Madrid: Rivadeneyera, 1869.

*Cataluña y la cuestión arancelaria, artículos publicados en "El Siglo" por un ex-ministro de Hacienda.* Madrid: Establecimiento Tipográfico de Gabriel Pedraza, 1881.

*Las clases obreras. Estudio completo de esta gravísima cuestión (indispensable para los principales y para los obreros).* Traducido y ordenado, con dos prólogos originales por B.V.G. Madrid: D. Adrian Garcés, n.d.

*Conferencias librecambistas.* Madrid: Imprenta de Manuel Galiano, 1863.

*Diario de las discusiónes y actas de las Cortes.* Cádiz: Imprenta Real, 1811.

*Diario de las Sesiones de las Cortes.* Madrid: Eco del Comercio, 1837.

*Diario de Sesiones de las Cortes Constituyentes.* Madrid: Imprenta Nacional, 1870.

*Diario de Sesiones de las Cortes Constituyentes.* Madrid: J. A. García, 1874.

*Diario de Sesiones de las Cortes Constituyentes* [1854–55]. Madrid: J. A. García, 1880.

*Diario de las Sesiones de Cortes. Congreso de los Diputados.* Vol. 4. Madrid: Imprenta de J. A. García, 1872.

*Diccionario de la lengua castellana.* La Academia Española. Madrid: La Imprenta Real, 1832.

*Diccionario de la lengua castellana.* La Academia Española. Madrid: Imprenta de Don M. Rivadeneyra, 1869.

Dulce, Domingo. "Informe del Excmo. Sr. D. Domingo Dulce." In *Información sobre reformas en Cuba y Puerto Rico.* New York: Hallet y Breen, 1867.

*Españoles y cubanos después de la separación de 1900.* Interview with D. Rafael M. de Labra by S. B. Madrid: Establecimiento tipográfico de Jaime Rafés, 1916.

*Exposición de Filipinas. Colección de artículos publicadose en "El Globo."* Madrid: El Globo, 1887.

Fernández de Castro, José Antonio. *Medio siglo de historia colonial de Cuba. Cartas a José Antonio Saco.* Havana: Ricardo Veloso, 1923.

Ferrer de Couto, José. *Los negros en sus diversos estados y condiciónes; tales como son, como se supone que son, y como deben ser.* 2nd ed. New York: Imprenta de Hallet, 1864.

Gallenga, A. *The Pearl of the Antilles.* New York: Negro Universities Press, 1970 [originally published 1873].

Garrido, Fernando. *Historia de las clases trabajadoras.* 3 vols. [1870]. Madrid: Biblioteca Promoción del Pueblo, 1972.

Gräell, Guillermo. *Historia del Fomento del Trabajo Nacional.* Barcelona: Imprenta de la Viuda de Luis Tasso, n.d.

Güell y Ferrer, Juan. *Escritos económicos.* Barcelona: Imprenta Barcelonesa, 1880.

Hartzenbusch, Eugenio. *Periódicos de Madrid.* Madrid: Imp., estereotipía y galvanoplastía de Aribau y Ca. 1876.

*Impugnación de las doctrinas librecambistas.* Madrid: Imprenta de Manuel Tello, 1862.

*Información sobre reformas en Cuba y Puerto Rico.* 2 vols. New York: Imprenta de Hallet y Breen, 1867.

*Junta General de la Sociedad Económica de Amantes del País de Puerto Rico.* Puerto Rico: Imprenta Fraternidad, 1822.

Krause, C. Cr. *Ideal de la humanidad para la vida.* Trad. Julián Sanz del Río. Madrid: Imprenta de Manuel Galiano, 1860.

Labra y Cadrana, Rafael María de. *La abolición de la esclavitud en el órden económico.* Madrid: Imprenta de J. Noguera, 1873.

———. *La abolición de la esclavitud en las Antillas españolas.* Madrid: Imprenta a cargo de J. E. Morete, 1869.

———. *La abolición y la Sociedad Abolicionista Española en 1873.* Madrid: Sociedad Abolicionista Española, 1874.

———. *A los electores de Sabana Grande (Puerto-Rico).* Madrid: Imprenta de M. G. Hernández, 1873.

———. "A mis electores de Cuba y Puerto-Rico." In *Mi campaña en las Córtes españolas de*

*1881 a 1883*, 1–43. Madrid: Imprenta de Aurelio J. Alavia, 1885.

———. *El Ateneo de Madrid. Sus orígenes, desenvolvimiento, representación y porvenir.* Madrid: Imprenta de A.J. Alaria, 1878.

———. *La brutalidad de los negros.* [1876]. Havana: Imprenta de la Universidad de la Habana, 1961.

———. *Mi campana en las Córtes españolas de 1881 a 1883.* Madrid: Imprenta de Aurelio J. Alavia, 1885.

———. *Carta que a varios electores del distrito de Infiesto (Oviedo) dirige su ex-diputado a Cortes.* Madrid: Imprenta de José Norguera, 1872.

———. *La Constitución de Cádiz.* Madrid: Imprenta de Alfredo Alonso, 1907.

———. *La crisis colonial de España. 1868–1898. Estudios de política palpitante.* Madrid: Tipografía de Alfredo Alonso, 1902.

———. *La cuestión colonial. 1868–1869. Cuba.–Puerto Rico.– Filipinas.* Madrid: Tipografía de Gregorio Estrada, 1869.

———. *La emancipación de los esclavos en los Estados-Unidos.* Madrid: Imprenta de Manuel G. Hernández, 1873.

———. *Estudios biográfico-políticos.* Madrid: Imprenta de "La Guirnalda", 1887.

———. "Introducción." *El problema colonial contemporáneo.* Madrid: Agustín Avrial, 1895.

———. *La mujer y la legislación castellana.* Madrid: Rivadeneyra, 1869.

———. "El negro Santos de Santo Domingo." In *Estudios biográfico-políticos.* [1880]. Madrid: Imprenta de "La Guirnalda," 1887.

———. *La pérdida de las Américas. Artículos publicados en "Los Conocimientos Utiles."* Madrid: Imprenta de Francisco Roig, 1869.

———. *Política y sistemas coloniales.* Madrid: Imprenta de J. Noguera, a cargo de M. Martínez, 1874.

———. *El Tratado de París de 1898 entre España y los Estados Unidos.* Madrid: Tipografía de Alfredo Alfonso, 1899.

Labra y Cadrana, Rafael María de, and Gabriel Rodríguez. *Una sesión de la Tertulia Radical de Madrid.* Madrid: Imprenta a cargo de Teodoro Lucuix, 1873.

Larra, José de. "¿Quién es el público y donde se encuentra?" In *Artículos,* ed. Enrique Rubio, 127–37. Madrid: Cátedra, 1988.

Ledrú, Andrés Pedro. *Viaje a la Isla de Puerto-Rico en el Año 1797.* Trans. Julio de Vizcarrondo. Puerto Rico: Imprenta Militar de J. González, 1863.

*El libro del obrero.* Barcelona: Narciso Ramírez, 1862.

Lorenzo, Anselmo. *El proletariado militante.* [1901, 1923]. Madrid: Alianza Editorial, 1974.

Madoz, Pascual. *Diccionario Geográfico-estadístico-histórico de España y sus posesiónes de Ultramar.* 16 vols. Madrid: Est. Literario-Tipográfico de P. Madoz y L. Sagasti, 1845–50.

Manzano, Juan Francisco. *Autobiography of a Slave/Autobiografía de un esclavo.* Intro. Ivan A. Schulman. Trans. Evelyn Picon Garfield. Detroit: Wayne State University Press, 1996.

Mesonero Romanos, Ramón de. *Manual de Madrid.* Madrid: Imprenta de D. M. de Burgos, 1831.

———. *Nuevo Manual Histórico-topográfico-estadístico y descripción de Madrid.* Madrid: Imprenta de la Viuda de D. Antonio Reyes, 1854.

———. *Panorama Matritense (primera serie de las escenas) 1832 a 1835.* Nueva edición, corregida y aumentada con notas. Madrid: Oficinas de la Ilustración Española y Americana, 1881.

Moret y Prendergast, Segismundo. *Influencía de la madre sobre la vocación y profesión de los hijos.* Madrid: Rivadeneyra, 1869.

————. "Perjuicios que causa el proteccionismo a las clases obreras." *Conferencias librecambistas,* 141–53. Madrid: Imprenta de Manuel Galiano, 1863.

Pi y Margall, Francisco. *La misión de la mujer en la sociedad.* Madrid: Rivadeneyra, 1869.

Portuondo, Bernardo. *Voto particular sobre la reforma social de Cuba.* Madrid: J.J. de las Heras, 1879.

*El proceso abolicionista en Puerto Rico: Documentos para su estudio.* 2 vols. San Juan: Centro de Investigaciónes Históricas, 1974.

*Proyecto de inmigración africana para las islas de Cuba y Puerto Rico y el Imperio de Brasil. Presentado a los respectivos gobiernos por los Sres. Argudín, Cunha Reis y Perdones.* Havana: Imprenta La "Habanera," 1860.

Quiñones, Francisco Mariano. *Historia de los partidos reformista y conservador de Puerto Rico.* Mayagüez: Tipografía Comercial, 1889.

Ramírez de Arellano, Rafael. *Instrucciónes al diputado Don Ramón Power y Giralt.* Río Piedras: University of Puerto Rico, 1936.

Rodríguez, Gabriel. "La idea y el movimiento antiesclavista en España durante el siglo XIX." In *El proceso abolicionista en Puerto Rico,* 1:462–63.

Romanones, El Conde de. *Rafael María de Labra y la política de España en América y Portugal.* Madrid: Gráfica Ambos Mundos, 1922.

Saco, José Antonio. *Carta de un patriota o sea Clamor de los Cubanos dirigido a sus procuradores a Cortes.* Cádiz: n.p., 1835.

————. *Colección de pápeles científicos, históricos, políticos y de otros ramos sobre la isla de Cuba ya publicados, ya inéditos.* 3 vols. Havana: Ministerio de Educación, 1960.

————. *L'Esclavage à Cuba et la révolution d'Espagne.* Paris: F. Dentu, 1869.

————. *Examen analítico del Informe de la Comisión Especial nombrada por las Cortes, sobre la exclusión de los actuales y futuros diputados de Ultramar, y sobre la necesidad de regir aquellos países por leyes especiales.* Madrid: Oficina de Tomás Jordan, 1837.

————. *Historia de la esclavitud de la raza africana en el nuevo mundo y en especial en los países Americo-hispanos.* Havana: Cultural S.A., 1938.

————. *Memoria sobre caminos en la isla de Cuba.* New York: Imprimido por G.F. Bunce, 1830.

————. *Mi primera pregunta. La abolición del comercio de esclavos africanos arruinará o atrasará la agricultura cubana?* Madrid: Imprenta de Don Marcelino Calero, 1837.

————. "Noticias del Brasil en 1828 and 1829 por el Pbro. R. Walsh, autor de un viage de Constantinopla &c." *Revista Bimestre Cubana* 2, no. 6 (April 1832), 173–230.

————. *Obras de Don José Antonio Saco.* 2 vols. New York: Librería Americana y Estranjera de Roe Lockwood e Hijo, 1853.

————. "Paralelo entre la Isla de Cuba y algunas colonias inglesas." [1837] *Idearío reformista.* Havana: Cuadernos de Cultura, 1935.

————. "La política absolutista en las provincias ultramarinas." *Revista Hispano-Americana* (Madrid), 27 April 1866.

————. *La vagancia en Cuba. Vigencia de Saco, por Rafael Esténger.* Havana: Minsterio de Educación, 1946.

Saez de Melgar, Faustina. *Memoria del Ateneo de Señoras.* Madrid: Imprenta de los Señores Rojas, 1869.

Sagra, Ramón de la. *Apuntes destinados a ilustrar la discusión del artículo adicional al proyecto de Constitución que dice "Las provincias de ultramar serán gobernadas por leyes especiales."* Paris: La Imprenta de Maulde et Renou, 1837.

Sanromá, Joaquín María. *Educación social de la mujer.* Madrid: Rivadeneyra, 1869.

———. *La esclavitud en Cuba.* Madrid: T. Fortanet, 1872.

———. *Política del taller.* Madrid: Imprenta de Víctor Saiz, 1876.

Schwabe, Salis, comp. *Reminiscences of Richard Cobden.* London: T. Fisher Unwin, 1895.

*A Series of Articles on the Cuban Question Published by the Editors of "La Verdad."* New York: Printed at the Office of *La Verdad,* 1849.

Sociedad Abolicionista Española. *Conferencias anti-esclavistas del Teatro Lope de Rueda.* Madrid: Sociedad Abolicionista Española, 1872.

Valiente, Porfirio. *Réformes dan les isles de Cuba et Porto-Rico.* Paris: A. Chaix et Cia., 1869.

Vázquez Queipo, Vicente. *Contestación a la carta de un cubano suscrita por D. José Antonio Saco.* Madrid: Imprenta de Martín Alegría, 1847.

———. *Informe fiscal sobre fomento de la población blanca en la Isla de Cuba y emancipación progresiva de la esclava.* Madrid: Imprenta de Martín Alegría, 1845.

Vega-Mar, Conde de. *Informe del excmo. Señor Conde de Vega-Mar, Senador del Reino, en contestación a los interrogatorios hechos por el Gobierno de S.M. sobre la información de las leyes especiales para las Islas de Cuba y Puerto Rico.* Madrid: T. Fortanet, 1868. AHN/U, leg. 3552, exp. 2.

*Velada celebrada en honor de D. Joaquín Ma. Sanromá.* Madrid: Establecimineto tipográfico de A. Avrial, 1895.

Villaverde, Cirilo. *Cecilia Valdés.* 2 vols. Havana: Editorial Pueblo y Educación, 1990.

———. *General Narciso López, the Cuban Patriot.* New York: n.d. [ca. 1850.]

## Secondary Works

Alarcón Caracuel, Manuel R. *El derecho de asociación obrera en España (1839–1900).* Madrid: Ediciones de la Revista de Trabajo, 1975.

Aldaraca, Bridget. "El angel del hogar: The Cult of Domesticity in Nineteeth-century Spain." In *Theory and Practice of Feminist Literary Criticism,* ed. Gabriela Mora and Karen S. van Hooft, 62–87. Ypsilanti: Bilingual Press/Editorial Bilingüe, 1982.

Althusser, Louis. *Lenin and Philosophy and Other Essays.* Trans. Ben Brewster. New York: Monthly Review Press, 1971.

Alvarez Junco, José. *La Comuna en España.* Madrid: Siglo XXI, 1971.

———. *El Emperador del Paralelo: Lerroux y la demagogía populista.* Madrid: Alianza Editorial, 1990.

———. *La ideología política del anarquismo español (1868–1910).* 2nd ed. Madrid: Siglo XXI, 1991.

Andrews, George Reid. "Spanish American Independence: A Structural Analysis." *Latin American Perspectives* 44 (1985): 105–32.

Anna, Timothy. "Instituional and Political Impediments to Spain's Settlement of the American Rebellions." *The Americas* 38 (1982): 481–95.

Appadurai, Arjun. *Modernity at Large: Cultural Dimensions of Globalization.* Minneapolis: University of Minnesota Press, 1996.

Anderson, Benedict. "Exodus." *Critical Inquiry* 20 (winter 1994): 314–27.

———. *Imagined Communities.* London: Verso, 1983.

Artola, Miguel. *La burguesía revolucionaria (1808–1874).* Madrid: Alianza Editorial, 1983.

Artola, Miguel, ed. *Los Ferrocarriles en España, 1844–1943.* 2 vols. Madrid: Servicio de Estudios del Banco de España, 1978.

Azcárate Rossell, Rafael. *Nicolás Azcárate, el reformista.* La Habana: Editorial Tropical, 1939.

Bahamonde, Angel, and José Gregorio Cayuela Fernández. "La creación de nobleza en Cuba durante el siglo XIX." *Historia Social* 11 (1991): 57–82.

———. *Hacer las Américas.* Madrid: Alianza Editorial, 1992.

Bahamonde, Angel, and Juan Toro. *Burguesía, especulación y cuestión social en el Madrid del XIX.* Madrid: Siglo XXI, 1978.

Bairoch, Paul. "European Trade Policy, 1815–1914." In *The Cambridge Economic History of Europe,* ed. Peter Mathias and Sidney Pollard, 8:1–160. Cambridge: Cambridge University Press, 1989.

Baker, Edward. *Materiales para escribir Madrid.* Madrid: Siglo XXI, 1991.

Baker, Thomas Hart, Jr. "Imperial Finale: Crisis, Decolonization, and War in Spain, 1890–1898." Ph.D. diss., Princeton University, 1977.

Balfour, Sebastian. *The End of the Spanish Empire, 1898–1923.* Cambridge: Cambridge University Press, 1997.

Barahona, Renato. *Vizcaya on the Eve of Carlism: Politics and Society (1800–1833).* Reno: University of Nevada Press, 1989.

Baralt, Guillermo. *Esclavos rebeldes: conspiraciónes y sublevaciónes de esclavos en Puerto Rico (1795–1873).* 3rd ed. Río Piedras, P.R.: Ediciónes Huracán, 1989.

Beck, Earl R. *A Time of Triumph and of Sorrow: Spanish Politics during the Reign of Alfonso XII, 1874–1885.* Carbondale: Southern Illinois University Press, 1979.

Bender, Thomas, ed. *The Antislavery Debate.* Berkeley: University of California Press, 1992.

Benet, Josep, and Casimiro Martí. *Barcelona a mitjan segle XIX: el moviment obrer durant el Bieni Progressista (1854–1856),* 2 vols. Barcelona: Curial, 1976.

Bergad, Laird. "Agrarian History of Puerto Rico, 1870–1930." *Latin American Research Review* 13 (1978): 63–94.

———. *Coffee and the Growth of Agrarian Capitalism in Nineteenth-Century Puerto Rico.* Princeton: Princeton University Press, 1983.

———. *Cuban Rural Society in the Nineteenth Century: The Social and Economic History of Monoculture in Matanzas.* Princeton: Princeton University Press, 1990.

———. "The Economic Viability of Sugar Production Based on Slave Labor in Cuba: 1859–1878." *Latin American Research Review* 24 (1989): 95–113.

———."Slavery and Its Legacies." *Latin American Research Review* 25 (1990): 199–213.

Bergad, Laird, Fé Iglesias, and María del Carmen Barcía. *The Cuban Slave Market, 1790–1880.* Cambridge: Cambridge University Press, 1995.

Bernal, Antonio M., and Michel Drain. "Progreso y crisis de la agricultura andaluza en el siglo XIX." In *Historia agraria de la España contemporánea,* vol. 2, ed. Garrabou et al., 412–42.

Bethell, Leslie. *The Abolition of the Brazilian Slave Trade.* Cambridge: Cambridge University Press, 1970.

Bethell, Leslie, ed. *Latin America: Economy and Society, 1870–1930.* Cambridge: Cambridge University Press, 1990.

Blackbourn, David, and Geoff Eley. *The Peculiarities of German History.* New York: Oxford University Press, 1985.

Blackburn, Robin. *The Overthrow of Colonial Slavery, 1776–1848.* London: Verso, 1988.

Blinkhorn, Martin. "Spain, the 'Spanish Problem', and the Imperial Myth." *Journal of Contemporary History* 15 (1980): 5–23.

Bolt, Christine, and Seymour Drescher, eds. *Antislavery, Religion and Reform: Essays in Memory of Roger Anstey.* Folkestone: Wm. Dawson and Sons, 1980.

Brading, David. *The First America. The Spanish Monarchy, Creole Patriots, and the Liberal State, 1492–1867.* Cambridge: Cambridge University Press, 1991.

Brau, Salvador. *Historia de Puerto Rico.* Río Piedras, P.R.: Editorial Edil, 1983.

Brubaker, Rogers. *Citizenship and Nationhood in France and Germany.* Cambridge: Harvard University Press, 1992.

Burdiel, Isabel. "Dret, compromís i violència en la revolució burguesa: la revolució de 1836." *Recerques* 22 (1989): 63–81.

Calhoun, Craig, ed. *Habermas and the Public Sphere.* Cambridge: MIT Press, 1993.

Cánovas Sánchez, Francisco. "Los partidos políticos." In *Historia de España. La era isabelina y el sexenio democrático (1834–1874),* 34:373–499 (Madrid: Espasa Calpe, 1981).

Carr, Raymond. *Spain, 1808–1975,* 2nd ed. Oxford: Clarendon Press, 1982.

Carrera Pujal, *La economía de Cataluña en el siglo XIX.* Vol. 1. Barcelona: Bosch, 1961.

Casanovas Codina, Joan. "Labor and Colonialism in Cuba in the Second Half of the Nineteenth Century." Ph.D. diss., State University of New York, Stony Brook, 1994.

Castells, Irene. *La utopía insurrecional del liberalismo.* Barcelona: Crítica, 1989.

Castro Alfín, Demetrio. "El Partido Demócrata, 1849–1868." In *El republicanismo en España,* ed. Townson, 59–85.

———. "Orígenes y primeras etapas del republicanismo en España", "El Partido Demócrata, 1849–1868." In *El republicanismo en España,* ed. Townson, 33–57.

Cayuela Fernández, José G. *Bahía de Ultramar: España y Cuba en el siglo XIX. El control de las relaciónes coloniales.* Madrid: Siglo XXI, 1993.

Cepero Bonilla, Raúl. *Azúcar y abolición.* Havana: Editorial de Ciencias Sociales, 1971.

Chaffin, Tom. *Fatal Glory: Narciso López and the First Clandestine U.S. War Against Cuba.* Charlottesville: University of Virginia Press, 1996.

Christiensen, E. *The Origins of Military Power in Spain, 1800–1854.* London: Oxford University Press, 1967.

Coll y Toste, Cayetano, ed. *Boletín Histórico de Puerto Rico.* [1916]. New York: Kraus Reprint, 1968.

Conrad, Robert E. *The Destruction of Brazilian Slavery, 1850-1888.* Berkeley: University of California Press, 1972.

Cooper, Frederick. "Race, Ideology, and the Perils of Comparative History." *American Historical Review* 101 (1996), 1122–38. Cooper, Frederick, and Ann Stoler. "Between Metropole and Colony: Rethinking a Research Agenda." In *Tensions of Empire,* ed. Cooper and Stoler, 1–56.

———. "Tensions of Empire: Colonial Control and Visions of Rule." *American Ethnologist* 16 (1989): 609–21.

Cooper, Frederick, and Ann Stoler, eds. *Tensions of Empire: Colonial Cultures in a Bourgeois World.* Berkeley and Los Angeles: University of California Press, 1997.

Cope, R. Douglas. *The Limits of Racial Domination: Plebeian Society in Colonial Mexico City, 1660–1720.* Madison: University of Wisconsin Press, 1994.

Corbitt, Duvon C. *A Study of the Chinese in Cuba, 1847–1947.* Wilmore, Ky.: Asbury College, 1971.

Corwin, Arthur. *Spain and the Abolition of Slavery in Cuba, 1817–1886.* Austin: University of Texas Press, 1967.

Costas Comesaña, Antón. *Apogeo del liberalismo en "La Gloriosa." La reforma económica en el Sexenio liberal (1868–1874)*. Madrid: Siglo XXI, 1988.

Costeloe, Michael. *Response to Revolution*. Cambridge: Cambridge University Press, 1986.

Cruz, Jesús. *Gentlemen, Bourgeois, and Revolutionaries: Political Change and Cultural Persistence Among the Spanish Dominant Groups, 1750–1850*. Cambridge: Cambridge University Press, 1996.

———. "Notability and Revolution: Social Origins of the Political Elite in Liberal Spain, 1800 to 1853." *Comparative Studies in Society and History* 36 (January 1994): 97–121.

Cruz Monclova, Lidio. *Historia de Puerto Rico (siglo XIX)*. 3 vols. University of Puerto Rico: Ediciones Universitarias, 1952–64.

*The Cuba Commission Report: A Hidden History of the Chinese in Cuba*. Intro. by Denise Helly and trans. by Sidney Mintz. Baltimore: Johns Hopkins University Press, 1993.

Cubano Iguina, Astrid. *El hilo en el laberinto: claves de la lucha política en Puerto Rico (siglo XIX)*. Río Piedras, P.R.: Ediciones Huracán, 1990.

Curet, José. "From Slave to 'Liberto': A Study on Slavery and Its Abolition in Puerto Rico, 1840–1880." Ph.D. diss., Columbia University, 1980.

———. *Los amos hablan. Unas conversaciónes entre un amo y su esclavo en 'El Ponceño' 1852–53*. Río Piedras, P.R.: Editorial Cultural, 1986.

Curtin, Philip. *The Atlantic Slave Trade: A Census*. Madison: University of Wisconsin Press, 1969.

Davin, Anna. "Imperialism and Motherhood." *History Workshop* 5 (1978): 9–65.

Davis, David Brion. *The Problem of Slavery in the Age of Revolution, 1770–1823*. Ithaca: Cornell University Press, 1975.

———. *The Problem of Slavery in Western Culture*. New York: Oxford University Press, 1966.

———. "Reflections on Abolitionism and Ideological Hegemony." *American Historical Review* 92 (October 1987): 797–812.

———. *The Slave Power Conspiracy and the Paranoid Style*. Baton Rouge: Louisiana State University Press, 1969.

———. *Slavery and Human Progress*. New York: Oxford University Press, 1984.

———. "Slavery and 'Progress.'" In *Anti-Slavery, Religion and Reform*, ed. Bolt and Drescher, 351–66.

Davis, Horace. *Nationalism and Socialism*. New York: Monthly Review Press, 1967.

De la Fuente, Alejandro. "Race and Inequality in Cuba, 1899–1981." *Journal of Contemporary History* 30 (1995): 131–68.

Deschamps Chapeaux, Pedro. "Flebotomianos y dentistas." *Contribución a la historia de la gente sin historia*. Havana: Editorial de Ciencias Sociales, 1974.

Díaz Quiñones, Arcadio. "El enemigo íntimo: cultura nacional y autoridad en Ramiro Guerra y Sánchez y Antonio S. Pedreira." *Op. Cit.*, no. 7 (1992): 9–65.

———. "Salvador Brau: la paradoja de la tradición autonomista." *La Torre* 7 (1993): 395–414.

Díaz Soler, Luis M. *Historia de la esclavitud negra en Puerto Rico*, 3rd edition. Río Piedras, P.R.: Editorial Universitaria, 1981.

Dietz, James. *An Economic History of Puerto Rico*. Princeton: Princeton University Press, 1986.

Domínguez, Jorge. *Insurrection or Loyalty: The Breakdown of the Spanish American Empire*. Cambridge: Harvard University Press, 1980.

Drescher, Seymour. "Brazilian Abolition in Comparative Perspective." In *The Abolition of Slavery and the Aftermath of Emancipation in Brazil*, ed. Scott et al., 23–54.

———. *Capitalism and Antislavery*. New York: Oxford University Press, 1987.

————. "Cart Whip and Billy Roller: Antislavery and Reform Symbolism in Industrializing Britain." *Journal of Social History* 15 (1981): 3–24.

————. *Econocide: British Slavery in the Era of Abolition.* Pittsburgh: University of Pittsburgh Press, 1977.

————. "Epilogue: Reflections." In *Fifty Years Later,* ed. Oostinde, 243–61.

————. "Eric Williams: British Capitalism and British Slavery." *History and Theory* 26 (1987): 180–96.

————. "The Long Goodbye: Dutch Capitalism and Antislavery in Comparative Perspective." *American Historical Review* 99 (February 1994): 44–69.

————. "Review of Robin Blackburn, *The Overthrow of Colonial Slavery, 1776–1848.*" *Social History* 15 (1990): 256–59.

————. "Two Variants of Anti-slavery: Religious Organization and Social Mobilization in Britian and France, 1780–1870." In *Anti-Slavery, Religion and Reform,* ed. Bolt and Drescher, 43–63.

————. "Whose Abolition? Popular Pressure and the Ending of the British Slave Trade." *Past and Present* 143 (1994): 136–66.

Duarte, Angel. *El Republicanisme català a la fi del segle XIX.* Vic: Eumo Editorial, 1987.

————. *Pere Coromines: del republicanisme als cercles llibertais (1888–1896).* Barcelona: Biblioteca Serra d'Or, 1988.

Eley, Geoff. *From Unification to Nazism.* Boston: G. Allen and Unwin, 1986.

————. "The British Model and the German Road: Rethinking the Course of German History before 1914," in Blackbourn and Eley, *The Peculiarities of German History.*

————. "Liberalism, Europe, and the bourgeoisie, 1860–1914." In *The German Bourgeoisie,* ed. David Blackbourn and Richard J. Evans, 293–317. London: Routledge, 1993.

————. "Nations, Publics, and Political Cultures: Placing Habermas in the Nineteenth Century." In *Habermas and the Public Sphere,* ed. Calhoun, 289–339.

————. *Reshaping the German Right.* 2nd ed. Ann Arbor, University of Michigan Press, 1991.

Eltis, David. *Economic Growth and the Ending of the Transatlantic Slave Trade.* New York: Oxford University Press, 1987.

Ely, Roland T. *Cuando reinaba su majestad el azúcar.* Buenos Aires: Editorial Sudamericana, 1963).

Espadas Burgos, Manuel. *Alfonso XII y los orígenes de la Restauración,* 2nd ed. Madrid: CSIC, 1990.

Estrade, Paul. "Los colonos yucatecos como sustitutos de los esclavos negros." In *Cuba, la perla de las antillas,* ed. Naranjo Orovio and Mallo Gutiérrez, 93–107.

————. *Les écrits de Betances dans la presse latino-américaine de Paris.* Paris: Publications de l'Équipe de Recherche de l'Université de Paris VIII, 1988.

Fernández, James D. *Apology to Apostrophe: Autobiography and the Rhetoric of Self-Representation in Spain.* Durham: Duke University Press, 1992.

Ferrer, Ada. "Social Aspects of Cuban Nationalism: Race, Slavery, and the Guerra Chiquita, 1879–1880." *Cuban Studies* 21 (1991): 37–56.

————. "To Make a Free Nation: Race and the Struggle for Independence in Cuba, 1868–1898." Ph.D. diss., University of Michigan, 1995.

Fields, Barbara Jeanne. *Slavery and Freedom on the Middle Ground: Maryland during the Nineteenth Century.* New Haven: Yale University Press, 1985.

————. "Slavery, Race and Ideology in the United States of America." *New Left Review* 181 (1990): 95–118.

Figueroa, Luis Antonio. "Facing Freedom: The Transition from Slavery to Free Labor in Guayama, Puerto Rico, 1860–1898." Ph.D. diss., University of Wisconsin, 1991.

Findlay, Eileen Jean. "Domination, Decency, and Desire: The Politics of Sexuality in Ponce, Puerto Rico, 1870–1920." Ph.D. diss., University of Wisconsin, 1995.

Foner, Eric. *Free Soil, Free Labor, Free Men: The Ideology of the Republican Party before the Civil War.* New York: Oxford University Press, 1970.

———. *Reconstruction: America's Unfinished Revolution, 1863–1877.* New York: Harper and Row, 1988.

Fontana, Josep. *Cambio económico y actitudes políticas en la España del XIX.* Barcelona: Crítica, 1975.

———. *La crisis del antiguo régimen.* 4th ed. Barcelona: Crítica, 1992.

———. *La quiebra de la monarquía absoluta (1814–1820).* Barcelona: Ariel, 1971.

Fradera, Josep M. *Cultura nacional en una societat dividida.* Barcelona: Curial, 1992.

———. "La importáncia de tenir colonies." In *Catalunya i ultramar,* ed. Fradera, 22–52.

———. *Indùstria i mercat.* Barcelona: Crítica, 1987.

———. *Jaume Balmes: Els fonaments racionals d'una política catòlica.* Vic: Eumo Editorial, 1996.

———. "La participació catalana en el tràfic d'esclaus." *Recerques,* no. 16 (1984): 118–39.

———. "Quiebra imperial y reorganización política en las Antillas españolas, 1810–1868." *Op. Cit.,* no. 9 (1997): 289–317.

———. "Why Were Spain's Special Overseas Laws Never Enacted?" In *Spain, Europe and the Atlantic world: Essays in Honour of John H. Elliott,* ed. Richard Kagan and Geoffrey Parker, 335–49. Cambridge: Cambridge University Press, 1995.

Fradera, Josep M., ed. *Catalunya i ultramar.* Barcelona: Museu Maritim, 1995.

Fradera, J. M., J. Millan, and R. Garrabou, eds. *Carlisme i moviments absolutistes.* Vic: Eumo Editorial, 1990.

Garcia, Balaña Albert. "Tradició liberal i política colonial a Catalunya." In *Catalunya i Ultramar,* ed. Fradera and Benadi, 78–106.

García, Osvaldo. *Fotografías para la historia de Puerto Rico, 1844–1952.* 2nd ed. Río Piedras, P.R.: Ediciones Huracán, 1993.

García Mora, Luis Miguel. "El Ateneo de Madrid y el problema colonial en las vísperas de la Guerra de Independencia Cubana." *Revista de Indias* 56 (1996): 429–49.

———. "Tras la revolución, las reformas: El Partido Liberal Cubano y los proyectos reformistas tras la Paz de Zanjón." In *Cuba, la perla de las Antillas,* ed. Naranjo Orovio and Mallo Gutiérrez, 197–212.

García Rovira, Ana María. *La revolució liberal a Espanya i les classes populars.* Vic: Eumo Editorial, 1989.

García Balaña, Albert. "Tradició liberal i política colonial a Catalunya. Mig segle de tempatives i limitacions, 1822–1872." In *Catalunya i Ultramar,* ed. Fradera and Bernardi, 78–106.

García Sanz, Angel. "Crisis de la agricultura tradicional y revolución liberal (1800–1850)." In *Historia agraria de la España contemporánea,* ed. Garrabou et al.

Garrabou, Ramón, Jesús Sanz, and Angel García Sanz, eds. *Historia agraria de la España contemporánea,* 2 vols. Barcelona: Crítica, 1985.

Genovese, Eugene. *Roll, Jordan, Roll: The World the Slaves Made.* New York: Vintage Books, 1974.

———. *The Slaveholders' Dilemma: Freedom and Progress in Southern Conservative Thought, 1820–1860.* Columbia: University of South Carolina Press, 1992.

————. *The World the Slaveholders Made*. New York: Pantheon, 1969.

Gil Novales, Alberto. "Abolicionismo y librecambio." *Revista de Occidente*, no. 59 (1968): 154–81.

Gómez Acevedo, Labor. *Sanz, promotor de la conciencia separatista en Puerto Rico*. 2nd ed. Río Piedras: Editorial Universitaria, 1974.

González, José Luis. *El país de cuatro pisos y otros ensayos*. Río Piedras, P.R.: Ediciones Huracán, 1989.

Gootenberg, Paul. *Between Silver and Guano: Commercial Policy and the State in Postindependence Peru*. Princeton: Princeton University Press, 1989.

————. *Imagining Development: Economic Ideas in Peru's "Fictitious Prosperity" of Guano, 1840–1880*. Berkeley and Los Angeles: University of California Press, 1993.

Gudmundson, Lowell. "Society and Politics in Central America, 1821–1871." In *Central America, 1821–1871*, ed. Gudmundson and Lindo-Fuentes, 120–25.

Gudmundson, Lowell, and Hector Lindo-Fuentes. *Central America, 1821–1871: Liberalism before Liberal Reform*. Tuscaloosa: University of Alabama Press, 1995.

Guereña, Jean-Louis. "Hacia una historia socio-cultural de las clases populares en España (1840–1920)." *Historia Social* 11 (1991): 147–64.

Guerra y Sánchez, Ramiro. *La Guerra de los Diez Años, 1868–1878*, 2nd ed. 2 vols. Havana: Editorial Pueblo y Educación, 1986.

————. *Manual de historia de Cuba*. Havana: Editorial de Ciencias Sociales, 1971.

Gupta, Akhil, and James Ferguson. "Beyond 'Culture': Space, Identity, and the Politics of Difference." *Cultural Anthropology* 7 (1992): 6–23.

Habermas, Jürgen. *The Structural Transformation of the Public Sphere*. Trans. Thomas Burger, with Frederick Lawrence. Cambridge: MIT Press, 1989.

Hale, Charles. *Mexican Liberalism in the Age of Mora, 1821–1853*. New Haven: Yale University Press, 1968.

————. "Political and Social Ideas." In *Latin America: Economy and Society, 1870–1930*, ed. Bethell.

————. *The Transformation of Liberalism in Late Nineteenth-Century Mexico*. Princeton: Princeton University Press, 1989.

Hall, Catherine. "The Economy of Intellectual Prestige: Thomas Carlyle, John Stuart Mill, and the Case of Governor Eyre." *Cultural Critique*, no. 12 (1989): 167–96.

Hall, Stuart. "When Was the 'Post-colonial'? Thinking at the Limit." In *The Post-Colonial Question: Common Skies, Divided Horizon*, ed. Iain Chambers and Lidia Curti, 242–60. London: Routledge, 1996.

Harrison, Joseph. *An Economic History of Modern Spain*. Manchester: Manchester University Press, 1978.

Helg, Aline. *Our Rightful Share: The Afro-Cuban Struggle for Equality, 1886–1912*. Chapel Hill: University of North Carolina Press, 1994.

————. "Race in Argentina and Cuba, 1880–1930." In *The Idea of Race in Latin America, 1870–1940*, ed. Richard Graham. Austin: University of Texas Press, 1990.

Helly, Denise. Introduction to *The Cuba Commission Report: A Hidden History of the Chinese in Cuba*. Trans. Sidney Mintz. Baltimore: Johns Hopkins University Press, 1993.

Hennessey, C. A. M. *The Federal Republic in Spain*. Oxford: Clarendon Press, 1962.

Héran, François. "Tierra y parentesco en el campo sevillano. La revolución agrícola del siglo XIX: los comienzos de una agricultura capitalista." In *Historia agraria de la España contemporánea*, vol. 2, ed. Garrabou et al., 443–76.

Herr, Richard. *The Eighteenth-Century Revolution in Spain.* Princeton: Princeton University Press, 1958.

———. *An Historical Essay on Modern Spain.* Berkeley: University of California Press, 1971.

———. *Rural Change and Royal Finances in Spain at the End of the Old Regime.* Berkeley: University of California Press, 1989.

———. "Spain." In *European Landed Elites in the Nineteenth Century,* ed. David Spring, 98–126. Baltimore: Johns Hopkins University Press, 1977.

Hirschman, Albert O. *Exit, Voice, and Loyalty.* Cambridge: Harvard University Press, 1970.

———. *The Passions and the Interests.* Princeton: Princeton University Press, 1977.

———. "The Principle of Conservation and Mutation of Social Energy." In *Direct to the Poor: Grassroots Development in Latin America,* ed. Sheldon Annis and Peter Hakin, 7–14. Boulder, Colo.: Lynne Rienner, 1988.

———. *Rival Views of Market Society and Other Recent Essays.* New York: Viking Books, 1986.

Hobsbawm, E. J. *The Age of Capital, 1848–1875.* New York: New American Library, 1979.

———. *The Age of Empire, 1875–1914.* New York: Vintage Books, 1989.

———. *The Age of Revolution, 1789–1848.* New York: New American Library, 1962.

———. *Nations and Nationalism since 1780.* Cambridge: Cambridge University Press, 1990.

Holt, Thomas C. "'An Empire over the Mind': Emancipation, Race, and Ideology in the British West Indies and the American South." In *Race, Region, and Reconstruction: Essays in Honor of C. Vann Woodward,* ed. J. Morgan Kousser and James M. McPherson, 283–313. New York: Oxford University Press, 1982.

———. "Explaining Abolition." *Journal of Social History* 24 (winter 1990): 371–78.

———. "Marking: Race, Race-making, and the Writing of History." *American Historical Review* 100 (February 1995): 1–20.

———. *The Problem of Freedom: Race, Labor, and Politics in Jamaica and Britain, 1832–1938.* Baltimore: Johns Hopkins University Press, 1992.

Hunt, Lynn. *The Family Romance of the French Revolution.* Berkeley: University of California Press, 1992.

Ibarra, Jorge. *Ideología mambisa.* Havana: Instituto Cubano del Libro, 1972.

Izard, Miquel. *Manufactureros, industriales y revolucionarios.* Barcelona: Crítica, 1979.

James, C. L. R. *The Black Jacobins.* 2nd ed. New York: Vintage Books, 1963.

Janué i Miret, Marició. *La Junta Revolucionaria de Barcelona de l'any 1868.* Vic: Eumo Editorial, 1992.

Jensen, Larry. *Children of Colonial Despotism: Press, Politics, and Culture in Cuba, 1790–1840.* Tampa: University of South Florida Press, 1988.

Jiménez de Wagenheim, Olga. *El Grito de Lares.* Boulder: Westview Press, 1985.

Juliá, Santos, et al. *Madrid. Historia de una capital.* Madrid: Alianza Editorial, 1995.

Kaplan, Temma. "Positivism and Liberalism." In *La Revolución de 1868,* ed. Lida and Zavala, 254–66.

Keane, John, ed. *Civil Society and the State: New European Perspectives.* London: Verso, 1988.

Kern, Robert. *Liberals, Reformers, and Caciques.* Albuquerque: University of New Mexico Press, 1974.

Kiernan, Victor. *The Revolution of 1854 in Spanish History.* Oxford: Clarendon Press, 1966.

King, James F. "The Colored Castes and American Representation in the Cortes of Cádiz." *Hispanic American Historical Review* 33 (1953): 33–64.

Kinsbruner, Jay. *Independence in Spanish America.* Albuquerque: University of New Mexico Press, 1994.

————. *Not of Pure Blood: The Free People of Color and Racial Prejudice in Nineteenth-Century Puerto Rico.* Durham: Duke University Press, 1996.

Kirkpatrick, Susan. *Las Románticas: Women Writers and Subjectivity in Spain, 1835–1850.* Berkeley: University of California Press, 1989.

Klor de Alva, Jorge. "The Postcolonization of the (Latin) American Experience: A Reconsideration of 'Colonialism', 'Postcolonialism', and 'Mestizaje.'" In *After Colonialism,* ed. Gyan Prakash, 241–75. Princeton: Princeton University Press, 1995.

Knight, Franklin. *Slave Society in Cuba During the Nineteenth Century.* Madison: University of Wisconsin Press, 1970.

Krieger, Leonard. *The German Idea of Freedom.* Boston: Beacon Press, 1957.

Kuethe, Allan J. *Cuba, 1753–1815: Crown, Military, and Society.* Knoxville: University of Tennessee Press, 1986.

Laclau, Ernesto, and Chantal Mouffe. *Hegemony and Socialist Strategy.* London: Verso, 1985.

Lewis, Gordon. *Main Currents in Caribbean Thought.* Baltimore: Johns Hopkins University Press, 1983.

Lida, Clara, and Iris Zavala, eds. *La Revolución de 1868. Historia, pensamiento, literatura.* New York: Las Americas Publishing Company, 1970.

Lluch, Ernest. "'La economía política': poema didático de B.C. Aribau." *Hacienda pública Española* 27 (1974): 187–99.

————. "La 'gira trionfal' de Cobden per Espanya (1846)." *Recerques,* no. 21 (1988): 71–90.

López Garrido, Diego. *La Guardia Civil y los orígenes del estado centralista en España.* Barcelona: Crítica, 1982.

López-Morillas, Juan. *The Krausist Movement and ideological change in Spain, 1854–1874.* 2nd ed. Trans. Frances M. López-Morillas. Cambridge: Cambridge University Press, 1981.

López-Ocón, Leoncio. *Biografía de "La América."* Madrid: CSIC, 1987.

Love, Joseph L., and Nils Jacobsen, eds. *Guiding the Invisible Hand: Economic Liberalism and the State in Latin America.* New York: Praeger, 1988.

Luis, William. *Literary Bondage: Slavery in Cuban Narrative.* Austin: University of Texas Press, 1990.

Lynch, John. *The Spanish American Revolutions.* New York: W.W. Norton, 1973.

*Madrid: Atlas histórico de la ciudad.* Centro de Documentación y Estudios para la Historia de Madrid. Madrid: Fundación Caja de Madrid and Lunwerg Editores, S.A., 1995.

Maluquer de Motes, Jordi. "La burgesia catalana i l'esclavitud colonial: Modes de producció i pràctica política." *Recerques,* no. 3 (1974): 83–136.

————. "The Industrial Revolution in Catalonia." In *The Economic Modernization of Spain,* ed. Sánchez-Albornoz, 169–90.

————. "Inmigración y comercio catalan en las Antillas Españolas durante el siglo XIX." *Siglo XIX* 2 (1987): 160–81.

————. "El mercado colonial antillano en el siglo XIX." In *Agricultura, comercio y crecimiento económico en la España contempóranea,* ed. Jordi Nadal and Gabriel Tortella, 322–57. Esplugues de Llobergat: Ariel, 1974.

————. *Nación e inmigración: los españoles en Cuba (ss. XIX y XX).* Colombres: Ediciones Júcar, 1992.

————. "El problema de la esclavitud y la revolución de 1868." *Hispania* 31 (1971): 56–76.

————. *El socialismo en España, 1833–1868.* Barcelona: Crítica, 1977.

Marichal, Carlos. *Spain (1834–1844). A New Society.* London: Tamesis Books Limited, 1977.

Martí, Casimiro. *Orígenes del anarquismo en Barcelona.* Barcelona: Teide, 1959.

Martínez-Alier, Verena. *Marriage, Class and Colour in Nineteenth-Century Cuba.* 2nd ed. Ann Arbor: University of Michigan Press, 1989.

Martínez-Fernández, Luis. *Torn between Empires: Economy, Society, and Patterns of Political Thought in the Hispanic Caribbean, 1840–1878.* Athens: University of Georgia Press, 1994.

Martínez-Vergne, Teresita. *Capitalism in Colonial Puerto Rico: Central San Vicente in the Late Nineteenth Century.* Gainesville: University Press of Florida, 1992.

May, Robert E. *The Southern Dream of a Caribbean Empire, 1854–1861.* Athens: University of Georgia Press, 1989.

Mayer, Arno. *The Persistence of the Old Regime: Europe to the Great War.* New York: Pantheon Books, 1981.

McDonogh, Gary W. *Good Families of Barcelona.* Princeton: Princeton University Press, 1986.

Midgley, Clare. "Antislavery and Feminism in Nineteenth-Century Britian." *Gender and Society* 5 (1993): 343–62.

———. *Women Against Slavery: The British Campaigns, 1780–1870.* London: Routledge, 1992.

Mintz, Sidney. *Caribbean Transformations.* Chicago: Aldine, 1974.

———. "The Culture History of a Puerto Rican Sugar Cane Plantation: 1876–1949." *Hispanic American Historical Review* 33 (1953): 239–44.

———. "Slavery and Forced Labor." In *Caribbean Transformations,* 82–94.

———. *Sweetness and Power: The Place of Sugar in Modern History.* New York: Penguin Books, 1985.

Mintz, Sidney, and Sally Price, eds. *Caribbean Contours.* Baltimore: Johns Hopkins University Press, 1985.

Morales Carrión, Arturo. *Auge y decadencia de la trata negrera en Puerto Rico (1820–1860).* San Juan: Instituto de Cultura Puertorriqueña, 1978.

Morato, J. José. *Lideres del movimiento obrero español 1868–1921.* Selección, presentación y notas de Víctor Manuel Arbeloa. Madrid: Editorial Cuadernos para el Diálogo, 1972.

Moreno Fraginals, Manuel. *Cuba/España, España/Cuba. Una historia común.* Barcelona: Crítica, 1995.

———. *El Ingenio.* 3 vols. Havana:Editorial de Ciencias Sociales, 1978.

———. *The Sugarmill.* Trans. Cedric Belfrage. New York: Monthly Review Press, 1978.

———. "Plantations in the Caribbean: Cuba, Puerto Rico, and the Dominican Republic in the Late Nineteenth Century," in *Between Slavery and Free Labor,* ed. Moreno Fraginals et al.

Moreno Fraginals, Manuel, and José J. Moreno Masó. *Guerra, migración y muerte (El ejército español en Cuba como vía migratoria.* Colombres: Ediciones Júcar, 1993.

Moreno Fraginals, Manuel, Frank Moya Pons, Stanley L. Engerman, eds. *Between Slavery and Free Labor: The Spanish-speaking Caribbean in the Nineteenth Century.* Baltimore: Johns Hopkins University Press, 1985.

Morgan, Edmund. *American Slavery, American Freedom.* New York: W.W. Norton, 1975.

Murray, David. *Odious Commerce: Britain, Spain and the Abolition of the Cuban Slave Trade.* Cambridge: Cambridge University Press, 1980.

Nadal, Jordi. *El fracaso de la revolución industrial en España, 1814–1913.* Esplugues de Llobergat: Ariel, 1975.

Naranjo Orovio, Consuelo, and Armando García González. *Racismo e inmigración en Cuba en el siglo XIX.* Madrid: Editorial Doce Calles, 1996.

Naranjo Orovio, Consuelo, and Tomás Mallo Gutiérrez, eds. *Cuba, la perla de las Antillas.* Madrid: Ediciones Doce Calles, 1994.

Naranjo Orovio, Consuelo, Miguel Puig-Samper, and Luis Miguel García Mora, eds. *La nación soñada: Cuba, Puerto Rico y Filipinas ante le 98.* Madrid: Editorial Doce Calles, 1996.

Náter Vázquez, Laura. "Los autonomismos: de la semilla al proyecto (1809–1887)." M.A. thesis, University of Puerto Rico, Río Piedras, 1991.

Navarro, Miguel Ángel Esteban. "De la esperanza a la frustración, 1868–1873." in *El republicanismo en España,* ed. Townson, 87–112.

Navarro García, Jesús Raúl. *Entre esclavos y constituciónes.* Sevilla: CSIC, 1991.

Oostindie, Gert, ed. *Fifty Years Later: Antislavery, Capitalism, and Modernity in the Dutch Orbit.* Pittsburgh: University of Pittsburgh Press, 1996.

Opatrny, Josef. *Antecedentes históricos de la formación de la nación cubana.* Prague: Charles University, 1986.

Pagden, Anthony. *Spanish Imperialism and the Political Imagination.* New Haven: Yale University Press, 1990.

Pagden, Anthony, and Nicholas Canny, eds. *Colonial Identity in the Atlantic World, 1500–1800.* Princeton: Princeton University Press, 1987.

Palacio Morena, Juan Ignacio. *La institucionalización de la reforma social en España (1883–1924).* Madrid: Ministerio de Trabajo y Seguridad Social, 1988.

Palomas, Joan, and Montserrat Bravo. "Víctor Balaguer, la diputació catalana i la lluita pel proteccionisme (1881–1890)." *Recerques,* no. 25 (1992): 31–52.

Pan-Montojo, Juan, ed. *Más se perdió en Cuba. España, 1898 y la crisis de fin de siglo.* Madrid: Alianza Editorial, 1998.

Paquette, Robert. *Sugar Is Made with Blood.* Middletown, Conn.: Wesleyan University Press, 1988.

Pateman, Carole. *The Sexual Contract.* Stanford: Stanford University Press, 1988.

Pedreira, Antonio S. "La actualidad del jíbaro." *Boletín de la Universidad de Puerto Rico* 6 (1935): 5–21.

Pérez, Louis A., Jr. "Between Baseball and Bullfighting: The Quest for Nationality in Cuba, 1868–1898." *Journal of American History* 81 (1994): 493–517.

———. *Cuba: Between Reform and Revolution.* New York: Oxford University Press, 1988.

———. *Cuba Between Empires.* Pittsburgh: University of Pittsburgh Press, 1983.

———. *Lords of the Mountain.* Pittsburgh: University of Pittsburgh Press, 1989.

Pérez de la Riva, Juan. *El barracón. Esclavitud y capitalismo en Cuba.* Barcelona: Editorial Crítica, 1978.

Pérez de la Riva, Juan, ed. *Correspondencia reservada del Capitan General D. Miguel Tacón.* Havana: Biblioteca Nacional José Martí, 1963.

Pérez Ledesma, Manuel. *El obrero consciente.* Madrid: Alianza Editorial, 1987.

———. "'Ricos y pobres: pueblo y oligarquía: explotadores y explotados'. Las imágenes dicótomicas en el siglo XIX español." *Revista del Centro de Estudios Constitucionales* 10 (1991): 59–88.

Picó, Fernando. *Amargo café: los pequeños y medianos caficultores de Utuado en la segunda mitad del siglo XIX.* Río Piedras, P.R.: Ediciones huracán, 1981.

———. *Historia general de Puerto Rico.* 5th ed. Río Piedras, P.R.: Ediciones Huracán, 1990.

———. *Libertad y servidumbre en el Puerto Rico del siglo XIX.* Río piedras, Ediciones Huracán, 1979.

Pike, Frederick. *Hispanismo, 1898–1936.* Notre Dame: University of Notre Dame Press, 1971.

———. "Making the Hispanic World Safe from Democracy: Spanish Liberals and *Hispanismo.*" *Review of Politics* 33 (July 1971): 307–22.

Piqueras Arenas, José Antonio. *La revolución democrática (1868–1974): Cuestión social, colonialismo y grupos de presión.* Madrid: Ministerio de Trabajo y Seguridad Social, 1992.

Piqueras, José Antonio, and Enric Sebastià. *Agiotistas, negreros y partisanos.* Valencia: Edicions Alfons el Magnànim, 1991.

Planas, Jordi. "Els propietaris i l'associacionisme agrari a Catalunya." *L'Avenç,* no. 171 (1993): 32–55.

Poey Baró, Dionisio. *La entrada de los Aldamistas en la Guerra de los Diez Años.* Havana: Editorial de Ciencias Sociales, 1989.

Poovey, Mary. *Uneven Developments: The Ideological Work of Gender in Mid-Victorian England.* Chicago: University of Chicago Press, 1988.

Poyo, Gerald. "Evolution of Cuban Separatist Thought in the Emigré Communities of the United States, 1848–1895." *Hispanic American Historical Review* 66 (1986): 485–507.

———. *"With All and for the Good of All": The Emergence of Popular Nationalism in the Cuban Communities of the United States, 1848–1898.* Durham: Duke University Press, 1989.

Prados de la Escosura, Leandro. *De imperio a nación: Crecimiento y atraso económico en España (1780–1930).* Madrid: Alianza Editorial, 1988.

Prakash, Gyan, ed. *After Colonialism: Imperial Histories and Postcolonial Displacements.* Princeton: Princeton University Press, 1995.

Przeworski, Adam. *Capitalism and Social Democracy.* Cambridge: Cambridge University Press, 1989.

Quiroz, Alfonso. "Loyalist Overkill: The Socioeconomic Costs of 'Repressing' the Separatist Insurrection in Cuba, 1868–1878." *Hispanic American Historical Review* 78 (1998): 261–305.

Ramos Mattei, Andrés A. *La hacienda azucarera: su crecimiento y crisis en puerto Rico (siglo XIX).* San Juan, P.R.: CEREP, 1981.

———. "La importación de trabajadores contratados para la industria azucarera puertorriqueña: 1860–1880." In *Inmigración y clases sociales en el Puerto Rico del siglo XIX,* ed. Scarano, 125–41.

———. "Technical Innovations and Social Change in the Sugar Industry of Puerto Rico, 1870–1880," in *Between Slavery and Free Labor,* ed. Moreno Fraginals et al., 158–78.

Reddy, William. *Money and Liberty in Modern Europe.* Cambridge: Cambridge University Press, 1987.

Ringrose, David. *Madrid and the Spanish Economy (1560–1850).* Berkeley and Los Angeles: University of California Press, 1983.

Riquer, Borja de. "El conservadurisme polític català: del fracàs del moderantisme al decencís de la Restauració." *Recerques* 11 (1981): 29–80.

Robert, Karen. "Slavery and Freedom in the Ten Years' War, Cuba, 1868–1878." *Slavery and Abolition* 13 (December 1992): 181–200.

Rodríguez, Mario. *The Cádiz Experiment in Central America, 1808–1826.* Berkeley: University of California Press, 1978.

Roediger, David. *The Wages of Whiteness: Race and the Making of the American Working Class.* London: Verso, 1991.

Sahlins, Peter. *Boundaries: The Making of Spain and France in the Pyrennees.* Berkeley: University of California Press, 1989.

Salvemini, Gaetano. *Mazzini.* Trans. I. M. Rawson. New York: Collier, 1962.

Sánchez-Albornoz, Nicolás, ed. *The Economic Modernization of Spain, 1830–1930.* Trans. Karen Powers and Manuel Sañudo. New York: New York University Press, 1987.

———. *España hace un siglo: una economía dual.* Barcelona: Ediciones Peninsular, 1968.

———. "El trasfondo económico de la Revolución." In *La Revolución de 1868,* ed. Lida and Zavala, 64–79.

San Miguel, Pedro. *El mundo que creó el azúcar. Las haciendas en Vega Baja, 1800–1873.* Río Piedras, P.R.: Ediciones Huracán, 1989.

Scanlon, Geraldine. *La polémica feminista en España (1868–1974).* Madrid: Siglo XXI, 1976.

Scarano, Francisco, "The *Jíbaro* Masquerade and the Subaltern Politics of Creole Identity Formation in Puerto Rico, 1745–1823." *American Historical Review* 101 (1996): 1398–1431.

———. *Puerto Rico: Cinco siglos de historia.* San Juan, P.R.: McGraw Hill, 1993.

———. *Sugar and Slavery in Puerto Rico: The Plantation Economy of Ponce, 1800–1850.* Madison: University of Wisconsin Press, 1984.

Scarano, Francisco, ed. *Inmigración y clases sociales en el Puerto Rico del siglo XIX.* 3rd ed. Río Piedras, P.R.: Ediciones Huracán, 1989.

Schmidt-Nowara, Christopher. "Imperio y crisis colonial." In *Más se perdió en Cuba. España, 1898 y la crisis de fin de siglo,* ed. Juan Pan-Montojo, 31–89. Madrid: Alianza Editorial, 1998.

———. "'Spanish' Cuba: Race and Class in Spanish and Cuban Antislavery Ideology, 1861–1868." *Cuban Studies* 25 (1995): 101–22.

Schorske, Carl. *Fin-de-siècle Vienna.* New York: Vintage Books, 1981.

Schumpter, Joseph. *Imperialism and Social Classes.* Trans. Heinz Norden. New York: Meridian Books, 1955.

Scott, Joan Wallach. *Gender and the Politics of History.* New York: Columbia University Press, 1988.

———. "'L'ouvrière! Mot impie, sordide . . .': Women Workers in the Discourse of French Political Economy, 1840–1860." In *Gender and the Politics of History,* 139–63.

Scott, Rebecca. "Defining the Boundaries of Freedom in the World of Cane: Cuba, Brazil, and Louisiana after Emancipation." *American Historical Review* 99 (February 1994): 70–102.

———. "Dismantling Repressive Systems: The Abolition of Slavery in Cuba as a Case Study." In *Development, Democracy, and the Art of Trespassing,* ed. Alejandro Foxley, Michael S. McPherson, and Guillermo O'Donnell. Notre Dame: University of Notre Dame Press, 1986, 269–81.

———. *Slave Emancipation in Cuba.* Princeton: Princeton University Press, 1985.

Scott, Rebecca, et al., eds. *The Abolition of Slavery and the Aftermath of Emancipation in Brazil.* Durham: Duke University Press, 1988.

Serrano, Carlos. *Final del Imperio. España 1895–1898.* Madrid: Siglo XXI, 1984.

Serrano Sanz, José María. "El proteccionsimo y el desarrollo económico en la Restauración. Reflexiónes para un debate." *Revista de Historia Económica* 7 (1989): 133–56.

Sewell, William H., Jr. *A Rhetoric of Bourgeois Revolution: The Abbé Sieyes and "What Is the Third Estate?"* Durham: Duke University Press, 1994.

———. "Toward a Post-Materialist Rhetoric for Labor History." In *Rethinking Labor History,* ed. Lenard Berlanstein. Urbana: University of Illinois Press, 1993, 15–38.

———. *Work and Revolution in France.* Cambridge: Cambridge University Press, 1980.

Shubert, Adrian. "'Charity Properly Understood': Changing Ideas about Poor Relief in Liberal Spain." *Comparative Studies in Society and History* 33 (1991): 36–55.

Smith, Bonnie G. *Ladies of the Leisure Class: The Bourgeoisies of Northern France in the Nineteenth Century.* Princeton: Princeton University Press, 1981.

Soldiván de Acosta, Jaime A. "Genelogía de Don José Julián de Acosta y Calbo." *La Revista del Centro de Estudios Avanzados de Puerto Rico y el Caribe* 8 (1989): 124–33.

Solé Tura, Jordi. *Constituciónes y periódos constituyentes en España (1808–1936).* Madrid: Siglo XXI, 1977.

Soliván de Acosta, Jaime A. "Genealogía de Don José Julián de Acosta y Calbo." *La Revista del Centro de Estudios Avanzados de Puerto Rico y el Caribe,* no. 8 (1989): 124–33.

Stedman Jones, Gareth. *Languages of Class.* Cambridge: Cambridge University Press, 1983.

Stein, Stanley, and Barbara Stein. *The Colonial Heritage of Latin America.* New York: Oxford University Press, 1970.

Stepan, Nancy. *The Idea of Race in Science: Great Britain, 1800–1960.* London: Macmillan, 1982.

Stoler, Ann. *Race and the Education of Desire: Foucault's History of Sexuality and the Colonial Order of Things.* Durham: Duke University Press, 1995.

———. "Sexual Affronts and Racial Frontiers: European Identities and the Cultural Politics of Exclusion in Southeast Asia." In *Tensions of Empire,* ed. Cooper and Stoler, 198–237.

Szporluk, Roman. *Communism and Nationalism: Karl Marx versus Friedrich List.* New York: Oxford University Press, 1988.

Tedde de Lorca, Pedro. "On the Historical Origins of Andalusian Underdevelopment." In *The Economic Modernization of Spain,* ed. Sánchez-Albornoz, 251–67.

Temperley, Howard. *British Antislavery, 1833–1870.* London: Longman's, 1972.

Termes, Josep. *Anarquismo y sindicalismo en España, 1864–1881.* Barcelona: Ariel, 1972.

Thopmson, E. P. *The Making of the English Working Class.* New York: Vintage Books, 1963.

Thomson, J. K. J. *A Distinctive Industrialization: Cotton in Barcelona, 1728–1832.* Cambridge: Cambridge University Press, 1992.

Thorne, Susan. "'The Conversion of Englishmen and the Conversion of the World Inseparable': Missionary Imperialism and the Language of Class in Early Industrial Britain." In *Tensions of Empire,* ed. Cooper and Stoler, 238–62.

Thornton, J. Mills, III. *Power and Politics in a Slave Society. Alabama, 1800–1860.* Baton Rouge: Louisiana State University Press, 1978.

Tomich, Dale. "The 'Second Slavery': Bonded Labor and the Transformation of the Nineteenth-Century World Economy." In *Rethinking the Nineteenth Century,* ed. Francisco Ramírez, 103–17. Stanford: Stanford University Press, 1988.

———. "Spaces of Slavery, Times of Freedom: Rethinking Caribbean History in World Perspective." *Comparative Studies of South Asia, Africa and the Middle East* 17 (1997): 67–80.

———. "World Slavery and Caribbean Capitalism: The Cuban Sugar Industry, 1760–1868." *Theory and Society* 20 (June 1991): 297–319.

Torras, Jaume. *Revolución liberal y rebeldía campesina.* Barcelona: Ariel, 1976.

Torres-Cuevas, Eduardo. *José Antonio Saco: la polémica de la esclavitud.* Havana: Editorial de Ciencias Sociales, 1984.

Tortella Casares, Gabriel. *Banking, Railroads, and Industry in Spain, 1829–1874.* New York: Arno Press, 1977.

———. *El desarrollo de la España contemporánea.* Madrid: Alianza, 1994.

————. *Los orígenes del capitalismo en España.* Madrid: Tecnos, 1973.

Townson, Nigel, ed. *El republicanismo en España (1830–1977).* Madrid: Alianza, 1994.

Trend, J. B. *The Origins of Modern Spain.* New York: Macmillan Company, 1934.

Trías, Juan J., and Antonio Elorza. *Federalismo y reforma social en España (1840–1870).* Madrid: Seminarios y Ediciones, 1975.

Trouillot, Michel-Rolph. *Silencing the Past: Power and the Production of History.* Boston: Beacon Press, 1995.

Van Aken, Mark. *Pan-Hispanism, Its Origins and Development to 1866.* Berkeley: University of California Press, 1959.

Varela Ortega, José. *Los amigos políticos. Partidos, elecciónes y caciquismo en la Restauración.* Madrid: Alianza Editorial, 1977.

————. "El proteccionismo de los trigueros castellanos y la naturaleza del Poder político en la Restauración." *Cuadernos de ICE* 5 (1978): 7–60.

Vázquez Sotillo, Nelly. "La represión política en Puerto Rico durante la administración de Miguel López de Baños (1837–1840)." M.A. thesis, University of Puerto Rico, Río Piedras, 1983.

Vilar, Pierre. "Spain and Catalonia." *Review* 3 (spring 1980): 527–77.

Villacorta Baños, Francisco. "Teoría y práctica del obrerismo democrático: el Fomento de las artes, 1847–1876." In *Madrid en la sociedad del siglo XIX,* 2:71–96. Madrid: Comunidad de Madrid, 1986.

Wade, Peter. *Blackness and Race Mixture: The Dynamics of Racial Identity in Colombia.* Baltimore: Johns Hopkins University Press, 1993.

Whitney, Robert. "The Political Economy of Abolition: The Hispano-Cuban Elite and Cuban Slavery, 1868–1873." *Slavery and Abolition* 13 (August 1992): 20–36.

Williams, Eric. *Capitalism and Slavery.* Chapel Hill: University of North Carolina Press, 1944.

Wolf, Eric. *Europe and the People without History.* Berkeley and Los Angeles: University of California Press, 1982.

Yáñez Gallardo, César. *Saltar con red: la temprana emigración catalana a América (1820–1870).* Madrid: Alianza, 1996.

# INDEX